The Second Indochina War

About the Book and Author

In the United States, discussion of the Vietnam War has tended to focus on the U.S. role, U.S. strategy, U.S. diplomacy, and the war's effects on American society. The tendency to hold U.S. domestic politics responsible for the war's outcome implies that events in Indochina were nothing more than a backdrop for an essentially American drama. In contrast, *The Second Indochina War* emphasizes the Vietnamese dimensions of a conflict in which all of Indochina—Vietnam, Laos, and Cambodia—was treated as a single strategic unit. The author contends that only from this perspective is it clear how the war began, why its scale outstripped U.S. expectations, and why the Communists prevailed.

Professor Turley gives a balanced account of events in, and views from, Washington, Saigon, and Hanoi. Drawing on years of research in primary documents and interviews conducted by the author in Saigon and Hanoi, the book focuses on the experience, strategies, leadership, and internal politics of the revolutionary side.

To set the scene, the author considers the legacies of colonial rule in Indochina and the origins of the U.S. commitment there. He recounts the development of the Saigon regime and explains the bases of revolution in the South, the key communist decisions, and the North's response to bombing. The major military campaigns are clearly described and analyzed, as are the negotiations that led to the Paris Agreement and its aftermath. Vietnam is the central focus, but the reader's attention is also drawn to the strategies and events that unified the conflict in all three countries of Indochina into a single war.

Concise yet comprehensive, *The Second Indochina War* is suitable for the general reader, as a text for courses on the war, or as supplementary reading for courses on Southeast Asian politics, U.S. foreign policy, revolutionary conflict, and Asian regional security. An annotated bibliography and chronology enhance its usefulness. Original material on communist internal debates and military campaigns, based on primary documents in Vietnamese, will also make this book a valuable resource for scholars of Southeast Asia.

William S. Turley, associate professor of political science at Southern Illinois University, has been researching Vietnamese communism since 1970, including extensive work in Vietnam. He has spent time in Southeast Asia as a Ford Foundation Research Associate at Saigon University (1972–1973) and a Fulbright Professor at Chulalongkorn University, Bangkok (1982–1984); his numerous publications include *Vietnamese Communism in Comparative Perspective* (Westview 1980).

The Second Indochina War

A Short Political and Military History, 1954–1975

William S. Turley

Westview Press • Boulder, Colorado

Gower • London, England

Published in 1986 in the United States of America by Westview Press, Inc.; Frederick A. Praeger, Publisher; 5500 Central Avenue, Boulder, Colorado 80301

Published in 1986 in Great Britain by Gower Publishing Company Limited, Gower House, Croft Road, Aldershot, Hampshire GU11 3HR

Library of Congress Cataloging-in-Publication Data
Turley, William S.
The second Indochina War: A Short Political and Military History, 1954–1975.
Bibliography: p.
Includes index.
1. Vietnamese Conflict, 1961–1975. 2. Vietnam—Politics and government—1945–1975. I. Title.
DS557.7.T87 1986 959.704′3 85-31518

ISBN (U.S.) 0-8133-0308-7
ISBN (U.K.) 0-566-05224-5

Printed and bound in the United States of America.

The paper used in this publication meets the minimum requirements of the American National Standard for Permanence of Paper for Printed Library Materials Z39.48-1984.

10 9 8 7 6 5 4 3 2 1

Contents

Tables, Figures, and Maps

Tables

Figures

Maps

Preface

Vietnam went to war for independence from France in 1946. Laos and Cambodia were soon drawn in, and the three countries of Indochina have been embroiled in conflict ever since. Two breaks in that conflict, however, divide it into three distinct periods. The first break was the defeat of France in 1954, which marked an end to the First Indochina War but left Vietnam partitioned. The second break was the victory of communist forces in all three countries of Indochina in 1975, which unified Vietnam and set the scene for confrontation with wary neighbors. In between these two breaks the United States sought to turn back communist-led struggles for revolution and national reunification by shoring up anticommunist regimes in Saigon, Vientiane, and Phnom Penh and by sending more than 2.5 million U.S. troops to South Vietnam. Though in many respects a continuation of the first war, the period from 1954 to 1975 was also a distinct phase. This phase has come to be known as the Second Indochina War.

Americans have tended to view that war as an essentially American drama. In popular consciousness, the words Vietnam War are as likely to trigger images of conflict in the U.S.

Congress, media, and streets as they are to call forth images of war in the padi fields of lands far away. If the countries, peoples, and terrain of Indochina have any place in these images at all, it is mostly as dim background against which U.S. soldiers fought valiantly but, in the end, vainly. These images reflect the haunting suspicion that the war's outcome was determined by what happened inside the United States, not in Indochina.

The present work grows out of my conviction that what happened in Indochina mattered. The historical momentum of social change and civil conflict in Vietnam, Laos, and Cambodia had its own dynamic, which the United States could influence but not unilaterally reshape to its own liking. The intention here is not to downplay the U.S. involvement, for the U.S. role is partly what sets the second war apart from the first one. U.S. politics, diplomacy, and military actions take up a large part of the discussion. Rather, the intention is to bring the Indochinese and U.S. contexts together in a single brief work. Special attention is paid, moreover, to the viewpoints and strategies of the ultimately victorious parties, particularly the Vietnamese Communists.

The latter emphasis is partly the reflection of the close attention I have given to Vietnamese communism and the Vietnamese communist military during fifteen years of academic research. From habit as well as conviction, I believe these subjects are important and intrinsically interesting. However, my treatment may differ in certain respects from what general readers—and not a few specialists—may have come to expect from histories of the war. Readers may find it odd, for example, that communist military strategies are not routinely ascribed here, as they are in other works, to the genius of General Vo Nguyen Giap. This is simply because Giap was not the grandmaster of strategy for the second war that he was in the first. Hanoi's strategy for the second war was made collectively, with significant civilian as well as military participation. Moreover, Giap was often at odds with the strategies adopted for the war in the South and lost power to influence them as the war progressed. The myth that Giap singlehandedly plotted all of Hanoi's military moves from 1941 to 1975 is one that should be laid to rest.

Another curiosity in the eyes of some may be this work's avoidance of the terms "Viet Cong" and "VC," which over a decade of reporting and discussion probably assured permanence in common English usage. Viet Cong, however, originally was a term contemptuous of the group it purported to designate and had no precise standard meaning. It has seemed better to call organizations as they called themselves, e.g., People's Liberation Armed Force instead of Viet Cong, and People's Army of Vietnam instead of North Vietnamese Army. Readers also may wish to know that the numbering of plenums of Communist party central committees starts all over again with each national congress. The Vietnamese Communists held congresses in 1935, 1951, 1960, and 1976.

Lastly, I should point out that in Vietnam traditionally and under colonial rule, three, not two, geographic and cultural regions were recognized: the north embracing the Red River Delta (Bac Bo in Vietnamese, Tonkin under the French), the center comprising the country's narrow waist (Trung Bo, or Annam), and the south anchored by the Mekong Delta (Nam Bo, or Cochinchina). In 1954, partition arbitrarily created two administrative zones, the North and the South, divided at the Ben Hai River and the 17th parallel. In the present work, the downcased terms north, center, and south refer to the traditional regions, and the capitalized terms North and South refer to the zones that existed from 1954 to 1975. To illustrate, a person born in central Vietnam, hence a central Vietnamese by birth, could have been a North or South Vietnamese by political affiliation depending on which side of the 17th parallel it was his fate to live during partition. I hope this exercise in precision eliminates rather than causes confusion.

In acknowledgments, it is customary for authors to absolve others of responsibility, but I wish to pin the blame, at least for conception, squarely on my dear friends Georges Boudarel and Bui Xuan Quang. It all began with their idea for the three of us to write separate volumes on all three of Indochina's wars (the first, the second, and the one ongoing) that could be integrated into a single set. Though that idea had to be shelved, it was their suggestion, advice, and encouragement that helped push me toward completion. I particularly benefited from Boudarel's unique knowledge of Vietnamese communism, which he shared in abundant conversation, correspondence, and comments on an early draft. My one regret is not to have had the space and time to answer every criticism or to follow every lead he provided.

From a practical standpoint the book owes its existence to the John F. Kennedy Foundation of Thailand and the Fulbright Program, which supported me in 1982–1984 as Visiting Professor in the American Studies Program of Chulalongkorn University, Bangkok. Due to the extraordinary generosity, kindness, and patience of the American Studies Program director, Professor Wiwat Mungkandi, I was able to devote most of my second year to writing about Indochina, at some expense to his and the Program's priorities. I shall be eternally grateful for the hospitality shown me by Professor Mungkandi, the Program's deputy director Professor Pratoomporn Vajarasthira and research associate Pranee Thiparat, Professors Kusuma Snitwongse and M. R. Sukhumbhand Paribatra of the Institute of Security and International Studies, and other faculty and staff of Chulalongkorn University too numerous to name, though I should like to mention Prapan Chimwongse, typist of my first draft.

The stay in Bangkok also made it feasible for me to make two extremely useful trips to Vietnam, one in March 1983 and another in April 1984, to gather material for several projects among which this book was one. My host in Hanoi was the Institute of International Relations in the Ministry of Foreign Affairs. Through the efforts of the Institute and its director, Mr. Pham Binh, I was able to interview diverse officials and to exchange views with officers in the Military History Institute of the People's Army in Hanoi. More than once did interviews go on longer than planned, and I am grateful for the time that busy individuals found to talk with me. Except for lodging and travel between Hanoi and Ho Chi Minh City that the Institute provided on my second visit, I made these trips at my own expense.

These visits were my first to Vietnam in a decade and my first ever to Hanoi. In 1972–1973, I had spent a year in Saigon as a visiting lecturer at Saigon University under the auspices of the Ford Foundation and the Bureau of Education and Cultural

Affairs of the Department of State. I conducted a number of interviews with defectors from communist forces, learned much from the late William C. Gaussman who was then editor of *Viet-Nam Documents and Research Notes,* and had occasional access to U.S. and Saigon government officials. I could not have done my work without the personal interventions of Le Thuc Lan and the assistance of Bui To Loan and Duong Tu Mai. Before then, in 1967–1968, I had used a State Department grant for study in Singapore to support a protracted stay in Saigon, where I had the good fortune to follow Jeffrey Race through some of the research for his book, *War Comes to Long An.* The subconscious residue as well as hard findings from those years almost certainly have had greater influence on the present work than may be apparent.

Back in the United States, William Duiker reviewed my draft and made a number of very helpful suggestions that I have attempted to deal with, though not necessarily to his satisfaction, in revision. Sue Davis and Angie Spurlock typed the final manuscript with unfailing good humor despite the pressures that I, pressured by the crisply competent editors at Westview, applied on them. To all of these people, and not least to my wife, Clarisse Zimra, who accompanied me to Bangkok and Hanoi and who has shown patience beyond her nature, I give my thanks.

INDOCHINA

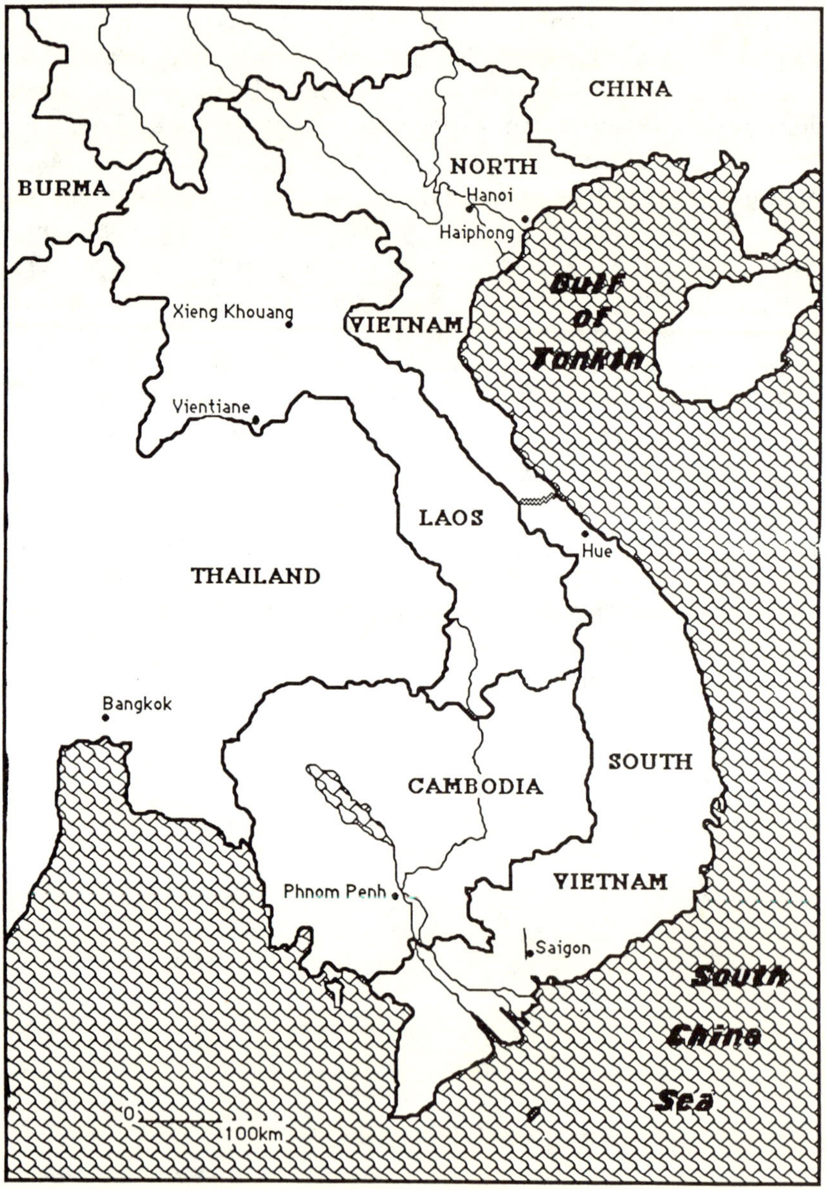
CHINA
BURMA
NORTH
Hanoi
Haiphong
Gulf
of
Tonkin
Xieng Khouang
VIETNAM
Vientiane
LAOS
Hue
THAILAND
Bangkok
SOUTH
CAMBODIA
VIETNAM
Phnom Penh
Saigon
South
China
Sea
0
100km

1

Legacies of Time

On March 29, 1973, the last American combat troop boarded a plane in Saigon, marking the end of U.S. involvement in the Second Indochina War. Although the fighting continued for another two years, the outcome was never seriously in doubt. From beginning to end, U.S. allies in Indochina were less disciplined, determined, and committed—though seldom less well armed—than their adversaries. U.S. intervention was in effect an attempt to reverse historical trends that were firmly established long before U.S. troops arrived. The United States was able to slow these trends but not, without unacceptable cost to itself, to halt them. For the war was not so much a new conflict as it was the resumption of an old, unfinished one. Of course U.S. leaders perceived their involvement on the side of beleaguered regimes as intrinsically different from the preceding French involvement. But an entanglement in Vietnamese history was inescapable for both France and the United States.

As popularly told, Vietnam's history is a litany of resistance to foreign domination. Formed in the Red River Delta, Vietnam fell under Chinese rule in 208 B.C.; the Vietnamese rebelled periodically over the next millennium, achieved independence in 938 A.D., defeated a Chinese attempt at reconquest in 1077, repulsed Mongol invasions in 1283 and 1287, and successfully resisted another Chinese occupation from 1407 to 1427. Out of this experience the Vietnamese fashioned a myth of national indomitability. Reality was murkier, of course, but the fact remains that the Vietnamese forged a strong collective identity early in their history, certainly long before Europeans appeared off their shores. A key element of that identity, in addition to a single language, a shared tradition, and a united territory, was an image of heroic resistance to foreign rule. Leaders who fulfilled this image could extract intense loyalty and enormous sacrifice from a broad spectrum of the population. Those leaders who succumbed to foreign pressure, collaborated with foreign rulers, or accommodated foreigners for personal gain suffered self-doubt and weak support. No foreign power could put its imprint on the Vietnamese without provoking a strong response.

Direct colonial rule began in 1858 with a series of French military thrusts. By 1883, the whole of Vietnam was under French control and administered as part of French Indochina. The takeover was resisted at each step, first by the Vietnamese imperial army, later by popularly supported rebellions led by local leaders. A major rebellion under the putative leadership of the boy-Emperor Ham Nghi, though instigated by the mandarinate (i.e., the Confucian intelligentsia), broke out in 1885. Significantly, however, these and other uprisings led by traditional elites occurred against Ham Nghi's wishes. Not only did these uprisings fail, they lacked imperial sanction. Traditional economic and community life were also undermined by colonial taxation, an intrusive colonial bureaucracy, the commercialization of agriculture, new patterns of landholding, and urbanization. As a result, by the end of the nineteenth century, the traditional Vietnamese order was discredited.

A new generation of the intelligentsia launched a search for other ways to come to terms with the West and Western colonial rule. This search led some to surrender to French tutelage, some to study abroad, and some to concoct or adopt doctrines strange to Vietnam, such as parliamentary democracy and Marxism. Though this search kept the flame of patriotism alive, it also fragmented the intelligentsia. Loosely united in a belief that Vietnam should be independent, the intelligentsia was deeply divided over which leader, party, or doctrine should reconstruct Vietnamese society in the postcolonial future.

It was against this background that Ho Chi Minh and a number of other young Vietnamese were attracted to socialism following the Soviet October Revolution. Particularly seductive was Lenin's "Thesis on the National and Colonial Question," which moved Ho to burst out: "Dear martyrs, compatriots! This is what we need, this is the path to our liberation!"[1] What Ho found appealing was Lenin's lucid, uncompromising critique of world imperialism. The "thesis" moreover was linked to a larger body of theory on organization, strategy, and tactics as well as to the program of the newly founded Communist Third International. By comparison, other doctrines then popular in patriotic circles seemed to him muddled, incomplete, and halfhearted. Thus Ho was launched on a revolutionary career. In 1930, he helped to organize the Indochinese Communist party (ICP). A decade later, thanks to demonstrated resolve, a conscious decision (after 1935) to stress patriotic themes, a trickle of cadres trained abroad, and an escape from the French suppression that destroyed rival groups, the ICP was the most effective of all Vietnamese organizations opposed to colonial rule.

In 1941, the party determined that it would seek independence through armed struggle, and it organized a national united front known as the *Viet Nam Doc Lap Dong Minh* (Vietnam Independence League), or Viet Minh for short. While other "nationalist" groups ceased activities, fled to China, or collaborated with the French, the Viet Minh prepared for armed resistance. Greatly assisted by the effects of a raging famine and Japan's surrender to the Allies, the Communists rode to power on the crest of a popular uprising known as the August Revolution of 1945. On September 2, party leaders declared independence for the Democratic Republic of Vietnam (DRV) encompassing all Vietnamese territory from the Chinese border to the farthest point south.

The August Revolution was a great watershed, for it signaled the collapse of colonial power, regardless of France's response. Though other groups contended for a share in the leadership, they appeared on the scene too late or with weak credentials. Like it or not, defense of Vietnam's newfound independence henceforward implied defense of the communist-led DRV. Tens of thousands of youths, many of them from the urban, educated middle classes, rallied to the Viet Minh. Membership in the party, just 5,000 before August, burgeoned, and total armed forces under Viet Minh control grew from 5,000 in August to 70,000 by the year's end.

The DRV had little time to consolidate this achievement, however, for France withheld recognition and reestablished control over Saigon, the country's largest city. France then entered negotiations with the DRV and agreed in March 1946 to recognize the DRV as a "free state" within the French Union. Further negotiations broke down, however, and fighting erupted in December. In the eight years of war that followed, the Viet Minh grew steadily in political and military strength, especially in rural areas. The victory of the Chinese Communist Revolution in 1949 provided the Viet Minh for the first time with a secure rear and source of supply. China also supplied some of the equipment that made possible the Viet Minh's decisive victory over the French at Dien Bien Phu on May 7, 1954. The nine-power Geneva conference, called to end the war in Indochina, held its first session the next day.

U.S. policy meanwhile had undergone a profound change. At the end of World War II, the United States had recognized French sovereignty over Indochina but had been reluctant to support France's war effort unless progress were made toward the establishment of an autonomous Vietnamese alternative to the DRV. As U.S. relations with the Soviet Union deteriorated into the Cold War and communist forces made gains in China, however, U.S. policy became increasingly concerned with the "containment" of communism. Thus, the establishment of the State of Vietnam in 1949 under French aegis (the "Bao Dai solution") removed U.S. objection to helping France, and U.S. aid began flowing to Vietnam in 1950. Finally, the outbreak of the Korean War transformed the French effort, in U.S. estimations, into part of the "free world's" effort to stem communist expansionism. U.S. aid, $10 million in 1950, rose to $1.1 billion by 1954; in that year, the United States underwrote 78 percent of France's war expenses.[2] Thus, long before the trauma of the 1960s, the United States had entered the war.

But the change in U.S. policy at the beginning of the decade was insufficient to reverse French military fortunes. By 1954, the French sought at Geneva only to withdraw, by a face-saving compromise if possible. Fortunately for France, both the Soviet Union and China were anxious at that time to avert a confrontation with the United States, and they pressured the DRV to make concessions. DRV leaders, too, feared deepening U.S. involvement. Contrary to their own assessment of what their battlefield victories entitled them, the Communists agreed to a military truce and regrouping of forces on either side of the 17th parallel. By a series of undertakings known collectively as the Geneva Agreements, the DRV was confined to territory north of that line, its capital in Hanoi. The State of Vietnam was to occupy the territory south of the line, its capital in Saigon. An International Control Commission consisting of representatives of India, Poland, and Canada was to oversee the ceasefire and regroupment.

The Final Declaration of the conference stipulated that the 17th parallel was a provisional military demarcation line, not a political or territorial boundary. Referring to the DRV and State of Vietnam as "representative authorities of Northern and Southern zones of Viet Nam," it provided that in two years, elections should be held to resolve political issues, particularly the issue of reunification. However, of the nine countries that attended the conference, only four (France, Great Britain, the Soviet Union, and China) gave the Final Declaration their unqualified endorsement. The Saigon regime denounced it, while the United States, in a separate statement, promised only to "refrain from the threat or the use of force to disturb" the accords and expressed a commitment to reunification through free elections supervised by the United Nations. It was a messy end to a messy war, a pause designed to let France withdraw, which weakly bound the participants to a lasting settlement.

The Vietnamese Communists for their part accepted partition with deep bitterness. The declaration gave them uncontested control of only half the country, though they had ruled it as a united one from August of 1945 to December of 1946, and the tide of battle had turned in their favor. The partition left a sizeable number of the party's loyal followers at the mercy of a vindictive, anticommunist regime in the South. Only the

Communists had any genuine interest in holding the promised elections on reunification.

Meanwhile the United States moved quickly to fill the vacuum left by France's retreat. The U.S. fear, expressed in the "domino theory," was that if the South fell to the Communists, Vietnam's neighbors would fall in succession or at least accommodate communist influence. The United States therefore took steps to make permanent the arrangements that the Geneva conference had declared should be temporary. The Southeast Asia Treaty Organization (SEATO), organized in September 1954, unilaterally offered protection to South Vietnam, which was prohibited by the Geneva Agreements from joining military alliances. The United States extended direct military assistance to the Saigon regime, including an advisory group whose numbers soon surpassed the limits placed at Geneva on such personnel. In June 1955, the United States asserted that it was not "a party to the Geneva armistice agreements,"[3] and that it supported Saigon's refusal to consult with Hanoi about elections on the grounds that elections could never be free in the North. In October, the United States approved the proclamation of a new constitution that established the Republic of Vietnam with a president holding almost dictatorial powers. As they watched the United States stake its prestige on a noncommunist South, the Communists realized, if they had ever doubted it, that elections on reunification would never be held. They also realized that the liberation of half the country from U.S. domination, as they saw it, might well require them to resume armed struggle.

Communist leaders knew that engaging in such a struggle risked retaliation from the world's greatest military power. Some flinched at the prospect, but when the moment of decision arrived, in 1959, most communist leaders were confident. There were several reasons for their confidence: (1) their victory over France in the First Indochina War; (2) their perception that in Saigon the United States had chosen an ally that was more a liability than an asset; (3) their conviction that the growing strength of liberation movements worldwide gradually would isolate, divert, and deplete U.S. power; and (4) the faith, which the triumph over France had done much to confirm, that the sheer will of politically motivated masses could prevail over a technologically superior adversary. Lastly, the Communists believed they had no choice but to incur the risk of U.S. response if they wished to "complete" Vietnam's independence.

As things turned out, the United States was able to prolong and intensify the war and to strengthen the South Vietnamese regime on whose side it had intervened. But the United States was unable in a few years to reshape what a century of colonial rule had wrought. That century, by 1954, had left Southern Vietnamese society—much more than Northern—deeply divided. The part of Vietnam that embraced the Mekong Delta, what the French called Cochinchina, had been the first region to fall under colonial rule. There the colonial economy had made the deepest inroads: it had linked villages to external markets, set the commercial city against the agricultural countryside, sharply increased debt and tenancy, and exacerbated inequalities. Nowhere else in Vietnam had so many people sought security in affiliation with millennial sects. To these sectarian groups were added, in 1954, a sizeable Catholic minority drawn from all three of Vietnam's traditionally recognized regions, the north, center, and south. The enlargement of the Catholic minority deepened the cleavages in South Vietnamese society. There was no "South Vietnamese" national consciousness, only a highly fragmented society, arbitrarily divided from its other half to facilitate France's retreat.

As time passed, the diverse fragments of South Vietnamese society sorted themselves into three broad political categories. On Saigon's side stood the former civil servants, military officers, and landowning elites who had no future under communism. Some fairly sizeable portion of the South's population also preferred this group to the Communists, though never unconditionally and seldom with enthusiasm. Leading the revolutionary side was the Communist party (with its Central Committee in Hanoi), which had broad support in the North and a branch in the South. In rural areas where the Viet Minh had been strong during the war against France, the party enjoyed active support or sympathy. The revolution also appealed to those peasants who perceived themselves as victims of predatory landlords and unjust government policies. Others such as a smattering of noncommunist intellectuals, monks, and discontented ethnic minorities aligned themselves with the revolution in reaction against government repression or the U.S. presence. Between these two groups, in various postures of neutrality, stood an array of splinter groups that dreamt of alternatives to both Saigon and the Communists. These groups articulated what was perhaps the sentiment of the majority of the population, but the groups had no organizational core, no outstanding leaders, and no coherent program. Foreign observers who dubbed these groups and the populations for which they stood the "Third Force" imputed to them a unity, power, and purpose they never possessed. They were simply the amorphous middle, pushed and pulled from both sides by Saigon and the Communists.

The war likewise encroached geographically upon all of Indochina. Though Vietnam, with nearly five times the population of Laos and Cambodia combined, was the natural epicenter of conflict, the major contestants treated all three countries as a single strategic unit. This perspective had come easily to the French, the colonial masters of the region. It had come later to the Vietnamese Communists, not from determination to succeed to French power as France and the United States supposed, but because French forces based in Laos and Cambodia had attacked their mountain redoubts. From that time onward, the Communists treated Indochina as a strategic unity and regarded denial of Laos and Cambodia to their enemies as fundamental to achieving objectives inside Vietnam. Thus, U.S. efforts to attack the Vietnamese Communists through Laos and Cambodia were certain to draw the United States more deeply into war all over Indochina. All that U.S. military strategy could do was to make the war bigger.

NOTES

1. Ho Chi Minh, "The Path Which Led Me to Leninism," in *Ho Chi Minh on Revolution,* Bernard B. Fall, ed. (New York: Praeger, 1967), p. 6.

2. Neil Sheehan et al., eds., *The Pentagon Papers* (New York: Bantam Books, 1971), p. 10.

3. Statement by Secretary of State John Foster Dulles at a press conference, June 28, 1955, quoted in *Viet-Nam Crisis: A Documentary History, Vol. I: 1940–1956,* Allan W. Cameron, ed. (Ithaca, N.Y.: Cornell University Press, 1971), p. 378. Dulles was certainly correct if by "armistice agreements" he meant only the truce document, which was negotiated and signed solely by the military representatives of France and the DRV. But his position was at least debatable if he meant to include the Final Declaration, which the United States had pledged to uphold. Though not bound by formal signature, the United States did strive during the 1950s to portray its support of Saigon as consistent with the Geneva Agreements and to disguise steps that were not.

2

Vietnam Between Two Wars

The Geneva Agreements gave combatants 300 days to assemble in "regrouping zones" and civilians the same 300 days to choose on which side of the 17th parallel they wished to live. As French forces regrouped in Northern ports, nearly 900,000 Vietnamese headed for the South. About two-thirds were Catholics, led by their priests and egged on by U.S.-supplied leaflets that said "Christ has gone to the South." The remainder for the most part were businessmen and former employees of the colonial administration who, like the Catholics, feared communist reprisals. Meanwhile, an estimated 87,000 People's Army troops and 43,000 civilians moved from the South to the North.

Among those who went north was Do Van Buu.[1] A twenty-year-old platoon commander in 1954, Buu had joined the Viet Minh at age fifteen. On October 26, 1954, Buu's unit and other elements of the People's Army 108th regiment boarded a Polish ship at Qui Nhon for regroupment in the North. Buu regrouped because his superiors told him to do so. Besides, he recalled, he was told he would be given an opportunity to continue his education and perhaps to meet Ho Chi Minh, and would return home in two years when elections reunified the country. On this last point, Buu had the personal word of the popular zone political commissar Nguyen Chanh, who addressed Buu's unit just before it boarded ship: "Comrades," Chanh said, "do not worry! If we do not return by peaceful means we will return by blood, but I assure you we will return to the South!"

Chanh's promise was kept . . . by blood. When Buu returned to the South in 1962, the peace that followed Geneva was long over, if it could be said to have existed at all.

THE RESURRECTION OF NGO DINH DIEM

In 1954, the Communists had reason to be confident, not so much because of the promised elections as because of conditions in the South. What passed for a government was a shambles. The "generals" had only recently elevated themselves from the noncommissioned ranks of French auxiliary forces to command an incompetent army. Regional commanders ignored instructions from the center, while in Saigon a rabble of personal cliques thwarted consensus or decision. The chief-of-staff, General Nguyen Van Hinh, openly vied for power with French encouragement. The bureaucracy, a colonial relic steeped in corruption and lethargy, administered little outside the province and district capitals. Wealthy, educated individuals who might have looked for salvation in an anticommunist regime showed more concern for their villas in France. Few people of talent saw much point in making a personal sacrifice for what seemed a lost cause.

Onto the bridge of this sinking ship stepped Ngo Dinh Diem, man of destiny in the eyes of few but quite possibly the only person with sufficient prestige and ability to organize an anticommunist regime in Saigon at that time. Born in Hue in 1901 to a Catholic family noted for its Confucian sense of duty to emperor and country, Diem's first ambition had been to be a priest, and as a result, he always would look upon government service as a calling.[2] After his graduation at the top of his class in 1921 from the French School of Administration in Hanoi, Diem joined the remnant imperial civil service of Annam. At the tender age of twenty-eight, he was appointed province chief, and in 1933, he leapt over many of his seniors to become minister of the interior to Emperor Bao Dai. In the latter position he worked with uncommon industry and integrity but soon resigned when French obstructionism and court intrigue undermined his efforts. Diem then withdrew from public life to read, pray, and prune roses. He sat out World War II, one of the nationalist figures whom the Japanese "protected" from the French, who suspected him of pro-Japanese sympathies. Ho Chi Minh offered him a position in the DRV government in 1946, but Diem, who blamed the deaths of a brother and a nephew on the Viet Minh, refused. In 1950, after four more years of seclusion in Hue, Diem left Vietnam, he claimed, under a Viet Minh death sentence for refusal to cooperate with the Viet Minh and travelled widely before settling at Maryknoll Seminary in Lakewood, New Jersey.

Up to this point, Diem's reputation had rested largely on his service in and resignation from Bao Dai's administration. The resignation in particular had given him standing as a patriot within a limited circle of elite nationalists. His subsequent retreat and seclusion, however, were gestures from Confucian tradition, not expressions of modern nationalist ideology. For Diem, the mandarin, political leadership meant rule by example, precept, and paternalism. His Catholic upbringing reinforced rather than replaced the Confucian tendency to base authority on doctrine, morality, and hierarchy. Utterly alien to him were the concepts of compromise, power-sharing, and popular participation. He was in fact the heir to a dying tradition, member of an elite that had been superbly prepared by birth, training, and experience to lead a Vietnam that no longer existed.

Diem returned to Vietnam from self-imposed exile to become premier of South Vietnam in July 1954. If, as alleged, the United States engineered his appointment in a move to supplant French influence, it could not have done so with much enthusiasm. Diem's U.S. backers were few, and the U.S. mission in Saigon, though charged with shoring up an anticommunist government, was divided over whether Diem was the man to head it. Because Diem lacked internal support, his prospects for staying in office seemed dim. The United States was not much less surprised than France when Diem, by divide-and-rule tactics, succeeded in eliminating his rivals in the government. Diem then turned on his remaining enemies, principal among which were the politico-religious sects.

Large parts of the countryside had remained under the control of these sects since the war. The largest, with some 2 million adherents, was the Cao Dai. Organized in crude emulation of the Catholic Church and professing a syncretic religion, the Cao Dai controlled the territory west of Saigon with an army of 25,000 men. The Hoa Hao, a millenarian Buddhist movement in existence only since 1939, held sway with an armed force of 15,000 men and 1 million followers over much of the Mekong Delta. Both sects enjoyed popular support in the areas they controlled, and both had flourished while the French had supported them as a counterweight to the Viet Minh and left them to manage their own affairs. Even Saigon had slid into the hands of a mafia-like sect called the Binh Xuyen, which ran gambling, prostitution, opium dens, protection rackets, and the police force. By war's end, these groups controlled sizeable fiefdoms that their leaders, grown rich and powerful on the proceeds, were loathe to relinquish to the new government.

These were potent adversaries for any leader as isolated as Diem. What saved him was intrasect rivalry and timely U.S. support. With some $12 million secretly supplied by the CIA, Diem bought off key Hoa Hao and Cao Dai leaders and absorbed some of their troops into his own army. Then in March 1955, Diem ordered the closing of the Binh Xuyen's gambling halls, brothels, and opium dens. Deprived of income, the Binh Xuyen precipitated a showdown in the streets of Saigon. Diem's shaky army held, and the Binh Xuyen were defeated.

Diem moved quickly to consolidate these victories by organizing a referendum in October 1955 on the question of whether to continue the constitutional monarchy under Bao Dai or establish a republic under himself. Some 450,000 registered voters in Saigon-Cholon were said to have cast 605,025 votes, 98 percent of them for Diem.[3] A year later, after another rigged election to satisfy U.S. demands for a nod toward democracy, a constituent assembly promulgated a constitution for the Republic of Vietnam (RVN) and installed Diem as president.

THE REPUBLIC OF VIETNAM

THE U.S. COMMITMENT

The U.S. commitment was not at first to Diem but to shoring up an anticommunist regime. General J. Lawton Collins, appointed U.S. ambassador to Saigon in December 1954, frankly doubted Diem was suitable to head the Saigon government and had agreed with the French High Commissioner Paul Ely that Diem should be jettisoned at the earliest possible moment.[4] But there had been no alternative, at least not one on which the United States and France could agree. This void permitted a clutch of people in the U.S. mission who did not share Collins' opinion to work quietly for Diem's survival. Probably the most enthusiastic of Diem's supporters was Colonel (later Major General) Edward G. Lansdale, the former advertising executive and air force officer turned secret agent who had helped Philippine President Ramon Magsaysay to suppress the Huk rebellion of 1945–1948. Immortalized in *The Pentagon Papers* as the mastermind of a plot to bring Hanoi to a standstill by sugaring its petrol supply, Lansdale was reputed at the time to be a counterinsurgency expert and skilled intelligence operative. It was Lansdale who headed off one coup against Diem by offering the plotters free trips to Manila; Lansdale who raised the money to bribe the sects; and Lansdale who journeyed into the jungle to offer the bribe. Lansdale's timely interventions probably staved off Diem's early fall. Before long, U.S. leaders committed to anticommunism felt they had no choice but to be committed to Diem as well.

To grasp why U.S. leaders felt bound to commit themselves to Diem in some fashion, it is necessary to recall that at that time in the United States anticommunism was at its peak, bolstered by a heightened sense of mission in Asia. The conquest of Japan and collapse of colonial power had confirmed U.S. presumptions of a "manifest destiny" to emancipate and protect the "free" peoples of Asia. The United States also perceived that Soviet-inspired revolutions posed a long-range threat to the free world, and this led U.S. policymakers to widen the strategy of "containment" and resist communist influence everywhere. At the time, this strategy had not seemed excessively ambitious, as the U.S. military presence in Asia was so superior that successful challenges to its supremacy were difficult to imagine. The Chinese Revolution and Korean War then aroused fears that the United States would stand alone against a joint Sino-Soviet threat if it did not demonstrate firm support for its allies, and so the United States supplied $3.5 billion in economic and military assistance to the French war in Indochina from

1950 to 1954. Meanwhile, at home, U.S. leaders found themselves boxed into virulent anticommunist postures by their own Cold War rhetoric and the McCarthyite red scare. No U.S. leader then or for years to come could have written off the already sizeable U.S. investment in "saving" Vietnam without inviting the charge of being "soft on Communism." Before Diem arrived on the scene, the United States was already committed, and that commitment could only deepen.

So it was that the United States set out to turn South Vietnam into an anticommunist bastion. To circumvent Geneva's prohibition of military alliances, the Southeast Asia Treaty Organization, in September 1954, unilaterally bestowed on Vietnam, Laos, and Cambodia the right to request protection from SEATO in the event of attack. In October, the United States commenced direct military assistance to the Saigon regime. The U.S. army training cycle and field manuals became the standards for Saigon's army. Because the Geneva Agreements had set strict limits on the number of foreign military personnel permitted in either half of Vietnam, the United States augmented its military assistance mission with personnel on "temporary duty" and "loan" that were not clearly proscribed by the Geneva Agreements. A Temporary Equipment Recovery Mission (TERM), ostensibly sent to dispose of surplus material (previously supplied to the French Union forces) with the approval of the International Control Commission, had as its "real assignment to aid in developing an adequate and effective South Vietnamese logistical system."[5] All major South Vietnamese forces had TERM personnel assigned to them for the purpose of developing military training courses, selecting officers for advanced training in the United States, and reorganizing the units along U.S. lines. By 1956, the U.S. Military Advisory Assistance Group (MAAG), the U.S. military aid mission, plus TERM personnel exceeded the limit placed on foreign military advisers at Geneva by 350.

The United States also provided growing amounts of economic, technical, and administrative aid. By 1956, South Vietnam was receiving $270 million per year, which made it the recipient of more U.S. aid per capita than any other country in the world except Laos and Korea. The United States, however, was too preoccupied with the strategic threat of communism to care much about how its client used this aid. Far from strengthening U.S. influence over Diem, the aid encouraged Diem to rule as he saw fit.

Diem gave in easily to his authoritarian and nepotistic instincts. Though his regime needed desperately to broaden its base, he relied for his main support on fellow Catholics, particularly recent arrivals from the North. One brother, Ngo Dinh Can, headed the regime's secretive cadre party; another brother, Ngo Dinh Nhu, served as the president's closest adviser. Nhu's wife virtually dictated legislation to the National Assembly. An Anti-communist Denunciation Campaign launched in 1955 to "reeducate" former Viet Minh was in fact a pretext for suppressing all forms of dissent. The number of politically motivated executions in the South during the 1950s probably exceeded the number in the North.[6] Meanwhile, with U.S. approval, Diem ignored DRV Premier Pham Van Dong's messages proposing consultations on reunification as stipulated at Geneva. By 1956, Diem's personal power was secure, and U.S. support was assured.

THE SOUTHERN REVOLUTION IN COMMUNIST STRATEGY

The Communists meanwhile had been preoccupied with consolidating their own regime in the North. Though much better equipped than Diem to do this, they too had their problems. The French had gutted basic services and sabotaged or dismantled industries as they withdrew from the North. Many skilled people had fled, and party cadres found their guerrilla skills inappropriate for the administration of cities. In the hills, ethnic minorities that had fought alongside the French held out against the government. Land reform and local administrative reorganization were completed in late 1956, but involved such "excesses" that the Central Committee felt compelled to offer self-criticism and to unseat the party secretary-general, Truong Chinh.[7] About the same time, Catholic residents of one district in Nghe An province staged a brief rebellion that required suppression by a People's Army division. A group of prominent writers and intellectuals, apparently inspired by de-Stalinization campaigns then under way in other communist countries, subjected party policies to scathing ridicule in two briefly published journals. This last incident was not negligible, as the critics included individuals, some from the military, who had long supported the revolution. Faced with such problems in the North, party leaders must have felt their hands were full and that reunification would have to depend on the elections promised at Geneva.

That certainly was Hanoi's public position, and Hanoi evidently was willing to hold the elections if Diem agreed. Party leaders, however, were not so unrealistic as to believe that Diem would agree to elections unless circumstances required him to do so. Saigon's representatives at Geneva, after all, had denounced the Geneva Agreements, and the United States had given only a tepid promise of noninterference. The Communists therefore placed their hopes for reunification in the difficulties they expected Diem would face. These difficulties, the Communists anticipated, would make it impossible for Diem to establish a stable government. He would have to invite "progressives" into the government who would demand that he implement the Geneva accords. Or the sects might stage a coup and precipitate chaos in which the party and its sympathizers would be able to gain power. Diem's refusal to discuss elections, party leaders calculated, would only reveal him as the enemy of "democracy" and "unity," thus isolating him and adding to his difficulties. If all this failed to bring about reunification, there were other options, and by early 1956, it was apparent to party leaders that the time had come to consider these.

The exact role of the party in what subsequently occurred was once a subject of sharp controversy. One theory, popular among critics of U.S. involvement, held that the revolution in the South began as a spontaneous uprising against a repressive regime and that the party only gradually gained predominance within it. The opposed theory, advanced by Washington and Saigon, was that the party masterminded everything from the beginning, and the upheaval was really "aggression from the North." Neither theory was satisfactory. The former exaggerated popular initiatives and ignored the party's role in creating the organizations that led the revolution to victory. The latter was blind to well-founded grievances on which the party capitalized and falsely depicted the party as a strictly Northern organization. Today, thanks to massive evidence that includes documents published in Hanoi,[8] it is possible to be quite precise about the party's objectives, strategies, and actions.

Somewhat less clear is the role played by the party's Southern membership in making key decisions. Some members who remained in the South after 1954 are known to have opposed the concessions made at Geneva. Those concessions required the southern branch of the party to bear all the risks of their implementation, while the North advanced peacefully to socialism. When Diem succeeded in eliminating his rivals and opened a vigorous campaign to exterminate Communists, a number of Southern members demanded that the party give higher priority to the "Southern revolution." At no time, however, did the Southern membership constitute a separate Communist party or make policy independently of the Central Committee in Hanoi.

In 1954, the party organization in the South numbered between 50,000 and 60,000 members. Many took advantage of the provisions of the Geneva Agreements to register with the government and take up a legal existence, while others continued to operate covertly. Natural attrition, a party program to weed out substandard members, and, increasingly, the depredations of Diem's police sharply reduced Southern membership. By 1956, party membership in the South was about 15,000.[9] With their numbers falling, morale worsening, and prospects for reunification dimming, some Southern cadres began to demand a new policy that would permit greater use of armed force. In March 1956, the Nam Bo regional committee (which was responsible for coordinating party activities in the provinces of former Cochinchina) recommended resuscitating Southern armed forces to a level of twenty regular battalions plus provincial and guerrilla units "to support other activities," that is, to provide a shield behind which cadres could continue their work.[10]

The head of the regional committee at the time was Le Duan, a member of the party Political Bureau and a long-time specialist in southern affairs. Born in 1908 in Quang Tri province, Duan had spent much of the 1930s in prison, along with other future party leaders, first in Hanoi and then on the island of Poulo

Condore (Con Son). By 1939, he was a member of the Central Committee and may have been implicated, while serving on the Saigon party committee, in the abortive Nam Ky uprising of November 1940 that resulted in the decimation of the hitherto strong southern branch. Returned to prison, he escaped or was released in 1945, resumed activity in the south, and was appointed head of the Central Committee Directorate for the South when this organ was created out of the Nam Bo regional committee in 1951. Though the directorate reverted to regional committee status at the end of the war with France, Duan remained in charge and built a reputation as the "flame of the South" for his ardent advocacy of reunification. His reward, when his views gained ascendancy, was election in 1960 to the post of party first secretary.[11]

Most party leaders were reluctant in 1956 to alter course significantly, however. They did not wish to jeopardize development in the North, which was then just beginning to show results. Nor did they wish to provoke the United States as long as assurance of support from North Vietnam's allies was not forthcoming. China was absorbed in its own reconstruction and was not inclined, after the Korean War, to let itself be dragged into another conflict. The Soviet Union for its part opposed revolutionary offensives that might require it to provide a strategic shield or draw it into confrontation with the United States.[12] The Soviets went so far as to delete "Indochina" from the agenda of the 1955 Geneva foreign ministers' meeting after that item had been placed there at the request of Vietnam. In 1957, the Soviet Union was to propose the admission of *both* North and South Vietnam to the United Nations—a "two Vietnams" policy that directly contradicted Hanoi's wishes. The Vietnamese party stood quite alone in its advocacy of reunification at that time.

After heated debate, the party reached an awkward compromise. The Central Committee, meeting in April 1956, bowed to the 20th Congress of the Communist party of the Soviet Union (CPSU) in allowing that socialism might be achieved by peaceful means, but it made an important reservation: "Where the bourgeois class still possesses a strong military and police apparatus and resolutely uses weapons to suppress the revolutionary movement, a fierce armed struggle to win political power will be unavoidable, so the proletarian class must prepare in advance."[13] A peaceful transition might be possible in some countries, the Vietnamese Communists agreed, but not in all, and it was obvious which situation they felt existed in the South.

The party's Political Bureau, meeting in June, nevertheless made clear that for a time the emphasis was to be on nonviolent action. The task of explaining this decision to Southern cadres fell to Le Duan. Once he was back in the South in August, Duan took up this task in a secretly circulated pamphlet, "Path to Revolution in the South."[14] Southern cadres, Le Duan wrote, were to make no immediate attempt to overthrow the Diem regime or to stage armed uprisings but rather were to rebuild their movement. A weak movement would be unable to take advantage of favorable political trends. Le Duan therefore instructed cadres to exploit contradictions that arose from Diem's suppression of popular aspirations and to employ the themes of "peace and reunification," "freedom and democracy," and "popular livelihood" in that process. The only permissible form of violence was "armed self-defense" when cadres' lives or the survival of party organs were at stake.

For a while, this approach seemed to work, thanks as much to Diem as to the party. Propaganda attacks by the party on Saigon's opposition to reunification and its dependence on the United States gained some sympathy from people who cared to listen. Probably more effective, however, were the party's attempts to mobilize public opinion against conscription, police surveillance, controls on movement, fraudulent elections, bureaucratic interference in local affairs, arbitrary uses of police power, and corruption—all of which had increased as Diem had consolidated his power. In rural areas, where roughly 1 million peasants were tenants, rents took 30–50 percent of tenants' crops, and landlessness and absentee landlordism were common, the party attacked inequities that government "reforms" did more to preserve than to correct. One such reform, in 1955, had sought to limit rent by requiring written contracts, but contracts forced peasants to whom the Viet Minh had given land to acknowledge that the land they tilled still belonged to the landlords. Another reform, in 1956, set a maximum landholding limit of 100 hectares that guaranteed little redistribution would ever take place. In such a setting, it took little for cadres to convince people, particularly where the Viet Minh had been strong before, that the government was their enemy and revolution their friend.

Yet the Communists were only briefly able to turn this state of affairs to their advantage. After a period of recovery in 1957 and 1958, the party's Southern branch headed into what members were to recall as its "darkest days." This was not the result of more enlightened government policies but rather of Diem's enhanced coercive capability. With the sects suppressed and U.S. assistance growing, Diem had more military, police, and administrative resources to turn against other threats. Gradually his regime penetrated areas from which it long had been excluded and imposed its will by sheer physical presence. Law 10/59, promulgated in May 1959 to punish virtually any kind of involvement with the revolutionary movement, led to sweeping arrests and intimidated the population into avoiding contact with political dissidents of any kind. Cadres not only found it unsafe to carry out their work or to recruit new supporters but also were themselves arrested or killed. As a result, many cadres left the party. Some entire party organs disappeared; most suffered serious losses. Go Vap and Tan Binh districts just outside Saigon, which together had 1,000 party members in 1954 and 385 in 1957, had only 6 in mid-1959. Total party membership in the South fell to about 5,000.[15] Although popular discontent in many areas rose to a point that would satisfy almost any definition of a "revolutionary situation," party members in the South were reluctant to act. They had to think of their survival. Many cadres demanded a change of policy, not just to capitalize on the discontent, but also, perhaps primarily, to save themselves from extinction.

A new party policy began to emerge in spring 1959. Meeting in March, the party Political Bureau issued a directive to establish a revolutionary base in the central highlands for the purpose of helping "political struggle advance to carrying out of limited guerrilla warfare."[16] This was a conditional call-to-arms, however. The 15th Plenum of the party Central Committee, meeting in

May, acknowledged that the struggle eventually would take a violent form, but authorized armed struggle to begin only in combination with political struggle as local circumstances required. This meant armed force could be used to defend party organs and to promote political work. It did not mean Southern organs were to commence a large-scale guerrilla or "people's war." They were instead to "prepare" for a "general uprising" in which armed force would play a secondary, supportive role.

However, the plenum also foresaw that "the uprising of the people in the South" might become a "protracted armed struggle" because of U.S. determination to support Saigon. In this case the Southern revolution might require external support, and the plenum instructed the Central Military Party Committee to set up Group 559, a special unit charged with moving people, weapons, and supplies overland from the North to the South. Group 759, for sea infiltration, appeared in July 1959, and Group 959, to supply the Laotian People's Liberation Army and "Vietnamese volunteers" fighting in Laos, came into being in September 1959.[17] These groups took shape slowly, numbering only a few hundred men each at first, but they formed the basis of what was to become a large and unique logistical complex.

Party leaders eschewed any sharp increase in armed activity, however. Neither the revolutionaries in the South nor the DRV wanted to provoke deeper U.S. involvement in the conflict. Nor were party leaders prepared openly to contradict Moscow's line on "struggle by peaceful means," so long as a largely political strategy leading toward "general uprising" could keep their hopes alive. The plenum therefore authorized just what was necessary to advance the revolution without prematurely exposing it to U.S. retaliation or Soviet criticism. But communist leaders obviously saw where things were headed and were determined to follow through.

THE ARMED STRUGGLE OPTION

Although the party emphasized political struggle until 1959, it had never completely abandoned the armed struggle option. In

1954, the party had left behind in the South enough weapons to arm 6,000 troops and kept intact a few units ranging in size from 50 to 200 men. These hard-core units, composed almost entirely of party members or members of the party's youth affiliate and well-equipped with a full range of light weapons, led a highly clandestine existence in the mountains of Quang Ngai, the U Minh forest, the Plain of Reeds, and swampy areas of the southeast.[18]

The party kept these forces in reserve, hoping no force of its own would be needed. Armed action was left to the sects. If sect forces did not overthrow Diem, party leaders had calculated, sect-inspired turbulence at least would provide a screen for the activities of the party. Though some cadres maintained informal contact with the sects, the leadership apparently considered direct support or cooperation unworkable, even unthinkable.[19] During the First Indochina War, the sects had spurned Viet Minh offers to form a united front or had sided with France; the party had ordered the execution of Hoa Hao leader Huynh Phu So in 1947; and party doctrine defined the sect leaderships as obscurantist, feudal, and anti-patriotic. But Diem's attacks on sect strongholds in spring 1955 sent some 2,000 Binh Xuyen and 500 Cao Dai troops scurrying into former Viet Minh resistance bases for sanctuary.[20] Occurring just before Diem was to declare his opposition to a reunification plebiscite, the flight of sect forces into the arms of the party presented an irresistible opportunity. By helping the sects, the party could keep up pressure on Diem without putting its own forces and innocence at risk.

Thus, in late April 1955, the Political Bureau approved a proposal to "win over" the remnants of the sect troops and their officers.[21] "Former resistance cadres" began training sect units, and some of these units acquired party members as officers. In late 1956, the party organized a General Staff along united front lines for these forces. Operating independently and under loose party guidance, remnant sect units staged a number of violent incidents from December 1956 through mid-1958. However, the party refused to supply the sect forces from its own caches or to merge them with its own secret units, and the sect forces deteriorated rapidly in the face of repression.

"The Resistance army of the religious sects," one semi-official account observed, "dwindled into a mere token force."[22] The party made one last attempt to salvage some sect remnants in late 1958 but concluded that these were too lacking in political reliability, discipline, and determination to serve the party's ends. As sect units disappeared, only a "small number" of sect troops, according to the party's official record, joined the revolutionary armed forces then being assembled in deep secrecy and on a small scale under the party's direct command.[23]

Since June 1956, the Political Bureau had emphasized that political struggle was to "create basic conditions for maintaining and developing armed forces."[24] In response to this policy, the Nam Bo party committee had begun organizing "armed propaganda forces" and had authorized the formation of the first battalion-size unit under party command in the South, Unit 250, which appeared in an old resistance base known as War Zone D in October 1957. By that time the party commanded thirty-seven companies scattered widely throughout the Mekong Delta, mostly in the west. In mid-1958, the Nam Bo party committee organized an Eastern Nam Bo Command to centralize control over that area's three companies of infantry and one of sappers(commandos with special training in demolitions) whose combined total was approximately 350 men.[25]

The party used these forces sparingly. When attacking outposts, the forces coordinated with sect units to mask their true identity. Usually, they only provided security for cadres engaged in political work, i.e., "armed propaganda," or killed "tyrant policemen" for political effect. A separate program, known only to high-level party organs, carried out selective assassinations of individuals considered dangerous to the party.[26] None of these activities met the party's definition of guerrilla war, armed uprising, or people's war.

Many party members in the South found armed action congenial and were impatient to begin. In the central highlands, the Quang Ngai province party committee requested permission to organize armed uprising among discontented ethnic minorities in the western mountains. Permission was granted, apparently to placate an insistent local leadership. In March 1959, the Quang Ngai committee assembled a 45-man guerrilla unit that spearheaded a rash of attacks and demonstrations in Tra Bong district (the "Tra Bong uprising") beginning in August.[27]

The situation was even more combustible in the Mekong Delta. Long-time southern party militant Nguyen Thi Dinh has written that in her native province of Ben Tre police repression and social inequity drove people and cadres alike to yearn for relief by violent means. In an interview with the author in March 1983, she claimed that the harsh repression of the Viet Minh and their families in 1958 and 1959 led to the execution of "thousands" and that the party had difficulty containing the popular demand for armed action. Cadres who were "too enthusiastic about military action" were pleased to learn that the 15th Plenum "had followed exactly the aspirations of the lower levels. . . ."[28] As in Quang Ngai, however, "uprisings," as distinct from sporadic unauthorized retaliation, did not begin in Ben Tre until after the plenum—January 17, 1960, to be exact.

Cadres who had waited for a new policy with such forbearance were quick to test its limits. After a kick-off attack on a trainee regiment of the Army of the Republic of Vietnam (ARVN) 5th division just seven kilometers outside Tay Ninh city on January 26, 1960, the frequency of armed incidents increased rapidly. Typically, small paramilitary units chased out or assassinated local authorities, and party cadres set up new hamlet and village administrations with peasant participation. Although party propaganda exaggerated the degree to which initiative lay with the masses, the ease with which handfuls of armed men put government officials to flight was significant. Not only were these officials unwilling to accept risks that had been the lot of communist cadres for years, they also found that they stood alone amidst a rural population, large portions of which regarded them, not the Communists, as the enemy. The true weakness of the government in the countryside stood revealed, and sizeable areas quickly fell under party control.

THE ORGANIZATIONAL COMPLEX

It was not credible in Vietnam or abroad, however, that such a movement could grow much further on the basis of unorganized mass yearnings and sectarian discontent alone. The party therefore approved plans at its 3rd Congress in September 1960 to set up an overt leadership organ for a "people's democratic national revolution" in the South. This organization, the National Liberation Front of South Vietnam (NLF), was unveiled at a Congress of People's Representatives held on December 20, 1960, in eastern Nam Bo (a "liberated area," in fact). Although thus proclaimed to exist, NLF was not to hold its first formal congress until 1962. The delay was caused, some intelligence analysts claimed, by the Communists' inability to recruit nonparty figures of sufficient stature to hold key posts, though in the end a suitable candidate for chairman was found in Nguyen Huu Tho, a dissident lawyer. What is certain is that the front's responsibility for rallying "broad revolutionary forces" was assigned to it by the party's Political Bureau in a directive dated January 31, 1961.[29] That directive also laid down basic strategy guidance that emphasized the need to strike an appropriate balance between political and military struggle in the South's three strategic areas. In jungles and mountainous areas, stress was to be placed on the military struggle; in lowland areas, approximately equal emphasis was to be given to political and military struggle; while in urban areas, the principal emphasis was to be on political struggle.

The unveiling of the NLF in 1960, fourteen months before its first plenary session, may have been a strategic move by the party to keep pace with events. Certainly the party was under pressure from Southern-based leaders to step up preparations. Revolutionary armed forces that had numbered perhaps 2,000 in 1959 exceeded 10,000 by the beginning of 1961.[30] The Political Bureau directive cited above noted that there was now "practically no possibility that the revolution will develop peacefully." The party needed the NLF to conceal its role in organizing for the conflict it now regarded as inevitable. Armed struggle henceforward was to be "placed on a par" with political struggle where circumstances permitted.

This still was not a call for "people's war," but it did signal an acceleration of the preparations for one. Events in Laos, as well as in South Vietnam, were forcing the Communists' hand. In Laos, following a mandate of the 1954 Geneva conference, the Royal Lao government and the Hanoi-backed Lao Communists (commonly referred to as the Pathet Lao) had reached agreement in November 1957 to form a neutral coalition government. Two Pathet Lao leaders had joined the cabinet of the neutralist Prince Souvanna Phouma, 1,500 Pathet Lao troops (one-quarter of their total) had been integrated into the Royal Lao Army, and Pathet Lao–supported candidates had won nine seats in partial elections for the National Assembly.

Up to this point Hanoi could only approve because these arrangements gave North Vietnam influence and security on its western flank, but this situation deeply perturbed Lao rightists who turned to Thailand and the United States for help. The United States provided encouragement and funds to rightists in the Lao Army, who then ousted Souvanna Phouma in July 1958 and subsequently arrested Pathet Lao members of the government. With Lao neutrality at an end, the Pathet Lao resumed military action, and the country slid into civil war. By August 1959, Thailand, as sensitive as the DRV to instability in Laos, had sent in troops, with U.S. approval, to help the rightists.[31] A U.S.-inspired coup in December further consolidated the rightists' hold on Vientiane, and the Royal Army attacked Pathet Lao strongholds. These developments, occurring just as the Vietnamese Communists were beginning preparations for armed struggle in the South, were a serious diversion for Hanoi. The Vietnamese could not stand idly by as their Lao clients suffered humiliation, nor could they afford to permit a U.S.-backed regime in Vientiane to menace their own access to the Lao mountains, a vital link between North and South Vietnam in the event of war.

The Pathet Lao responded by evicting the Royal Army from Sam Neua province in September 1960 and from Phong Saly province and the Plaine des Jarres in January 1961. In fact, the Pathet Lao had some help. Vietnamese publications now openly admit that "Vietnamese volunteer troops" fought "in coordination with" (actually, at the head or in place of) the Pathet Lao.[32] The effect was to consolidate communist bases from which to promote revolution in both Laos and South Vietnam. Thus, the United States and its Laotian clients supplied the Vietnamese and their Laotian clients with a pretext, if one were needed, for securing a logistical corridor through Laos to the borders of South Vietnam.

On February 15, 1961, communist military cadres met in War Zone D to transmit the Political Bureau's instructions to unify all armed units into a single People's Liberation Armed Force (PLAF). The party military committee for the Nam Bo region was designated the Liberation Army Command of South Vietnam.[33] Tran Luong, leader of the party in southern central Vietnam at the time of the Tra Bong uprising and a full member of the party Central Committee, became the command's first head. More Central Committee members, including a clutch of People's Army (PAVN) generals with Southern experience, began arriving from the North shortly after September 1961 when the Nam Bo and Trung Bo party committees merged to reconstitute the Central Committee Directorate for the South (*Trung uong cuc mien nam*), which had been in operation from 1951 to 1954. As its name implied, COSVN (the directorate's widely known acronym in mistranslated English) was a forward element of the party's Central Committee, i.e., an extension of the Central Committee constituted to provide authoritative direction at a distance from the "rear." By the time the NLF opened its 1st Congress on February 16, 1962, COSVN exercised control through the Liberation Army Command over about 17,000 PLAF troops.

These were the forces that came to be known as the Viet Cong, or VC for short. Actually, no revolutionary organization in the South ever called itself by this name. Diem concocted the term, a contraction of *Viet-nam Cong-san,* meaning Vietnamese Communist, and used it to disparage a broad spectrum of his enemies.

The most important fact, however, is that with very slender resources the party was able to recover so quickly from the "dark days" of 1959. It did this, in large measure, simply by authorizing Southern cadres to protect themselves with armed force and to spearhead "local uprisings" where Saigon authorities were vulnerable. A modest increment in support given by the North also helped, as we will see. These steps would not have produced the results they did had it not been for the growing popular resentment of Diem's personal dictatorship in the cities and the social and economic inequities that his regime sustained in the countryside. Diem and his elite landholding and bureaucratic supporters supplied the "contradictions" for the party to exploit; thus, the party was able to attract nonparty supporters, a few of whom appeared in the NLF leadership.

Organizations like the NLF and the PLAF did not spring like wildflowers from the tinder-dry padi fields, however. "Former resistance cadres" living in the South did not found the NLF on their own initiative. Nor did Diem's many opponents spontaneously coalesce to form it. Tinder-dry though the fields were, decisions on how and when to put them to the torch were made by the party Central Committee. The NLF was just what its name declared—a front, nominally a coalition but in practice a facade. Both the NLF and the PLAF were formed and chose leaders in accordance with party directives.

Ironically, the move to armed struggle reflected party leaders' abiding hope that reunification could be attained by some means short of war. What they had in mind was not Saigon's voluntary acceptance of negotiations and elections—they were too realistic, especially after 1956, for that—but an accumulation of popular antipathy to the Diem regime, helped along by the party's "political struggle." They hoped these circumstances would lead to a mass uprising, a coalition government, and a transition to reunification under party rule. This hope grew partly out of a faith that something like the August Revolution could be made to happen again, partly out of a need to reconcile conflicting strategic requirements. On the one hand, the party needed to maintain good relations with an ally bent on "peaceful coexistence" and avoid provoking the United States. On the other hand, it had to save the party's Southern branch from extinction in order to keep alive the hope of reunification. These requirements could be reconciled only by minimizing the North's involvement and maximizing Southern self-reliance. It was in the party's interest to rely as far as possible on popular political pressures in the South to build toward the desired event. A situation similar to what the party envisioned did begin to unfold in 1963, but it occurred largely outside the party's control.

NOTES

1. Da Van Buu is a pseudonym. Buu was interviewed by the author in Saigon in 1973.

2. See Denis Warner, *The Last Confucian* (New York: Macmillan, 1963), pp. 84–106; Frances Fitzgerald, *Fire in the Lake* (Boston: Atlantic Monthly Publications, 1972), pp. 80–84, 98–99; and on Diem's wartime role, see Huynh Kim Khanh, *Vietnamese Communism 1925–1945* (Ithaca, N.Y.: Cornell University Press, 1982), pp. 245, 295, 295fn9.

3. Bernard Fall, *The Two Viet-Nams* (Boulder, Colo.: Westview, 1985), p. 257.

4. George C. Herring, *America's Longest War: The United States and Vietnam, 1950–1975* (New York: John Wiley, 1979), pp. 52–53.

5. James Lawton Collins, Jr., *The Development and Training of the South Vietnamese Army, 1950–1957* (Washington, D.C.: Department of the Army, 1975), pp. 4, 7.

6. Alexander Kendrick, in *The Wound Within* (Boston: Little, Brown, 1974), p. 112, cites a figure of 75,000 for the South. Regarding the North, see note 7.

7. The errors of excess mentioned in party sources were mainly the result of rigid application of class criteria. Although somewhere between 3,000 and 15,000 people were executed, some on trumped-up charges, the slaughter of 500,000 described in anticommunist propaganda never took place. See Edwin E. Moise, "Land Reform and Land Reform Errors in North Vietnam," *Pacific Affairs* 49 (Spring 1976), p. 78.

8. War Experience Recapitulation Committee of the High-Level Military Institute, *Cuoc khang chien chong My cuu nuoc 1954–1975: nhung su kien quan su* [The Anti-U.S. Resistance War for National Salvation 1954–1975: Military Events] (Hanoi: People's Army Publishing House, 1980), translated by the Joint Publications Research Service JPRS no. 80,968 (Washington, D.C.: GPO, June 3, 1982). Hereinafter text is cited as *The Anti-U.S. Resistance War,* with page numbers for the JPRS translation.

9. The figure is from an internal party document cited in Carlyle A. Thayer, "Southern Vietnamese Revolutionary Organizations and the Vietnam Workers' Party: Continuity and Change, 1954–1974," *Communism in Indochina: New Perspectives,* J. J. Zasloff and M. Brown, eds. (Lexington, Mass.: Heath, 1975), p. 34. For detailed discussion of the party's fortunes in this period, see Thayer, pp. 33–46, and Jeffrey Race, *War Comes to Long An* (Berkeley: University of California Press, 1972), pp. 27–43, 80–104.

10. Department of State, *Working Paper on the North Vietnamese Role in South Vietnam: Captured Documents and Interrogation Reports* (Washington, D.C.: Department of State, May 1968), item 19.

11. I am indebted to Paul Quinn-Judge for key facts used in this sketch.

12. Gareth Porter, "Vietnam and the Socialist Camp: Center or Periphery?" in *Vietnamese Communism in Comparative Perspective,* W. S. Turley, ed. (Boulder, Colo.: Westview Press, 1980), pp. 225–264.

13. Plenum resolution quoted in *The Anti-U.S. Resistance War,* p. 16.

14. Jeffrey Race collection of Vietnamese documents, document no. 1002, Center for Research Libraries, Chicago.

15. Republic of Vietnam, Joint General Staff J-2 intelligence report, "Study of the Activation and Activities of R" (Saigon, July 17, 1969), p. 16. Also see Thayer, "Southern Vietnamese Revolutionary Organizations," pp. 42–43.

16. *The Anti-U.S. Resistance War,* pp. 28–29.

17. Ibid.

18. Race, *War Comes to Long An,* p. 36.

19. Ibid. Also see Jayne Werner, "Vietnamese Communism and Religious Sectarianism," in Turley, *Vietnamese Communism,* pp. 122–128.

20. Ta Xuan Linh, "How Armed Struggle Began in South Viet Nam," *Vietnam Courier* (March 1974), p. 21; also see Werner, "Vietnamese Communism and Religious Sectarianism," in Turley, *Vietnamese Communism,* pp. 122–128.

21. *The Anti-U.S. Resistance War,* p. 11.

22. Linh, "How Armed Struggle Began," p. 21.

23. *The Anti-U.S. Resistance War,* p. 12.

24. Political Bureau resolution quoted in *The Anti-U.S. Resistance War,* p. 16.

25. Ibid., pp. 22, 24.

26. The "extermination of traitors" (tru gian) program is described in Race, *War Comes to Long An,* pp. 82–83.

27. Pham Thanh Bien, Hong Son, and Do Quang Trinh, "Ve cuoc khoi nghia Tra-bong va mien Tay Quang-ngai mua thu 1959" [On the Tra Bong and Western Quang Ngai Uprising in Autumn 1959], *Nghien cuu Lich su* [Historical Research] (September-October 1972), pp. 19–20; also see Ta Xuan Linh, "Armed Uprisings by Ethnic Minorities along the Truong Son," *Vietnam Courier* (October 1974), p. 19.

28. Nguyen Thi Dinh, *No Other Road to Take,* Mai Elliott, trans. (Ithaca, N.Y.: Cornell University Southeast Asia Program Data Paper no. 102, 1976), p. 62.

29. *The Anti-U.S. Resistance War,* pp. 45–46.

30. Figures are from U.S. intelligence sources cited in *The Pentagon Papers,* Senator Gravel edition (Boston: Beacon, 1971), vol. 2, p. 43.

31. Information from a Thai military source.

32. Nguyen Viet Phuong, "Bo doi Truong son va he thong duong Ho Chi Minh" [The Truong Son Army and the Ho Chi Minh Road System], *Nghien cuu Lich su* [Historical Research] (March-April 1979), pp. 22–30.

33. *The Anti-U.S. Resistance War,* p. 46.

3

Fateful Decisions

The aged monk Quang Duc assumed the lotus position in the middle of a Saigon street. Calmly, without a trace of emotion, Duc sat straightbacked while two assistants drenched him with petrol. Accounts differ as to whether it was Duc or another monk who touched the match to his robes, but within a minute the human bonfire toppled over dead. It was June 11, 1963. In the next two months, four more monks followed Duc into self-immolation. Ostensibly protests against religious discrimination, the burnings were in fact the spearhead of a mass protest against the tyranny of the Diem regime. By November 2, it was Diem who was dead.

The political turmoil in South Vietnam presented the United States with hard choices. First for lack of alternatives, then with genuine enthusiasm, the United States had backed Diem to the hilt. But as his regime had degenerated into a family despotism and as his enemies had grown in number, Diem came to be seen by U.S. policymakers as the problem. The Buddhist protest movement of 1963 only revealed in graphic terms what had been fact all along: Though the Diem regime did not actively persecute Buddhists as its detractors claimed, it was dominated by Catholics, favored Catholics, and like the Catholic colonial regime before it, it was hopelessly alienated from a population that was 90 percent non-Catholic. But popular alienation was a condition to which Diem and his family were oblivious. Diem denounced the Buddhists as communist-inspired, and Madame Nhu, his sister-in-law, applauded what she called "monk barbeques" (a phrase reported in many news dispatches at the time) with morbid glee. Madame Nhu's husband, Ngo Dinh Nhu, advised Diem to suppress the Buddhists as mercilessly as he had suppressed the sects. Diem, manipulated by Nhu, attempted to do so. The result taxed U.S. patience with Diem but not with the project of "saving" Vietnam. The U.S. commitment was too firm; its reputation was too conspicuously on trial for the United States to steal away, or so the vast majority of U.S. leaders believed, especially the man who succeeded Dwight Eisenhower as president.

KENNEDY'S WAR

John F. Kennedy took office as president of the United States on January 20, 1961. As a senator, Kennedy had been one of the Catholics to whom Francis Cardinal Spellman had introduced Ngo Dinh Diem during the latter's stay in the United States. Kennedy also had worked with the so-called "Vietnam lobby" to promote Diem's candidacy for the premiership in 1954.[1] A vociferous opponent of assisting the French at Dien Bien Phu, by 1956 Kennedy was arguing at a conference sponsored by the American Friends of Vietnam that "Vietnam represents the cornerstone of the Free World in Southeast Asia, the keystone in the arch, the finger in the dike" against the "red tide of Communism," a model of "political liberty" and an "inspiration to those seeking to obtain and maintain their liberty in all parts of Asia—and indeed the world."[2]

On taking office, the Kennedy team saw Vietnam, as it saw the world, in Cold War terms. It mattered not whether the men in Washington were Republicans or Democrats; they were legatees of the U.S. postwar preoccupation with a communist challenge and the U.S. mission to lead the "free world" against it. Although Sino-Soviet frictions had not yet bloomed into a full-fledged dispute, local communist-led insurgencies still appeared, from Washington, to be the advancing tentacles of a hegemonic, monolithic bloc. When Soviet Premier Nikita Khrushchev declared, just two weeks before Kennedy's inauguration, that Moscow would support "wars of national liberation," Kennedy's advisers concluded that a new communist global offensive was about to begin. This was a challenge to which the United States, in Kennedy's view, had no choice but to respond. Accepting without question the assumptions of "containment" strategy, Kennedy called upon his countrymen to be "watchmen on the walls of freedom."

The United States already had staked its reputation and hundreds of millions of dollars on Saigon, and the new president was under pressure to show resolve. Bowing to the rule that no president, especially a new one, could afford to appear weak, Kennedy told Walt W. Rostow, his personal adviser and an energetic proponent of intervention, "I can't take a 1954 defeat today."[3]

The most important difference between Kennedy and his predecessor was how each met the communist challenge. The Eisenhower administration had relied on the threat of "massive retaliation" with nuclear weapons to deter the Soviet Union from supporting revolutionary adventures outside its borders. The Kennedy men, particularly the bright young "whiz kids" brought into the Department of Defense by Defense Secretary Robert McNamara, rightly criticized "massive retaliation" as a muscle-bound strategy. Massive retaliation left the United States no choice but nuclear war to defend Europe, and it provided no realistic means to cope with "brush fire wars" in the Third World in which the Soviet Union might be only indirectly involved, if at all. Kennedy's men posed as an alternative a "flexible response." This doctrine called for the development of an array of options, conventional and unconventional as well as nuclear. With Kennedy's blessing, Pentagon strategists, the intelligence services, and the "think tanks" began churning out ideas for "counterinsurgency" in unconventional, limited war. The president himself took a personal interest in the creation of the Special Forces, or Green Berets, an elite unit of professionals trained specifically to combat insurgent irregulars by irregular means.

Indochina besieged Kennedy even before he settled into the Oval Office. Eisenhower had stressed Laos in his briefing of the new president, and recommendations by the military and intelligence communities for dispatch of troops to prop up the Vientiane rightists awaited him. Thanks to the Bay of Pigs fiasco in April, however, Kennedy had grown wary of schemes hatched in the Pentagon and the CIA and chose instead to negotiate. A Geneva conference on Laos convened in May. But, having adopted the soft option for Laos, Kennedy felt he had to be firm elsewhere, especially in Vietnam, both to reassure Diem and to warn Moscow. Despite his misgivings, Kennedy turned for support to advisers like Rostow who recommended deeper involvement.

As delegates assembled in Geneva to discuss reestablishing a neutral coalition government in Laos, Kennedy quietly sent 100 more military advisers and 400 Special Forces troops into Vietnam. This seemingly small step had enormous symbolic importance, as it went beyond mere abuse of the Geneva ceiling on military missions: Kennedy's action openly breached the accords reached at Geneva. With this move, Kennedy buried what little was left of the Geneva Agreements.

Needing opinion on further measures, Kennedy dispatched Vice President Lyndon Johnson to Saigon in May, the economist Eugene Staley a few months later, and the dual team of Walt Rostow and General Maxwell Taylor, the president's personal military adviser, in October. All came back with reports of a deteriorating situation and recommendations to enhance support for Diem. Most important was the Rostow-Taylor report, which recommended placing U.S. advisers at all levels of the Saigon government and military, developing a Civil Guard and Village Self-Defense Corps, and dispatching an 8,000-man "logistic task force" under the guise of flood control assistance. There were contrary opinions, but when Khrushchev reaffirmed his commitment to wars of national liberation at the Vienna summit in June, the rising pitch of Cold War rhetoric drowned objections out. Kennedy, rejecting negotiations as a sign of weakness yet averse to sending troops, made what a former U.S. diplomat has identified as the first of ten "fateful decisions" that dragged the United States deeper into Vietnam.[4] He authorized an increase of aid and advisers. The number of advisers in South Vietnam, less than 800 when Kennedy took office, grew to 3,000 in

December 1961 (including an operational U.S. Army helicopter unit) and to 11,000—the equivalent of a full division—in late 1962.

Kennedy's decisions did not live up to his bold rhetoric, however; they were improvisational, incremental, tentative, and temporizing. They were designed to keep Diem from collapsing and to silence the critics of inaction, not to end the widening conflict. Wanting neither negotiations nor war, Kennedy, like his successors, based his policy on what one of his own advisers was later to describe as "wishful thinking": if this or that reform could be extracted from Diem, if a little more aid were given, if a little more time could be bought, things might get better.[5] "Better," of course, meant reversing revolutionary gains and putting the Saigon regime on a course toward stability and strength. No serious consideration was given to negotiated settlement, communist participation in a coalition government, or simply pulling out and leaving Saigon to its fate. The hope that things would get better and the view that abandoning Saigon would do irreparable damage to the credibility of U.S. commitments in other parts of the world prevailed over the misgivings.

At the time, Kennedy's decisions were not unpopular. The vast majority of Americans had yet to see that the war in Vietnam could disrupt their own lives. That included youth, who, swept along by the idealist activism of the Kennedy administration, joined the Peace Corps and the struggle for black civil rights. Not yet faced with dispatch to the jungles, they largely ignored Kennedy's lurching steps into Vietnam.

THE COMMUNIST MILITARY CHALLENGE

When Kennedy took office, Vietnam's tribulations had yet to enter U.S. consciousness as a war. The Communists devoted a good deal more time to organization and propaganda than to armed attacks. But in September 1961, they did manage to seize a provincial capital just eighty kilometers from Saigon. Revolutionary armed forces grew briskly. U.S. intelligence estimated that the number of "regular" troops under communist command grew from 4,000 to 10,000 during 1960 alone. By late 1961, the People's Liberation Armed Force, nominally the NLF's "main force," numbered 17,000. These troops were to grow to 23,000 in 1962, 25,000 in 1963, and 34,000 in late 1964. In addition to this body of full-time fighters, village self-defense and regional forces numbered about 3,000 in 1960 and an estimated 72,000 in late 1964. Thus, the total number of revolutionary armed forces, according to U.S. estimates, rose from about 7,000 in 1960 to 106,000 in 1964.[6] A secret assessment by COSVN, the communist high command in the South, placed the total in January 1964 at 140,000.[7] By either estimate, these forces grew rapidly, and with 28 percent of the regulars counted by COSVN as party members, they were firmly under the party's control.

In the beginning, most of the units were platoon-sized and took orders from party committees at the district and province levels. Lacking the necessary command elements and training to act in coordination, such units could do little more than mount hit-and-run attacks on isolated outposts and provide security for party organs and roving propaganda teams. By mid-1962, however, three main force regiments had appeared in the mountainous provinces of central Vietnam designated Military Region 5.[8] The process of grouping independent platoons and companies into larger units then began in earnest.

Main force units, it must be stressed, were but the tip of an iceberg. In the communist strategy, armed forces were to be organized into three categories: a guerrilla militia, regional forces, and main forces. In some ways the most important forces were the militia, or the village "self defense" forces, whose duties were to set booby traps, plant punji stakes, harass patrols and convoys, and support nighttime raids on small outposts. The militia also provided local party organs with police, intelligence, and a mechanism to recruit and train village youths for "promotion" to the higher force categories. Thus the militia were the foundation of a three-tiered pyramid; they were not only extremely lethal in the tiny engagements that comprised most of the fighting but also vital to the creation of the forces above them.

The fact that these forces had to be built largely from scratch made it essential for the Communists to obtain popular cooperation and community sanction, particularly for the formation of village militia. This was done through "political struggle" conducted by party and front cadres who worked individually, in teams, or through networks of family and friends to deepen sympathy for the revolution. Their methods went beyond mere propaganda on the themes of reform, justice, and peace to direct personal appeal to individuals who were likely to feel disadvantaged or mistreated by existing political, social, and economic arrangements. (Persons, and their relatives, who had fought for the Viet Minh—and suffered because of it—were the first contacted.) In addition to manipulating patriotic sentiment and traditional animosity toward the capital, cadres offered specific benefits (for example, land, village self-government, education and positions of status for the poor, execution of a hated local figure) in exchange for active support. Villagers naturally had to defend the gains thus won and so had reason to make significant sacrifices for the revolution. Political struggle moreover extended into the ranks of Saigon's army and bureaucracy in the form of "enemy and military proselytization" that sought, through propaganda and messages conveyed by intermediaries, to demoralize civil servants and ARVN troops or to encourage them to desert or defect.

The development of Southern insurgent forces no doubt benefited from Northern support as well, but by how much was not obvious. Until the Central Committee's 15th Plenum in May 1959, as we have seen, party policy was an important factor *restraining* the use of armed force by the party's Southern branch. The first effect of change in that policy was to unleash forces that were indigenous to the South. However, infiltration of arms and cadres from the North also played a role. Leadership cadres, numbering a few hundred, had moved both ways between North and South ever since 1955. From 1957 to 1958, the party recruited members of ethnic minority groups inhabiting Military Region 5 to improve the lines of communication through the mountains[9] and to guide the small groups of infiltrators that began moving from North to South following the May 1959 15th Plenum.[10] The PAVN's Group 559, discussed in the previous chapter, took over the organization and support of this trickle, which quickly increased. The total number of "confirmed" and

Table 3.1
"Confirmed" and "probable" infiltrators from the North, 1959–1964

1959–1960	4,582
1961	6,295
1962	12,857
1963	7,906
1964	12,424
Total	44,064

Source: Working Paper on the North Vietnamese Role in South Viet-Nam: Captured Documents and Interrogation Reports (Washington, D.C.: Department of State, May 1968), introduction, Table 1.

"probable" Northern infiltrators as estimated by U.S. intelligence is shown in Table 3.1.

A picture of the first team of infiltrators striding along a jungle trail now hangs in Hanoi's Military History Museum where the guide proudly declares that they were troops of the People's Army marching to the South in May 1959. In January 1960, the PAVN turned its base at Son Tay into a training ground for infiltrators, and shortly thereafter the 324th division was designated an infiltration training unit.

The 324th division was a fully integrated combat unit of the People's Army. It was not, however, a "Northern" unit in terms of the regional origins of its men, for it was composed of regroupees—the men who had gone North from the South in 1954. The overwhelming majority of people who went South between 1959 and 1964 were from this pool. The regroupees, of course, had been born south of the 17th parallel and so were best equipped by accent and experience to mingle with the Southern population. Many returned to their home villages to contact families and friends and to resurrect old resistance networks. The regroupees were also an elite group: Most of the men held officer or senior noncommissioned officer ranks in the PAVN or were trained political cadres. Over half were party members. More than one-third of the men who had regrouped in the North in 1954 returned South from 1959 to 1964, at which point the pool of regroupees still fit for infiltration dried up.[11] Highly motivated and well-trained, the regroupees supplied an invaluable nucleus of disciplined, skilled cadres. They undoubtedly played a crucial role in the party's recovery from the "dark days" of 1959.

But the regroupees did not supply as much of the movement's rank-and-file as did the South itself. The total number of regroupees sent to the South amounted to 40 percent of the U.S. estimate and 30 percent of the COSVN estimate of total Southern revolutionary armed forces in 1964. Due to attrition and nonmilitary assignment, the regroupees' actual proportion in this total had to be much lower. The number of combatants recruited in the South up to 1964, as distinct from the regroupees, was at least 60,000 and probably near 100,000. This rapid growth in the number of Southerners who were willing to bear weapons for the revolution attested to the sympathy with which many people listened to the Communist's message, though the regroupees played a role in putting that message across.

The movement from North to South also led inexorably to expansion of the logistical support, or "transportation groups," set up in 1959. One of these, Group 759, was responsible for the maritime route and sent its first ship, the *Phuong Dong 1,* to the Ca Mau peninsula in September 1962. From then until February 1965, when its operations were discovered in Phu Yen province, the group's 50-to-100-ton ships carried nearly 5,000 tons of weapons to the South.[12]

But the most important supply line was Group 559's land route, quickly dubbed the Ho Chi Minh Trail by the western news media. This route followed the communications-liaison lines that had linked Viet Minh bases up and down the Annamite Cordillera during the war against France. In August 1959, Group 559 delivered its first load of weapons, weighing 280 kilograms, in western Thua Thien province.[13] Fear of discovery, however, drove the group to map new routes down the western flank of the cordillera, known as the Truong Son range in Vietnamese, inside Laos and Cambodia. The "trail" soon developed into a web of footpaths, roads, and waterways down which flowed a steady stream of troops, cadres, equipment, and weapons.

Through the relative security of sparsely settled mountains and triple-canopy jungles, men and women with packs weighing up to 50 kilograms and bicycles reinforced to carry 100 to 150 kilograms began to wend their way. One Hero of the People's Army is said over a period of four years to have transported 55 tons a distance of 41,025 kilometers, in effect walking around the earth under a load equal to his own weight.[14]

It was this lightly protected, clandestine movement that came under attack by the Royal Lao Army, at the instigation of the United States, following the rightist coup in Vientiane. PAVN forces supporting the Pathet Lao then pushed the Royal Lao Army out of the highlands and consolidated control over half the country. The Vietnamese thus gained unimpeded use of the Laotian portions of routes 8, 9, and 12. By the end of 1961, the trail had doubled its capacity, and in June 1962, the Central Military Party Committee issued orders to develop capacity for mechanized transport over new routes still further to the west. Engineering regiments soon joined Group 559 to help build roads, and in 1964, the group moved forty times as much tonnage as in all previous years—51 percent by mechanized means—despite the U.S. bombing of Pathet Lao zones since May of that year.[15] More and more, supplies moved by truck, though people still walked much of the distance.

It was a hard trip. Infiltrators and supplies reached the jump-off point of Vinh, capital of the North's Nghe An province, by truck and train. From there they proceeded by a route that cut sharply around the western end of the demilitarized zone or by three other routes that swung deeper into Laos. Inside Laos, movement was by foot, oxcart, bicycle, and when the routes extended toward the west, by riverboat. On foot with an occasional short truck ride, the trip from Vinh to the border of South Vietnam took an average of two months (three for those who had to travel the 1,000 kilometers from Vinh to the southernmost way station). Monsoons from May to September turned the trails to mud, slowed motor transport to a crawl, and brought fatigue and disease. An estimated 15–17 percent of the troops moving down the trail fell behind their units, mostly due to malaria.[16]

The support system within the trail complex consisted of "military stations" (*binh tram*) and other camps scattered about a day's march apart. These stations numbered about sixty in

1969. The typical station, staffed by fifteen to twenty people and buried in jungle just off a narrow path to escape aerial detection, provided infiltrators with food, quarters, medicines, and guidance to the next station. When infiltrators reached a trail terminus—usually a base area hard on the border of South Vietnam—they were given a PLAF designation or assigned to existing PLAF units. Supply convoys were turned over to rear service units for transport the remaining short distance to the war zone.

THE "SPECIAL WAR"

The rapid growth of revolutionary armed forces and Saigon's growing isolation from the countryside did not go unnoticed in Washington. At the same time that he increased the numbers of U.S. military advisers, Kennedy authorized these advisers to accompany Saigon army units on combat operations down to the company level. As the number of advisers mounted to 11,000 in late 1962, the United States also began providing helicopter transport and air cover. Although only one U.S. adviser had died in combat before Kennedy took office, now American deaths and casualties occurred regularly.

Kennedy's hope in waging a "special war," however, was to keep U.S. forces in the background, to support and build Saigon, not do its fighting. This aim, in a sense, was only a logical extension of the military assistance program that had been in existence for years. By fall of 1959, thanks largely to U.S. assistance, the Army of the Republic of Vietnam had grown to seven standard divisions, a five-battalion airborne group, eight independent artillery battalions equipped with U.S. guns, and four armored cavalry squadrons. A small air force and navy also had emerged. One of Kennedy's first acts as president had been to offer Diem an additional $42 million for the expansion and training of the ARVN in exchange for a promise of reform (the reform never came to pass). Subsequent aid allotments helped the ARVN raise its force level by late 1962 to about 220,000 men. Armed, equipped, and trained in the U.S. style, the ARVN was prepared by the United States to meet a Korea-type attack across the demilitarized zone. (The North also had received Soviet and Chinese assistance to reorganize and refit its army and with the help of a draft instituted in 1960 had a six-division force of about 200,000 men.)

But Kennedy sought to do more than just prepare the ARVN for conventional defense. He also pushed the idea of "counterinsurgency," which, stripped of doctrinal pretensions, meant carrying the war to the guerrillas on more than just military terms. In the name of counterinsurgency, the U.S. Special Forces were sent into the central highlands to conduct civic action among the ethnic minorities. Small teams of Green Berets lived among the "montagnards" and organized them into Civilian Irregular Defense Groups (CIDG) to attack the Communists in their previously impregnable mountain redoubts. U.S. military advisers trained not only the ARVN but also supervised the rapid expansion of a village Civil Guard. Programs in psychological warfare, village administration, technical assistance, and propaganda were established. New tactics based on helicopter mobility and new weapons, including napalm, were devised to seize the initiative.

The military side of this effort enjoyed some success. In spring and summer 1962, the ARVN went on the offensive and dislodged communist forces from their most exposed positions. But the Communists quickly adapted to the ARVN's new firepower and mobility. They learned how to bring down helicopters with small arms, how to wait in hiding and destroy the helicopters as they landed, and how to ambush the landing parties at their moment of greatest vulnerability. ARVN commanders reverted to the tactics of caution, refusing to risk troops in battle except behind a barrage of airpower and artillery. Where the ARVN did not retreat, it fell back on methods that drove people into refugee camps or the arms of the revolution.

The U.S. overhaul of Saigon's defense establishment also had some ominous side effects. As the ARVN General Tran Van Don put it, U.S. preoccupation with invasion from the North deflected attention from "the real threat . . . at village level in the form of . . . highly disciplined guerrilla units . . . where cumbersome conventional units could not operate effectively. The French had already proved this to us. We wondered why we had to repeat the mistake for the Americans." Even more portentous was the effect of U.S. supervision on the initiative of the ARVN command. Asked what his military doctrine was, Chief of the General Staff General Cao Van Vien told Don, *"As long as the conduct of the war remains an American responsibility, we have no doctrine of our own."*[17]

Meanwhile, this period also witnessed the rise and fall of the strategic hamlet program. Modelled after the resettlement scheme that Brigadier Sir Robert K.G. Thompson had used with success in the Malayan "emergency," and on Sir Robert's advice, reorganization of hamlets was meant to cut off the revolutionaries from the food, intelligence, and recruits they needed to survive and fight. This approach required rebuilding, and in some cases relocating, entire rural communities on which insurgents depended for support.

Little heeding Sir Robert's injunction to plan carefully and apply the concept selectively, Ngo Dinh Nhu took the program under his personal direction in mid-1961 and announced the grandiose objective of organizing between 11,000 and 12,000 strategic hamlets, enough to shelter the entire rural population. Local officials soon had peasants moving their hamlets to new sites or fortifying old ones. The official claim of 7,200 hamlets built by July 1963 was an exaggeration, but no doubt a very large number of the South's rural communities did feel some impact of the program.[18] Communist internal documents identified the program as a significant challenge, and Madame Nguyen Thi Dinh admitted to this author that for a time "it did create some difficulties for us."[19]

But Vietnam was not Malaya. The Malayan Communist Party, composed mainly of ethnic Chinese, had been isolated by ethnicity from the majority Malays. The Malayan scheme had had to separate the insurgents only from about 500,000 ethnic Chinese squatters who were the insurgents' main base of support. The Vietnamese strategic hamlet program, by contrast, attempted to separate the entire rural population from its revolutionary kin by forced draft. Peasants were ordered to move or rebuild their hamlets, without incentive, compensation, or pay, often at a new location far from ancestral graves. Nothing in the program, such as meaningful land reform, bound the peasants to the hamlets or to the government. Much in it aroused their resentment. As Saigon lacked the military resources to police every hamlet by force, communist cadres soon reestablished contact with the people. Many people so resented the program that they welcomed the cadres into their midst more warmly than ever before.

U.S. efforts to save Saigon without sending troops came to naught in the padi fields of My Tho province during January 1963. There, near the hamlet of Ap Bac eighty kilometers southwest of Saigon, an ARVN force of 2,000 men encountered about 300 to 400 PLAF troops. Though the ARVN force called airplanes, helicopters, armed personnel carriers, and U.S. advisers to its assistance, it suffered 165 casualties and lost 5 helicopters, while the PLAF escaped with less than 12 dead. The implication was obvious to the U.S. and communist commands alike: the PLAF could defeat the ARVN, despite the ARVN's U.S. arms, equipment, and advice. The U.S. strategy of "special war" was bankrupt.

THE COUP

A change of strategy lay over a year in the future, however. For the rest of 1963, the war in the countryside churned on while attention shifted to the cities. Deeply displeased by political infighting that distracted ARVN commanders from military duties, the Kennedy team was itself divided over what to do. Upon returning from an inspection trip, counterinsurgency expert General Victor Krulak reported to the president at a meeting of the National Security Council on September 6, 1963, that Diem was a much-loved figure who only needed more U.S. support to win the war. But State Department official Joseph Mendenhall, who had accompanied Krulak, disagreed. According to Mendenhall, Diem was almost universally detested and an obstacle to victory. "Were you two gentlemen in the same country?" Kennedy asked.

U.S. frustration with Diem was mounting. The Kennedy administration had urged Diem to placate his enemies, broaden his government, and crack down on corruption, but to no avail.

The more the administration pressured him, the more he cut himself off from its advice. Diem's deepening intransigence was due not just to his natural obstinacy or to brother Nhu's malevolent conspiracies, though these played a part. It also was due to his belief that he could not survive the appearance of caving in to foreign, in this case U.S., pressure. This was the legacy of Vietnam's age-old resistance to China, its struggle for independence from France, and, perhaps most poignantly, of Diem's realization that in the contest for legitimacy, his own claim, in contrast to that of the Communists, was still weak. For Diem to have accepted U.S. advice would have confirmed his opponents' charge that he was a "puppet." To bolster his own claim as a rightful ruler, he had not only to turn aside foreign advice but, if possible, appear defiant. As long as Washington believed that without Diem things would be worse, the puppet pulled the strings and the United States was frustrated.

Every defect of the regime became a focus of popular protest in the South: the arrest and torture of prominent people, the silencing of dissent, the replacement of elected village chiefs with ones appointed from Saigon, the appointment of Catholics from central provinces to administer Mekong Delta districts, the enrollment of civil servants in brother Nhu's dictatorial Revolutionary Personalist Workers (Can Lao) party, the construction (ordered by Madame Nhu) of a monument to two national heroines carved in her likeness, the allocation of government funds for Madame Nhu's personal use, a ban on dancing, the widespread corruption, and so forth. With Buddhist monks in the vanguard, demonstrations, most of which took place in Saigon, became an almost daily occurrence.

Buddhism, however, was a secondary issue for most of the people who took part in the demonstrations and for many of the monks as well. Though Diem was indeed guilty of favoring his coreligionists and of incorporating Catholic elements into an official state ideology, the monks' cries of "persecution" were contrived to win sympathy more for political than for religious objectives. Protest leaders unabashedly identified Buddhism with nationalism to capitalize on the growing isolation of the Diem regime. As one bonze put it, "The campaign to overthrow the Ngo Dinh Diem regime in 1963 not only succeeded in mobilizing the people to the defense of Buddhism but also awakened the nationalist consciousness of the masses. In every Buddhist the idea of Buddhism and nationalism are intertwined and cannot be easily separated. Many non-Buddhist elements also took part in the Buddhist campaign, not because they wanted to support the Buddhists but because they realized that the Buddhist campaign was consistent with the people's aspirations."[20] In the guise of "defending Buddhism," the monks articulated a broad popular yearning to get rid of Diem, eliminate U.S. influence, restore traditional morality, and establish national harmony. Their ultimate political goal was national reunification under a coalition government.

At the core of the movement was a militant faction of the Unified Buddhist Church. Numbering perhaps 100,000 members, about 10 percent of the South's Unified Buddhists, this faction owed its dynamism to skillful organization and the charismatic leadership of the bonze Thich Tri Quang. Born, ironically, in the same village of central Vietnam as Ngo Dinh Diem, Tri Quang had sided with the Viet Minh against the French and Japanese and considered himself a revolutionary noncommunist patriot.

The United States advised appeasement, but Diem, on Nhu's advice, invoked the truncheon. On June 11, Quang Duc immolated himself, and on August 21, Nhu's Special Forces ransacked the pagodas. Many of the 1,400 people arrested were bonzes. The pagoda raids convinced key ARVN officers that Diem had to go. The last straw was an attempt by Nhu to implicate the army in the raids. Fearing that U.S. military aid could be in jeopardy, Chief-of-Staff Tran Van Don contacted Lieutenant Colonel Lucien Conein, a French-speaking CIA agent whose activities in Indochina dated back to 1944. Don assured Conein that the ARVN had not been involved in the pagoda raids and indicated that planning for a coup was under way. As it happened, Washington had just sent a new ambassador to Saigon to replace Frederick Nolting, who had come to be regarded as too "pro-Diem." Nolting's replacement was the enormously self-confident patrician, Henry Cabot Lodge. Lodge carried plenipotentiary powers, and he already had decided that Diem was going to be his main problem. Reports that Diem's brother Nhu was in contact with Hanoi through a third party hardened Lodge's conviction. In fact, Nhu's contact was Mieczyslaw Maneli, head of the Polish delegation to the International Control Commission, with French Ambassador Roger Laloulette carrying Nhu's messages to Maneli.

Accounts of what followed differ mainly over the degree of U.S. involvement. According to General Don, the plotters kept their plans to themselves until the last moment and acted without prompting from the United States.[21] But it is well established that the generals sought reassurance through Conein that the United States would support a new government. On August 28, in a cable to President Kennedy, Lodge recommended showing that support: "We are launched on a course from which there is no respectable turning back: the overthrow of the Diem government. There is no turning back because there is no possibility that the war can be won under a Diem administration. The chance of bringing off a generals' coup depends on them to some extent: but it depends at least as much on us. We should proceed to make all-out effort to get the generals to move promptly." Against the advice of General Paul Harkins, the embassy military assistance chief who had argued that Diem should be given a chance to get rid of Nhu, Lodge asserted that "such a step has no chance of getting the desired result and would have the very serious effect of being regarded by the Generals as a sign of American indecision and delay."[22] Kennedy promptly approved Lodge's recommendation and accepted full responsibility for the consequences.[23] Subsequently, Lodge maintained a conspicuous distance from Diem, hints of U.S. displeasure with Diem were broadcast by the Voice of America, and on October 5, Kennedy approved a list of aid cuts knowing this would encourage a coup.[24] The generals, who were as dependent on U.S. aid as Diem, apparently interpreted the threatened aid suspension as a virtual order to stage a coup.[25]

The circle of plotters quickly widened. One key leader, General Duong Van "Big" Minh, had begun his military career under the French and had risen swiftly by commanding the troops that crushed the sects. But he had lost Diem's trust in proportion to his gain in personal popularity, and Diem had divested him of any real authority by making him his personal military adviser. The other key conspirator, General Tran Van Don, had been born in France and had fought for France in Europe as well as Indochina. Swept up like so many young men by patriotic enthusiasm for the August Revolution, Don had volunteered to fight for the Viet Minh but had been refused a command because of his French citizenship. He had then salvaged a military career by joining General LeClerc's headquarters staff. When the French created a separate Vietnamese army under Bao Dai, Don had joined what was to become the ARVN. By 1963, as chief of the general staff, he too had earned Diem's distrust. Both Minh and Don were southern Buddhists.

Minh and Don recruited General Tran Thien Khiem, one of the generals most trusted by Diem and commander of the 7th division. Other members of the coup group—some of whom one day would mount coups of their own—included Major General Ton That Dinh, commander of the 3rd corps around Saigon and a favorite of Diem's brother Ngo Dinh Can; General Nguyen Khanh, commander of the 2nd corps and a notorious opportunist; General Do Cao Tri, commander of the 1st corps; Colonel Do Mau, chief of military security; Colonel Tran Ngoc Huyen, the devout Catholic commandant of Dalat Military Academy; General Le Van Kim, another Viet Minh reject who had carved out a career as an aide to Admiral Thierry d'Argenlieu; Lieutenant Colonel Nguyen Cao Ky, the French-trained chief of a C-47 transport squadron; and a Catholic colonel from central Vietnam named Nguyen Van Thieu.

Except for lack of ties to the old aristocratic mandarinate of Annam, the coup group differed little in social background or outlook from other stalwarts of the Diem regime. The officers were mostly products of French education and bourgeois families, holdovers of the colonial system who made up the South's anticommunist elite. An important hallmark of this elite was a self-serving obtuseness about conditions in which the vast majority of their countrymen lived. General Don believed that most of the land was owned by individuals in small plots "on a highly democratic basis,"[26] though his own father had owned 2,700 lush acres of Long Xuyen province where the average farm holding was 5 acres and 79 percent of all farm families owned no land of their own.[27] Genuinely revulsed at the treatment of the Buddhists, the officers were piqued at least as much by Diem's efforts to establish his personal control over the army. They had no idea what to do with power once they had seized it.

At 1:30 in the afternoon of November 1, Colonel Thieu's troops surrounded the presidential palace. At 4:30 P.M., while the palace guards held off the attack, Diem called Ambassador Lodge and the following conversation took place.

DIEM: Some units have made a rebellion and I want to know what is the attitude of the USA?

LODGE: I do not feel well enough informed to be able to tell you. I have heard the shooting, but am not acquainted with all the facts. Also it is 4:30 A.M. in Washington and the U.S. Government cannot possibly have a view.

DIEM: But you must have some general ideas. After all, I am a Chief of State. I have tried to do my duty. I want to do now what duty and good sense require. I believe in duty above all.

LODGE: You have certainly done your duty. As I told you only this morning, I admire your courage and your great contributions to your country. No one can take away from you the credit for all you have done. Now I am worried about your physical safety. I have a report that those in charge of the current activity offer you and your brother safe conduct out of the country if you resign. Have you heard this?

DIEM: No. (Pause.) You have my telephone number.

LODGE: Yes. If I can do anything for your physical safety, please call me.

DIEM: I am trying to reestablish order.[28]

Later that evening, Diem and Nhu escaped by a side entrance. Found hiding in a suburban church the next morning, they were bundled into an armored personnel carrier and shot by two of General Minh's aides.[29] Kennedy received the news of Diem's assassination with horror. But Washington had committed itself too deeply not to support Minh's Military Revolutionary Council. When Minh himself was overthrown three months later by

General Nguyen Khanh, Washington approved because it believed Minh had "neutralist" tendencies and might seek an accommodation with the Communists.[30] Though Minh's "neutralism" appears to have been little more than a casual interest in French President De Gaulle's proposal for compromise and negotiations,[31] only vigorous prosecution of the war was acceptable to Washington.

The other assassination, that of President Kennedy on November 22, 1963, made no difference in U.S. policy. Kennedy's successor, Lyndon Johnson, simply took over the Kennedy team, which went on planning for counterinsurgency on a bigger scale and, if necessary, for intimidation of the North. Having just begun to flex their muscles, U.S. leaders tended to regard any proposal for something less than outright victory as defeatist.

THE COMMUNIST RESPONSE

The turbulence that preceded Diem's fall certainly diverted attention from the countryside. The construction of strategic hamlets ceased, ARVN units avoided combat, and development programs ground to a halt. The reduced pressure, combined with the crescendo of protest in the South, made it easier for the party to find recruits for the PLAF and local guerrilla forces. The size of the party's Southern branch also grew, from the "dark days" of 1959, when it had approached extinction, to nearly 70,000 by late 1963.[32] Though Diem's fall deprived the Communists of a rallying point and left them briefly perplexed, the military government soon proved itself to be unstable, weakly committed to reform, and heavily dependent on the United States. The revolutionary momentum picked up again. However, party leaders realized that the generals would be more receptive than Diem to an expanded U.S. role in the war and that without greater external assistance the Southern revolution could lose the initiative.

It was against this background that the Central Committee convened its 9th Plenum in December 1963. This was a crucial moment for the Vietnamese Communists, both in regard to the South and in their relations with the Soviet Union and China.

The Southern revolution needed greater Northern support, especially if the United States intervened. But the Sino-Soviet split had widened, with Moscow opposed to offensives that risked confrontation with the United States. If Hanoi increased support for the Southern revolution, it would in effect put itself on China's side in the dispute, lose its Soviet backing, and heighten chances of U.S. retaliation. Yet this was a risk that Party First Secretary Le Duan, in his keynote speech to the plenum, made clear the party was prepared to take.[33]

The move tested the party's unity. Despite the party's decision in 1959 to extend limited support to the Southern revolution, a strong faction of risk-avoiders had warned ever since against endangering the North's development. In presenting the resolution of the 3rd National Congress of the party in September 1960, Truong Chinh had maintained that liberation of the South had to be carried out "by the Southern people themselves." In contrast, Le Duan had asserted that this was "not only a task of the Southern people, but also of the entire people, of the South as well as of the North."[34] Gradually, Truong Chinh and others had fallen in line as Le Duan, relying on the unassailable theme of patriotism, had shamed them into acquiescence. From that time onward, the party was irrevocably committed by ethos, emotion, and allegiance to accept any risk and make any sacrifice on behalf of Southern "liberation."

In a secret resolution,[35] the plenum adopted a long-range contingency plan that was to serve as the basic strategic guideline for the entire course of the war. The resolution noted that the symbolic defeat of the "special war" at Ap Bac left the United States facing a stark choice between further defeat or introducing its own ground combat troops. The latter step would transform the conflict into a "limited war." The Saigon government, the plenum surmised, might then develop into a neocolonial dependency able to withstand the pressure of the largely indigenous Southern revolution. This was unacceptable not only because of the obstacle it could pose to reunification but also because of what it implied over the long term for the security of the North.

It was necessary, the resolution therefore concluded, to prepare for a protracted people's war similar to the resistance against

France. Guerrilla warfare was to be the principal mode of attack "for a long time to come," but main forces were to be built up for the purpose of "annihilating" regular ARVN units. The strategic key was the "coordinated struggle" of armed and political movements in the three "strategic zones" of the mountains, lowlands, and cities. Main forces in mountain bases were to reinforce the mixed political-armed struggle of the lowlands, from which support could be extended to the largely political struggle that was supposed to take place in the cities. All of these struggles in combination were to divide, distract, deplete, and tie down the materially superior, more numerous enemy. At a suitable moment, a "general offensive and uprising" of the urban population coordinated with armed attack by troops coming from the countryside would "overthrow the enemy's central government." A separate section of the resolution entitled "The Mission of North Viet-Nam" argued that the North would have to "bring into fuller play its role as the revolutionary base for the whole nation," with scale and timing made contingent on U.S. action.

The 9th Plenum, Le Duan frankly admitted, was the scene of heated debate. Disunity, he said, had been caused by members who were "influenced by modern revisionism" or "held rightist views."[36] These were code words that clearly revealed the divisive effect of the Sino-Soviet dispute, which had allowed advocates of caution to find support in the Soviet line on peaceful coexistence while the majority took comfort from China's vociferous anti-U.S. posture. In addition, "rightist views" included those of party members who recoiled from the prospect of exposing the North to U.S. retaliation. This provoked the counterargument by Lieutenant General Tran Van Tra, who had fought the French in the South, that it was the Southern people who would bear the greatest hardships in what was, he said, a defense of the entire nation.[37] Another old Southern resistance commander, Major General To Ky, castigated "some people" who exaggerated U.S. tactical power and underestimated U.S. strategic vulnerability.[38]

The ripples of dissent continued to widen as the full implications of the 9th Plenum became apparent. According to a well-informed Hanoi source, the head of the Philosophy Institute,

Hoang Minh Chinh, addressed a thirty-page letter to Le Duc Tho supporting the Soviet position on ideological issues. For circulating a copy of the letter among his associates, Chinh was slandered in order to destroy his reputation, and then he was arrested. A number of other figures who disagreed too openly with policy also were imprisoned. (Released in 1975, Chinh noted the Soviet tilt of Hanoi's policy, announced "You see, I was right," and was arrested again.)

The military was little exercised by ideological issues but was divided over how to carry out its mission. The PAVN had been engaged since 1958 in a far-reaching program of modernization and reorganization that was intended to strengthen the PAVN's ability to defend the North by conventional means. Formal ranks and insignia had been handed out, new technical branches had been created, and a draft had been instituted. The training curriculum now included material on "modern" weapons and tactics, which younger officers interpreted as suggesting that the earlier doctrine of "people's war" was obsolete. Officers who were loathe to pit the semi-modernized PAVN against the United States also opposed reverting to "people's war" in the South. At least three officers, including a senior colonel named Le Vinh Quoc, reportedly could not reconcile themselves to the doctrinal reversal and requested transfer to the Soviet Union; there Quoc joined the Red Army and attained the rank of major general. But the fissures of dissent slammed shut when Ho Chi Minh, at a Special Political Conference held on March 27–28, 1964, issued a call for unity and sacrifice in the face of what lay ahead.[39]

Ho must have known what was in store. Since February, the CIA had upgraded an earlier program of sporadic commando raids, sabotage, and psychological warfare against the North into one of sustained harassment (the upgraded program was code-named OPLAN-34a). Diplomatic moves had come to naught. In April, Northern-born PAVN regulars, not just Southern regroupees, began special training for the march south. About that time also, the Political Bureau member charged with overseeing the enhanced effort, Nguyen Chi Thanh, returned from the South to report that war with the United States was unavoidable but that, with the North's support, it could be won. Hanoi was primed for the next U.S. move.

Three separate events that seemed related in Hanoi catalyzed actions on both sides. On the 1st and 2nd of August, U.S.-supplied Laotian T-33s bombed two villages in the North's Nghe An province. About the same time, South Vietnamese naval units shelled the islands of Hon Me and Hon Ngu. On the 2nd and 4th, two U.S. destroyers, the *Maddox* and the *C. Turner Joy,* exchanged fire with North Vietnamese torpedo boats while gathering intelligence eight nautical miles off the North's coastline (and four nautical miles from its offshore islands). Despite ambiguities in the encounter, President Johnson seized on this incident as a pretext to extract special war powers from the U.S. Congress.[40] Passed with only two dissenting votes, the Tonkin Gulf Resolution gave Johnson a basis for claiming congressional support for an undeclared war; with his "approval rating" in opinion polls jumping from 42 percent to 72 percent, he claimed to have the support of the American people as well.

It was at this juncture that Hanoi dispatched the first whole unit of Northern-born regulars to the South. Rather than dispersing among PLAF units as the regroupees had done, this unit stayed together as the independent 808th battalion. The PAVN 95th regiment departed the North in October and entered the South in December. Three more regiments were detected entering the South between then and May 1965, bringing the number of Northern-born regulars in the South to perhaps 6,500.[41]

Hanoi quite probably had grown impatient waiting for the United States to make the first move. The PLAF had been overrunning an average of one district capital each week, but having reached a plateau of military development and lacking a strong organization in the cities, the revolution, according to COSVN's military committee, had been unable in the course of 1964 to "exploit thoroughly the opportunity to create a new situation."[42] U.S. actions subsequent to the Tonkin Gulf incident, however, more than satisfied Hanoi's need of pretext.

In February 1965, the United States launched airstrikes against the North in reprisal for PLAF attacks on U.S. installations at Pleiku and Qui Nhon; the airstrikes followed plans Johnson had approved two months earlier. In March, "reprisal airstrikes" were upgraded to a program of sustained air war known as Operation ROLLING THUNDER. The arrival that month of two marine battalions to protect the airfield at Danang raised the U.S. force level to 27,000. Further arrivals in April and May brought the level to 46,000 and in June to 74,000. The United States was ready to fight, and the "limited war" long anticipated by the Communists was about to begin.

NOTES

1. Robert Scheer and Warren Hinkle, "The Vietnam Lobby," *Ramparts* (July 1967), pp. 16–25.

2. John F. Kennedy, "America's Stake in Vietnam," *Vital Speeches* 22 (August 1, 1956), p. 618.

3. Quoted in Murray Marder, "Our Longest War's Tortuous History," *The Washington Post*, January 28, 1973.

4. Paul M. Kattenburg, *The Vietnam Trauma in American Foreign Policy, 1945–1975* (New Brunswick, N.J.: Transaction Books, 1980), pp. 108–109.

5. James C. Thompson, "How Could Vietnam Happen? An Autopsy," *Atlantic Monthly* (April 1968).

6. Department of Defense, *United States-Vietnam Relations* (Washington, D.C.: GPO, 1971), book 2, Table 1, IV.A.5, p. 25.

7. "Bao cao: tinh hinh mien Nam tu cuoi nam 1961 den dau nam 1964" [Report on the Situation in South Vietnam from Late 1961 to Early 1964]. In author's possession.

8. War Experiences Recapitulation Committee of the High-Level Military Institute, *The Anti-U.S. Resistance War for National Salvation 1954–1975: Military Events*, trans. by the Joint Publications Research Service, JPRS no. 80,968 (Washington, D.C.: GPO, June 3, 1982), p. 52.

9. Information according to a former PAVN officer who had been attached to the Military Region 5 command staff, interviewed by the author in 1973.

10. Dan Hong, "An Outline History of the Ho Chi Minh Trail," *The Ho Chi Minh Trail* (Hanoi: Foreign Languages Publishing House, 1982), p. 10.

11. J. J. Zasloff, *Origins of the Insurgency in South Vietnam, 1954–1960: The Role of the Southern Vietminh Cadres* (Santa Monica, Calif.: Rand Corporation, RM-5163/2, May 1968).

12. *The Anti-U.S. Resistance War,* p. 32.
13. Hong, "An Outline History," p. 14.
14. Ibid., p. 16.
15. Nguyen Viet Phuong, "Bo doi Truong son va he thong duong Ho Chi Minh" [The Truong Son Troops and the Ho Chi Minh Trail System], *Nghien cuu Lich su* [Historical Research] (March-April 1979), p. 24.
16. Combined Intelligence Center Vietnam, Study ST70-05, "North Vietnam Personnel Infiltration into the Republic of Vietnam," U.S. Military Assistance Command Vietnam, J-2, Saigon, December 16, 1970, pp. 24–30.
17. Tran Van Don, *Our Endless War* (San Rafael, Calif.: Presidio Press, 1978), p. 150. Emphasis is in the original.
18. See Milton E. Osborne, *Strategic Hamlets in Viet Nam* (Ithaca, N.Y.: Cornell University Southeast Asia Program Data Paper no. 55, April 1965), pp. 32–35.
19. Interview with the author, Hanoi, March 30, 1983.
20. Thich Nhat Hanh, *Vietnam: Lotus in a Sea of Fire* (New York: Hill and Wang, 1967), p. 45.
21. Don, *Our Endless War,* p. 98.
22. *The Pentagon Papers,* Senator Mike Gravel edition (Boston: Beacon, 1971), vol. 2, pp. 738–739.
23. Michael Maclear, *The Ten Thousand Day War* (London: Thames Methuen, 1981), p. 70.
24. Roger Hilsman, a Kennedy aide, cited in George C. Herring, *America's Longest War: The United States and Vietnam, 1950–1975* (New York: John Wiley, 1979), p. 104.
25. Maclear, *Ten Thousand Day War,* p. 81.
26. Don, *Our Endless War,* p. 25.
27. Jeffrey Race, *War Comes to Long An* (Berkeley: University of California Press, 1972), pp. 58–60.
28. *The Pentagon Papers,* p. 268.
29. The assassinations were carried out on orders from Minh, according to Don, *Our Endless War,* p. 112.
30. *The Pentagon Papers,* p. 304–305.
31. Don, *Our Endless War,* pp. 134–135.
32. "Bao cao."
33. "Mot vai van de trong nhiem vu quoc te chu Dang ta" [Some Problems Concerning Our Party's International Tasks], *Lich su Dang Cong san Viet Nam, Trich van kien Dang* [History of the Vietnam Communist Party: Excerpts from Party Documents] (Hanoi: Marx-Lenin Textbook Publishing House, 1979), vol. 3, pp. 265–313.

34. Le Duan, "Leninism and Vietnam's Revolution," in *On the Socialist Revolution in Vietnam* (Hanoi: Foreign Languages Publishing House, 1965), vol. 1, p. 48.

35. A copy of this resolution, which was captured in the South, is translated in *Viet-Nam Documents and Research Notes* [hereinafter cited as VNDRNs], no. 96 (Saigon: U.S. Mission, July 1971).

36. Talk by Le Duan at the 9th Plenum, *Hoc Tap* [Study and Practice,], February 1964, translated in VNDRNs, no. 96.

37. Tran Van Tra, speech commemorating the third anniversary of the NLF, in *Quan doi nhan dan* [People's Army], December 19, 1963, p. 1.

38. *Quan doi nhan dan* [People's Army], December 21, 1963, p. 4.

39. "Bao cao tai Hoi nghi chinh tri dac biet" [Statement to the Special Political Conference], *Lich su Dang Cong san Viet-Nam,* vol. 3, pp. 214–331.

40. A detailed account of these events can be found in Wallace J. Thies, *When Governments Collide: Coercion and Diplomacy in the Vietnam Conflict, 1964–1968* (Berkeley: University of California Press, 1980), pp. 41–52.

41. Combined Intelligence Center Vietnam, Research and Analysis Study ST76-013, "Update: The NVA Soldier in South Vietnam," U.S. Military Assistance Command, J-2 (Saigon, October 18, 1966), p. 2.

42. "Nghi quyet quan uy mien Nam-1-1965" [Resolution of the Party Military Committee, Southern Region, January 1965]. In author's possession.

4

Americanization

America seemed omnipotent then," wrote former Marine Philip Caputo of his dispatch to Vietnam in 1965. "The country could still claim it had never lost a war, and we believed we were ordained to play cop to the Communists' robber. . . . We saw ourselves as the champions of 'a cause that was destined to triumph.'"[1] In the mid-1960s, such were the convictions of just about every American involved in the war from President Johnson down to the lowliest grunt. Many believed that the revolution would dissolve before the mere display of U.S. power. If it did not, the United States was confident it could crush the revolution with its overwhelming armed might. That had always been the American way of war, and it had always prevailed.

Although the U.S. conceit totally ignored how the Communists might respond, it was not entirely fanciful. When a unit of U.S. combat marines landed near Qui Nhon in June 1965, the squad of local guerrillas that had been sent out to observe them, unbeknownst to the marines, turned and ran. Every revolutionary from the lowliest guerrilla to the party first secretary knew that victory could not come by pushing U.S. soldiers into the sea. Nor could it come just by surviving the onslaught. The United States had to be made to withdraw of its own accord. This, the Communists knew, could only be done by thwarting the U.S. expectation of success, forcing Washington to admit the bankruptcy of each in a dwindling set of options, until only the option of withdrawal remained.

In the beginning, however, U.S. intervention rescued Saigon from a desperate situation. It almost certainly saved the ARVN from imminent collapse. In achieving these results, U.S. intervention transformed the conclusion of a civil and revolutionary conflict into a lethal international war of long duration.

WESTMORELAND'S STRATEGY

"It was apparent," a senior U.S. military adviser was to write, that in 1964 "the South Vietnam government could not prevent the enemy from taking over the country."[2] No sooner had Diem been ousted than Saigon's new military rulers had fallen to bickering among themselves. The ARVN's morale, never good, went into steep decline. The government, already shaky and unpopular, was reluctant to enforce the draft that had been in effect since 1957, and prospects for expanding the ARVN were poor. In 1964, 73,000 men deserted. Paramilitary and auxiliary units, fruits of U.S. advice and assistance during the preceding four years, were disbanding or going over to the other side. The U.S. advisory mission had to concede in mid-1964 that the initiative had passed to the revolution. With growing urgency, the United States began late that year to draw up plans for the introduction of its own ground combat troops.

The man chosen for this task, Lieutenant General William C. Westmoreland, was descended from men who had fought for the South in the U.S. Civil War. Graduate of West Point in 1936, artillery officer in North Africa and Europe, regimental commander in Korea, silvery-maned and jut-jawed, Westy was a general by predestination. He was also the creature of the new U.S. army, a vast bureaucratic establishment in which management skills and respect for routine counted more than grasp of strategy or tactical brilliance. In this bureaucracy, Westmoreland had risen steadily thanks to influential patrons and the skillful use of talented staff assistants. Deputy commander of the U.S. Military Assistance Command–Vietnam (MACV) since January 1964, Westmoreland took over full command from General Paul Harkins in June.

By comparison with the Pollyannaish Harkins, Westmoreland was a grim realist. Told to request whatever he needed to win the war, he outlined a two-phase plan. In a first phase (lasting through 1965), he proposed to build a logistical base for a large force. In the second phase, U.S. forces would search out and destroy the Communists' main force units, especially in remote or thinly inhabited areas where U.S. firepower and mobility could be brought to bear against PAVN base areas and troop concentrations. Meanwhile the ARVN, strengthened by an enhanced assistance program, would concentrate on pacification in the more densely populated lowlands. The combination, Westmoreland theorized, would give the PAVN no choice but retreat if it wished to avoid defeat, leaving the ARVN to take care of what Southern revolutionary forces remained. Though reluctant to fix a timetable for victory ("incredible," he said of an earlier Harkins' prediction of six months), Westmoreland ventured to suggest that if his requirements were met, it might be possible to begin withdrawing U.S. troops by late 1967.[3]

The Westmoreland strategy relied partly on the sheer magnitude of U.S. resources. U.S. forces in South Vietnam rose from approximately 80,000 men in 1965 to a peak of 543,000 in 1969. (Australia, New Zealand, Thailand, and the Philippines sent small contingents, while South Korea sent 50,000 men.) A vast complex of infantry support bases sprang up all over South Vietnam. Some 2,000 aircraft (exclusive of helicopters) were posted to Guam, the Philippines, Thailand, and carriers at sea. A seemingly endless supply of artillery, tanks, jeeps, trucks, and other equipment crossed the Pacific.

The combination of these resources gave Westmoreland his strategic equation: mobility + firepower = attrition. A network of fortified hilltop "firebases" covered almost every nook and cranny with artillery fire. Under that protection, infantry patrols were to fan out and engage the enemy. Battalion-strength, heliborne reaction forces stood ready to join the fray and, with the help of artillery and airpower, to pulverize the enemy at low cost in casualties to themselves. Thus Westmoreland hoped to inflict losses on the Communists that they would find intolerable while keeping U.S. losses at a level that the U.S. Army—and people—would accept.

The intended targets of "search and destroy" were the Communists' armed forces, particularly their main force units. Effective attack required finding the exact location of an elusive enemy, for which purpose the United States had developed technology and techniques never before tested in counterinsurgency warfare. Portable radar, infrared spotting scopes, and urine-detecting "people sniffers" were to pinpoint trails, bivouacs, and units. Fifty thousand tons of herbicides would be dumped on millions of hectares, clearing away half of the South's jungle cover. In areas declared "free fire zones" and presumably devoid of civilian inhabitants, artillery and aircraft were authorized to "harass and interdict" suspected enemy supply lines at will. By a combination of both well-aimed and random shots, communist forces were to be kept on the move, on the defensive, and run-to-ground.

Westmoreland not unreasonably considered defeat of the immediate military threat to be his first priority. However, his strategy imposed a U.S. design on the war. Control over resources gave the United States the decisive voice in planning. The leaders and army whom the United States came to rescue were, in effect, shunted aside. The desire to "win hearts and minds" and build a viable government was often declared, but in practice these efforts were relegated to "the other war," a term that aptly located them on the periphery of Westmoreland's perceptions. Like French commanders before him, Westmoreland's instinct was to militarize the conflict, for this was all he and the organization he commanded had been trained to do. Pushed far enough, however, his was a strategy whose sheer disruption of society as well as battlefield destruction had potential to confront the Communists with dilemmas they had never known.

HANOI'S SOUTHERN COMMAND: UPGRADING ARMED STRUGGLE

As Westmoreland prepared to put U.S. forces into combat, the Communists set their own plans in motion. Up to that time, COSVN, the Central Committee's forward element in the South, had been headed by Nguyen Van Linh, a native of Hanoi who had spent almost all of his revolutionary career in the South. Linh's principal assistants were Vo Van Kiet, a native of Vinh Long province who had led Viet Minh forces in the Mekong Delta and remained in the South after 1954, and Vo Chi Cong from Quang Tri province who was vice chairman of the NLF. All three men had been secretly elected to the Central Committee in 1960. Because the political struggle was paramount, COSVN's small military section consisted of personnel who had led guerrillas against France and formed the Eastern Interzone Command in 1956.

To equip COSVN for the coming armed struggle, the Central Committee assigned another member, Lieutenant General Tran Van Tra, in 1963. A native of Quang Ngai province and a party member since 1938, Tra had been appointed commander and political officer of the Saigon-Gai Dinh special zone as well as southern regional commander in 1950. He had regrouped to the North in 1954, became a deputy chief of the PAVN general staff in 1955, and was said by defectors to have gone abroad for training. Taking over as head of COSVN's Central Military Committee in 1963, Tra began to organize a command staff for the lower half of the South (or B2) that fell under COSVN's jurisdiction.[4] Just to the north, another regroupee general from Quang Ngai, Nguyen Don, arrived about the same time to set up a command for Military Region 5 (B1).

Meanwhile, in Hanoi, some officers had wanted to avoid confrontation with the United States as long as the PAVN was at a severe firepower disadvantage and could not count on Soviet largesse. But following the 9th Plenum, the inauguration of OPLAN-34a raids in February 1964, and Ho Chi Minh's call-to-arms in March, they were given no choice but to fight whether the PAVN had the means or not. As Northern-born regulars began training for infiltration in April, the army adopted a new training regimen. Based on a Chinese model, this regimen stressed psychological exercise to convince the troops that human factors were superior to material ones and thus that revolutionary men could prevail over U.S. weapons.[5] The party's Political Bureau also sent one of its own members who had conspicuously identified himself with this approach on a clandestine mission to the South to draft a strategic plan. Upon his return in late

COMMUNIST MILITARY ZONES IN SOUTH VIETNAM
(1973–1975)*

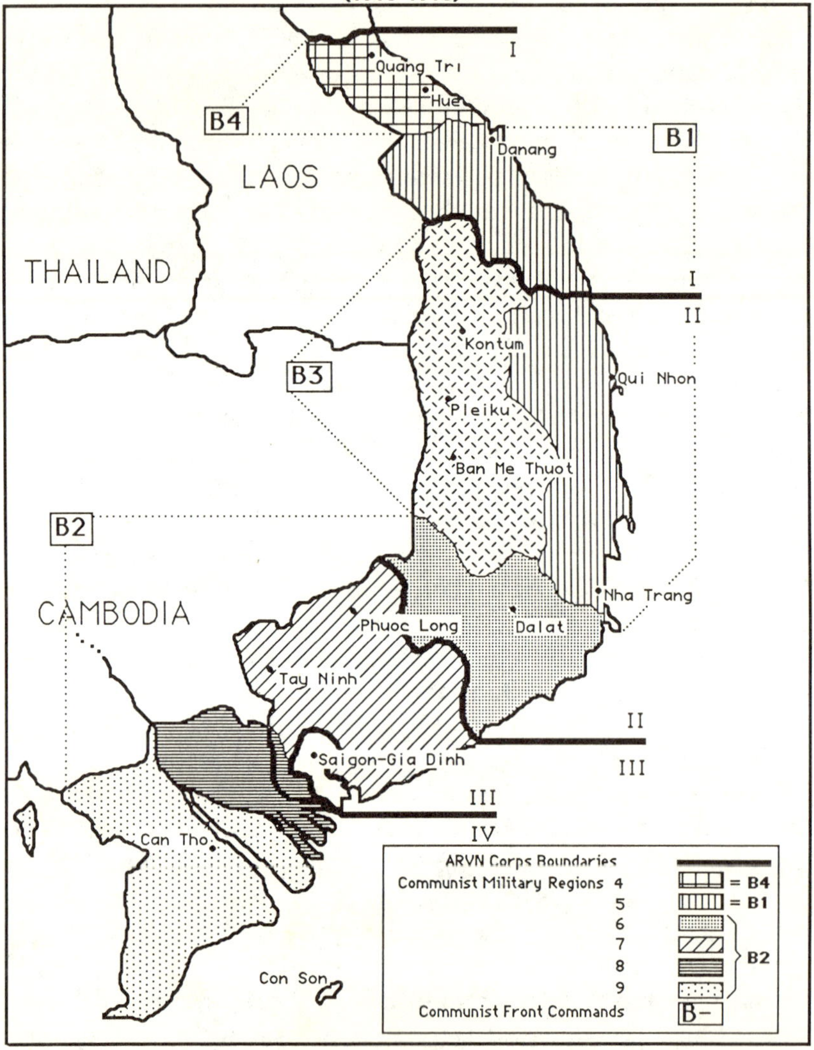

Based on a map in Lt. Gen. Tran Van Tra, *Nhung chang duong cua "B2-Thanh dong," tap V, Ket thuc chien 30 nam.* Ho Chi Minh City: Van Nghe Publishing House, 1982, and fn. 1, p. 7.

*Consolidation and adjustment of communist regions took place several times during the 1960s.

1964, the Political Bureau approved his recommendations, and early the following year, he crossed back into the South to implement them.[6]

If Westmoreland was predestined to be MACV commander, Nguyen Chi Thanh was even more the inevitable COSVN chief. Born in 1914 to a poor peasant family in Thua Thien province, Thanh had participated in tenant farmer strikes at age seventeen and had joined the party in 1937. One year later, he had been elected secretary of the Thua Thien province party committee. A commanding presence, infectious enthusiasm, and organizational talent had soon brought him to the attention of party hierarchs, who invited him to the party conference at Tan Trao in 1945, elected him to the Central Committee, and placed him in charge of the resistance in Central Vietnam. In 1950, he had been appointed head of the army's General Political Directorate (GPD), and in 1951, he had won a seat in the Political Bureau. In 1959, he had been given the PAVN's highest rank, general-of-the-army (*dai tuong*), an honor that by law only the president, Ho Chi Minh, could bestow, and that had made him the sole equal in rank of Vo Nguyen Giap, the minister of defense and architect of the Dien Bien Phu victory. Perhaps due to differences with Giap, but also because of plans for the South, Thanh had left the GPD in 1961 in order to concentrate on preparations for the unification struggle. He was one of the party's most vehement spokesman for reunification at any price. Though Giap remained influential as a member of the Political Bureau, real control over reunification strategy already was firmly in the hands of Party Secretary General Le Duan supported by Le Duc Tho, Pham Hung, and Nguyen Chi Thanh.

Accompanying Thanh on the journey south was Major General Tran Do, an alternate member of the party Central Committee, of northern origin and experience. On arriving at COSVN headquarters, Thanh took over as first secretary of both the party and military committees, with Do serving as his deputy. Other PAVN officers and subordinates followed to flesh out the military command structures in COSVN headquarters and in regional organs.

The influx of PAVN officers into the South invited speculation by many observers that the Southern revolution was being taken over by the North and Northerners. In fact, however, the "Southern revolution" all along had been a project of the Communist party, which had members from all regions and certainly defined its mission in national not regional terms. (A People's Revolutionary Party, unveiled as an ostensibly separate Communist party for the South in 1963, was simply a name given to the party's Southern branch. It was ceremonially "reunified" with the parent party in 1976 and never mentioned again.) Moreover, the first PAVN generals sent from the North, with few exceptions, were either Southern regroupees or Northerners who had fought in the South during the first war. Northerners without Southern experience began to join these in significant numbers only when the supply of regroupee officers ran out—about 1964—which was the same time that requirements for regular trained officers increased. That Thanh displaced Nguyen Van Linh and Tran Van Tra in COSVN's top posts merely reflected Thanh's higher party rank. To be sure, there were tensions between individuals and between Hanoi and the Southern-based leadership, as there were *within* Hanoi and *among* Southern-based leaders. But these were symptoms of normal wrangling within an otherwise cohesive organization, not of fragmentation or "Northern takeover."

The essence of Thanh's recommendation was to proceed with the strategy outlined at the 9th Plenum. The PLAF had been unable during 1964 to deal the ARVN a "decisive blow" despite the latter's "involvement in seven coups d'etat," as a chagrined COSVN military affairs committee noted.[7] Yet the ARVN's steady weakening presented opportunities for attack that were not to be passed up. At the same time, any of the three options contemplated by the United States—attacking the North, intensifying the "special war," and transforming the conflict into a "limited war" by introducing "hundreds of thousands" of U.S. troops—could create difficulties. To keep up their own momentum and at the same time tie down the United States in a war confined to the South, the Communists decided it was necessary to accelerate the formation of main forces in the lowlands and proceed with infiltration of regular PAVN units from the North. Both of these moves required increasing supply over the Ho Chi Minh Trail and into the central highlands.

As early as November 1953, party leaders had recognized that "only by developing into the central highlands is it possible to obtain the most strategic position in the South."[8] So in May 1964, the Political Bureau had elevated the western subregion of Military Region 5 into a full-fledged front command. Four months later, a detachment from Region 5 set up a Central Highlands Front Command (B3) to build bases where major supply trails spilled into the South's hilly midriff.[9]

THE TURNING POINT

But war came first to the lowlands. There the PLAF had begun to form mobile units and to receive new weapons during 1964. Having depended for most of its weapons and ammunition on what it captured from the ARVN, the PLAF began that year to receive AK-47 assault rifles, 7.63-mm machine guns, RPG-2 rocket launchers, 82-mm mortars, and 57-mm and 75-mm recoilless rifles, most of Chinese manufacture. Some PLAF foot soldiers soon held a firepower advantage over their ARVN counterparts whom the United States had equipped with World War II surplus. Standardization of equipment also facilitated the formation of larger units.

By late 1964, COSVN felt ready to launch a campaign with units of battalion and regimental size. On December 4, elements of two PLAF regiments attacked the hamlet outposts of Binh Gia village, a predominantly Catholic settlement about seventy kilometers southeast of Saigon. The attacks drew a strong response from heliborne ARVN ranger and marine units, but the PLAF held its ground. A month later, when the dust settled, it appeared that some 1,500 PLAF troops had killed 10 percent of the 2,000-man ARVN force, shot down three helicopters, and wounded six U.S. crewmen. U.S. advisers on the scene conceded victory to the PLAF. In this and similar actions across the country, the ARVN was losing an average of one infantry battalion each week, and senior U.S. officials believed they saw evidence of a shift to the "third stage" of "mobile warfare" prescribed in the military writings of Mao Zedong.

Actually, the Communists had learned in the Red River Delta campaign of 1951–1952 not to lock themselves into the three-stage-war straitjacket. Premature onslaughts on French positions had taught them to distrust strategies of mechanistic progression, especially when an interventionary superpower stood behind their enemy.

Lacking a vast territory like China's in which to maneuver, the Communists sought compensation in coordinated pressures of all kinds at as many locations as possible. Their concept of a campaign was to combine political and armed action at highly dispersed locations, thereby intensifying disruptions large and small at all points. Still, the Binh Gia battle convinced the U.S. command that the PLAF had achieved tactical superiority over the ARVN and that only U.S. troops could cope with the new "stage" the war had entered.

RESCUE MISSION

As the United States mulled over its options during spring 1965, few doubted that Saigon was headed for defeat. The new military leadership of Air Vice Marshall Nguyen Cao Ky and General Nguyen Van Thieu, in power since Ky and Thieu had ousted General Khanh in February, inspired no more confidence than its predecessors. The rising number of army desertions (a total of 113,000 in 1965, an increase of more than 50 percent over the previous year) had dashed U.S. hopes of setting the ARVN quickly on its feet. Even earlier, in January, Defense Secretary Robert McNamara and National Security Adviser McGeorge Bundy had advised President Johnson to consider sending U.S. troops into action, and a powerful group within the administration, headed by Westmoreland, the Joint Chiefs of Staff, and Walt Rostow, was pushing for intensification of the air war against the North. Sustained air attacks began in March but failed to obtain communist concessions or to weaken the communist offensive in the South.

At a meeting in Honolulu in April, the Joint Chiefs, McNamara, and Lodge's replacement as ambassador, General Maxwell Taylor, agreed to increase the number of troops to 82,000 in order to protect airbases and hold "enclaves" along the coast. But the 27,000 U.S. troops in Vietnam already had permission to go on combat patrols, and neither Westmoreland nor the ARVN generals could see the sense of a purely defensive U.S. role. "The Communists," said General Thieu, "controlled seventy-five per cent of the countryside. We controlled only the chief towns. We had the impression we would be overrun. There was a crucial need for American troops."[10] Ambassador Taylor was reluctant to approve a much larger presence for fear this would only further reduce the ARVN's incentive to fight, but by midyear, he too agreed there was no alternative. In July, Westmoreland submitted a request for 179,000 troops, and on the 28th, President Johnson announced that the force level would rise to 125,000 troops.

By August, the U.S. command felt ready to begin offensive operation. To kick off the campaign with a big victory, the command sought a communist stronghold that would be susceptible to complete destruction. The area chosen was the Batangan peninsula, located twenty-five kilometers south of the U.S. Marine base at Chu Lai. The villages of the peninsula had supported the Viet Minh during the resistance and had been a revolutionary base for at least two years before the marines arrived. Three of the villages, anchored by a hamlet called Van Tuong, were tightly organized guerrilla communities, riddled with tunnels, concrete reinforced bunkers, trenches, mine fields, and food and weapons caches. The terrain, marked by rocky hills and terraced padi fields, completed this fortress, in which hid a well-organized local militia and an estimated 2,000-man PLAF regiment.

The peninsula seemed to afford the U.S. command an opportunity to bottle up a sizeable communist force and to exterminate it with overwhelming firepower. Opening Operation STARLIGHT on August 18, a battalion of heliborne marines cut the peninsula at its neck, three companies made an amphibious landing on the outer shore, and a blocking force took up positions along one edge. Nearly 6,000 marines pressed the defenders against the sea while Phantom and Skyhawk jets, two destroyers, and ground artillery ploughed the cordoned area with napalm, rockets, and bombs.

As a display of firepower, the attack was impressive. In its wake the marines claimed to have found 599 "VC" bodies and to have taken 122 prisoners. But they reluctantly revealed that they had 200 dead and wounded of their own, and they had difficulty persuading reporters that all of the Vietnamese bodies were "VC." Despite capture of only 127 communist weapons and escape by three-quarters of the PLAF regiment, General Westmoreland cited the battle as proof that U.S. troops could defeat "any Viet Cong or North Vietnamese forces they might encounter."[11]

COSVN's General Thanh, however, pointed to the battle as evidence that "the Southern Liberation Army is fully capable of defeating U.S. troops under any circumstances, even though they have absolute superiority of . . . firepower compared with that of the liberation army."[12] Partly morale-boosting braggadocio, Thanh's boast had a serious side. An account of the battle reported years later in the PAVN newspaper, *Quan doi nhan dan* (People's Army), emphasized that the defenders had taken advantage of the rough terrain to set up crossfires that offset the marines' firepower superiority and then had broken out of the encirclement. What counted to the Communists was not so much the tally of bodies as the fact that the PLAF and local guerrillas had engaged U.S. troops at a time and place chosen by U.S. commanders, yet had lived to fight another day. Indeed, almost as soon as the marines withdrew, the Batangan peninsula reverted to the status it had held before Operation STARLIGHT.

Years later, long after the Batangan villages had witnessed a succession of efforts to "pacify" them, a U.S. civilian official filed a confidential report that read in part:

> For more than five years the Batangan Peninsula has symbolized VC influence in Quang Ngai and has posed a threat not only to the people of Binh Son and Son Tinh districts but to neighboring districts including the city of Quang Ngai itself. It provided a source of supply, recruits, food and weapons to the 48th main force battalion as well as other VC units. While it is true that U.S., Korean and ARVN forces conducted periodic operations in this area, the VC merely faded away until the operation terminated and then returned to their base which remained virtually intact.[13]

The report went on to call the efforts toward establishing control over the peninsula since 1968 a "success story" of the war. But it acknowledged the continued operation of the PLAF 48th battalion and argued that U.S. support was still needed if the ARVN were to completely pacify the area.

U.S. attention, however, was on the highlands, where it was feared in 1965 that the Communists were preparing to "cut the country in two." Actually, all major links except air had been cut long ago, and only the Communists moved on the ground at will. What the Communists had decided to do was to meet the United States head on, and this implied a need to preempt strategic positions and push supply lines beyond the lower end of the Ho Chi Minh Trail. The only existing road link between the Cambodian bases and road networks in the lower highlands, Route 19, passed through the Ia Drang valley on its way to Pleiku. There, in late October, three PAVN regiments mounted attacks on ARVN camps and outposts of the montagnard Civilian Irregular Defense Group. The U.S. 1st cavalry division, an entirely airmobile unit that had just barely had time to establish a base at nearby An Khe, rushed to the rescue.

U.S. troops swept around the valley in their helicopters, chasing, blocking, surrounding, and engaging any PAVN units they could find. The PAVN adapted by focusing fire on helicopter landing zones, attacking only at close quarters or at night, and cutting up small U.S. detachments. But in the end, after a series of engagements that occurred over the period of a month, U.S. forces were able to count nearly 1,800 PAVN dead on the battlefield, at a cost of 300 casualties to themselves.

As 1965 came to a close, the Communists could point to success in pushing Special Forces and CIDG camps out of the A Shau Valley, attacking the Danang airfield, and mounting assaults against outposts all over the South. They also succeeded during the fall in grouping PLAF regiments to form two divisions (the 9th and 5th) in the Mekong Delta and two more (the 3rd and 2nd) in the midst of populous central provinces. But they had been unable to prevent U.S. forces from gaining a foothold in the highlands or from penetrating some areas where revolutionary forces previously had been safe from attack. The idea of dispersing into guerrilla formations gained support, forcing

General Thanh to defend his strategy of preserving the initiative at any price. In a speech to COSVN cadres in mid-1966, Thanh admitted that the United States had only begun to tap its potential, but he maintained that big unit warfare was necessary if the revolution were to remain on the offensive. Dispersing the big units to wage guerrilla warfare would sacrifice all that had been won and be tantamount to defeat. "If we want to take the defensive position," he said, "we should withdraw to India."[14]

On the question of tactics, however, Thanh appeared willing to compromise. Many PAVN commanders had come south with their heads full of conventional doctrine, some of it learned from Soviet manuals and from training abroad. Thanh could agree with old guerrilla cadres that "modern tactics might be irrelevant in combat with large U.S. units. Better, he said, to find a "special way of fighting the Americans," the way "a tiger leaps at his prey"—in other words, short, swift, surprise assaults at close quarters and then rapid disengagement to avoid the full impact of U.S. firepower. Better too, he added, to strengthen all forms of political struggle among the people and within the enemy's armed force as a complement to the armed struggle. But under no circumstances was he willing to slacken the main force offensive or adopt a solely guerrilla-based strategy.[15]

THE BIG SWEEPS

By mid-1966, Westmoreland had completed his support base and begun the campaign of massive attrition. The number of U.S. troops in Vietnam stood at 350,000, which combined with 315,000 ARVN regulars and an equal number of auxiliaries brought the total number of armed personnel on Saigon's side to more than 1 million. On the revolutionary side, there were 114,000 main forces (including 46,300 PAVN regulars) and 112,000 guerrillas for a total of 225,000 according to U.S. estimates. Captured communist documents claimed there were 320,000 people in guerrilla and local militia forces for a total of 435,000 in all troop categories.[16] As we now know from testimony given by General Westmoreland in his suit against

CBS news in November 1984, the discrepancy was due to U.S. exclusion and Communist inclusion of "part-time" local militia in these figures. Even by the more generous count, however, communist armed forces in the South were outnumbered nearly three-to-one. Though well equipped with light arms, communist troops lacked the heavy weapons, armed vehicles, transport, and airpower that their enemies enjoyed in abundance.

Communist strategies hoped to redress the unfavorable military balance with a favorable political one. Not even the prospect of more U.S. troops perturbed dialecticians who saw in the growing U.S. presence an opportunity to whip up a patriotic backlash. Anticipating a rise in anti-U.S. sentiment, a Central Committee plenum in December 1965 had called for a "people's war of national resistance." In addition, the plenum had reaffirmed support for main force offensives in order to deliver a "decisive victory in a relatively short period of time." What this implied was a two-tiered strategy, according to which conventional attacks would be intensified to convince the United States soon that Westmoreland's strategy could never produce an acceptable outcome (and thus lead to a "decisive victory in a relatively short period of time"), while a "people's war" waged by guerrillas, political cadres, and the masses would be developed to preserve the option of protracted war.

One of the party's fondest dreams seemed about to materialize in spring 1966 when the ARVN I Corps command broke off from Saigon, and another wave of Buddhist dissidence erupted in Hue and Danang. The ensuing turmoil presented an opportunity that the Communists, though they had done little to create it, rushed to exploit. The PAVN 324B division slipped into Quang Tri province, and a new military region covering Quang Tri and Thua Thien provinces (the Tri-Thien Region, or B4) under Hanoi's direct command (bypassing COSVN) appeared in April.[17] Thinking that Hanoi was preparing to seize these two provinces, the United States installed a string of combat and fire support bases all along Route 9 from Dong Ha to the Laotian border. Work began on an anti-infiltration system, popularly known as the McNamara Line or Electric Fence, that consisted of a strip of sensors, infrared intrusion detectors, electronic warning devices, and minefields. Pitched battles within

ROUTE 9

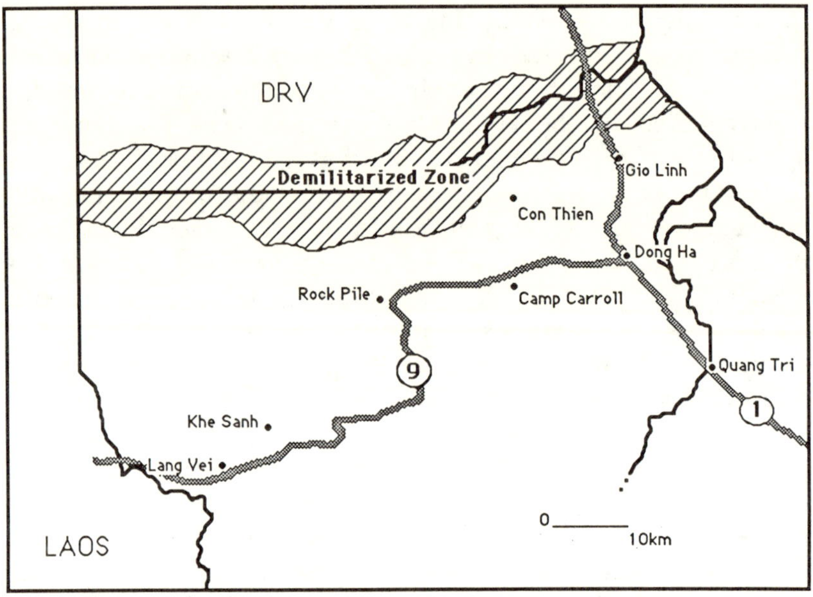

range of PAVN artillery and anti-aircraft weapons raged at Con Thien, Gio Linh, Camp Carroll, Rock Pile, and Khe Sanh. Bitter fighting left U.S. and ARVN troops in control of the high ground, and the U.S. command claimed to have held off the "invading North Vietnamese."[18]

The Communists had flexible objectives, however, and military seizure of the two provinces was a distant second to diverting attention from the Tri-Thien lowlands and loosening Saigon's hold over Hue and Danang so that the wave of dissent could erupt into mass uprising. But party organs in the cities were too weak to exploit the situation; "We lost an opportunity to win an even greater victory," Le Duan was to say.[19] Meanwhile, the offensive in these provinces also sought to drain resources away from Westmoreland's accelerating campaign of attrition further south.

There the United States planned the largest "search and destroy" operations of the war, against the Iron Triangle, a base area thirty-five kilometers northeast of Saigon (known to the

Communists as War Zone D) and a staging area adjacent to the Cambodian border (War Zone C) that the United States believed sheltered COSVN headquarters.

Believing the Communists were preparing to swarm out of these bases and attack population centers, U.S. and ARVN forces launched probes into War Zone C during April 1966. These probing forces stumbled into the PLAF 9th division (whose presence was suspected but whose location was unknown) and PAVN 101st regiment, and an operation code-named ATTLEBORO was mounted to exterminate the communist forces. Altogether, ATTLEBORO involved 2,000 U.S. and ARVN troops, 1,600 tactical air sorties, and the dropping of 12,000 tons of bombs (one-third by B-52s). U.S. commanders credited ATTLEBORO with a very favorable "kill ratio" of nearly one-to-fifteen, the capture of large stocks of rice, weapons, and supplies, and the foiling of communist plans to attack the major population centers near Saigon and in the Mekong Delta.[20]

The PLAF commands, however, noted with approval that elements of its 9th division and auxiliaries had fought 100 different engagements over a period of nearly two months in what it called the Tay Ninh Campaign."[21] Despite some "depletion," "revolutionary forces" had escaped extermination and put up resistance until the last enemy troops had withdrawn. The PLAF assessment conceded that heliborne U.S. and ARVN troops had been able to seize strong tactical positions, but scoffed at them for not following through with infantry assaults. Aerial bombardment had had insignificant effect, it claimed, and ATTLEBORO had neither exterminated communist forces nor denied them the use of War Zone C. Even the United States had to admit that it had not found COSVN headquarters.

Nevertheless, the United States thought it had hit upon an effective technique and mounted a similar operation, CEDAR FALLS, against the Iron Triangle in January 1967. This operation, immortalized in Jonathan Schell's book *The Village of Ben Suc,*[22] sought to destroy forever a complex of tunnels, bunkers, and "combat hamlets" that reputedly were home to the PLAF 272nd and 265th regiments and administrative headquarters for the Saigon–Gia Dinh military region.

Ben Suc, a Viet Minh base during the first war, had been an outpost for an ARVN battalion from 1955 to 1964. The PLAF had routed the battalion, and Ben Suc, to the evident satisfaction of its 6,000 inhabitants, had become a solid NLF village. Fearing breaches of security, the United States did not inform South Vietnamese authorities of Operation CEDAR FALLS until it was about to be launched. The population was evacuated, aircraft and artillery bombarded the dense jungle, and sixty-ton Rome Plow bulldozers cut giant swaths through the brush. Tunnel and bunker complexes were blown up. Finally, the plows flattened Ben Suc. U.S. Army engineers planted 10,000 pounds of explosives in the tunnels underneath and blew what remained of Ben Suc from the face of the earth.

Like ATTLEBORO, CEDAR FALLS produced a large number of "VC" bodies and substantial quantities of confiscated supplies. According to the U.S. general in command, the operation was "a decisive turning point in the III Corps area . . . and a blow from which the VC in this area may never recover."[23] In fact, CEDAR FALLS did demolish the area's physical structures and remove its population. But it missed the bulk of communist main forces headquartered there—they had slipped away as soon as the operation began—and left vengeful villagers sweltering in hastily constructed refugee camps.

With barely a pause, U.S. and ARVN forces returned to War Zone C to search for the communist forces that ATTLEBORO supposedly had crushed three months earlier. JUNCTION CITY, as the new operation was named, also sought to destroy COSVN headquarters (again) and make the area permanently insecure for the Communists. It, too, relied on sudden helicopter deployments, large infantry sweeps, and lavish use of firepower. It, too, ended with announcement of a high "body count" and large quantities of seized weapons, supplies, and documents. The PLAF's assessment, however, claimed that the majority of engagements had occurred at communist initiative or on terms that communist units had been willing to accept. Four regiments, it noted, had been able to attack continuously throughout the entire period of the operation,[24] and COSVN and PLAF 9th division headquarters remained as elusive as ever.

In the end, ATTLEBORO, CEDAR FALLS, and JUNCTION CITY failed to deny the use of War Zone C and the Iron Triangle to the Communists. Lacking sufficient forces to occupy either area permanently, U.S. commanders had to admit that communist troops and cadres soon returned to their positions.[25] But the operations did inflict heavy losses and showed that the Communists no longer enjoyed unimpeded use of what had been secure base areas.

STALEMATE

By mid-1967, the situation was in a stalemate. With 425,000 troops and an enormous logistical base, U.S. forces were not to be evicted from South Vietnam; they had even pushed some PAVN support facilities into Laos and Cambodia. U.S. pressure of quite a different kind also had put an end to coups in Saigon and paved the way in September for the election of Nguyen Van Thieu as president. The ARVN, deployed mainly in static defense and "pacification," was no longer on the verge of collapse.

On the other hand, revolutionary forces retained the capability for offensive action. The PAVN still roamed the mountains, and a growing volume of material was moving over an improved Ho Chi Minh Trail. In provinces directly below the demilitarized zone, U.S. camps were under almost continuous attack by PAVN units supported by heavy artillery and anti-aircraft weapons. Guerrilla and regional forces, undiminished in size, were still able to hit outposts and ambush convoys in most parts of the countryside at will.

Against this background, General Westmoreland returned to Washington in November to reassure a restive Congress that although the Communists had not been defeated, the end was in sight. Actually, his strategy was beginning to reveal some crucial vulnerabilities. The vast size of the U.S. presence and the destructiveness of U.S. tactics may have seemed necessary to cope with an emergency and to limit U.S. casualties, but they had self-defeating side effects. The big sweeps and lavish firepower that produced a high "body count" also caused civilian casualties, drove peasants off the land, and deepened the resentment of a dislocated population. U.S. money and bases created jobs, but they also exacerbated corruption and moral decline, to the abhorrence of most Vietnamese. U.S. assistance helped to train, equip, and expand the ARVN, but it deepened ARVN dependence on U.S. supply and ill-prepared it to fight alone.

Moreover, Defense Secretary McNamara had concluded in late 1966 that the United States simply was not able to "attrit" enemy forces at a rate exceeding their replacement. As of mid-1967, the North had sent less than 2 percent of its male labor force into combat. The communist political organization in the South remained effective at recruiting troops for local guerrilla and regional forces. Communist forces also were able to control their casualties by choosing the place and time of combat, a fact that revealed which side really held the strategic initiative.[26] Meanwhile, the United States was spending $2 billion per month on the war, and with more than 5,000 U.S. soldiers dead in 1967 alone, the toll was rising. The Communists were taking much higher casualties, but they had never had any delusions, once the United States had intervened, that the war would be "limited" for them.

While the big unit battles soaked up attention and resources, U.S. officials largely ignored the political dimensions of the conflict. A coherent "new model" pacification program did not get under way until mid-1967. This program sought to achieve territorial security by reforming administration at the hamlet level, stimulating economic revival, and gradually turning responsibility for protection of the rural population over to local forces recruited from the population itself. However, aside from its late inception, the promised new order suffered in comparison with the one that many peasants already knew well—that of the Communists. It was administered from "outside" the village by officials at the district and provincial levels, not by local people; its incentives (medical care, educational facilities, a police presence) demanded no particular response in return; and it did not (until 1970) include land reform. The U.S. Embassy, in fact, opposed land reform on the grounds that this would upset the landlords, cause them to withdraw support from the Thieu government, and lead to the government's collapse.[27] The battle for "hearts and minds" was going nowhere.

In addition, a new political front had appeared within the United States itself. Dissent, after gestating in pacifist and civil rights groups, had broken out on university campuses in 1965. An "anti-war movement" of diffuse aims and no formal leadership had spread outward from the few elite universities where it had begun. The vast majority of dissenters simply abhorred the destruction in Vietnam and wanted to withdraw from a war in which they could see no vital U.S. interest at stake. A few activists saw the movement as an opportunity to unmask social evils and lead the way to reform. It was no accident that the stridency of the movement rose in proportion to demands of the draft. Though the movement provoked the antipathy of older, conservative segments of society, by 1967, it also was attracting support from establishment figures.

Perhaps more important, and quite apart from the "movement," the war had begun to corrode the reflexive patriotism of ordinary citizens. The problem, as many saw it, was not with U.S. purpose or decency, but with policies that held little promise of quick and decisive victory. Major newspapers that had supported the war shifted to opposition. Public opinion polls showed popular support for the war dipping below the 50 percent mark in mid-1967. By October, the polls showed that only 28 percent of the people supported the way President Johnson was conducting the war. Inside the administration, Defense Secretary McNamara registered his disillusionment, recommended lowering objectives, and quietly resigned. But Johnson remained determined to see the war through and dug in to fight his critics.

The Communists observed this sharpening of "contradictions" with satisfaction. For the military stalemate, bearable to them, was unacceptable to the United States. As a global power the United States had obligations elsewhere that ruled out endless involvement in an inconclusive war. Under conditions of stalemate, the United States eventually would have to withdraw. Therefore, to the Communists, deadlock was a sufficient condition for eventual victory.

Moreover, communist forces had retained the initiative despite a firepower handicap, and they were steadily upgrading their own conventional warfare capability. While the U.S. effort was approaching its peak, the communist effort had room to grow. Yet, U.S. strategists remained convinced that they could turn the stalemate into something favorable either for negotiations or for the development of the ARVN and Saigon, and they still had potential to enlarge the war in pursuit of these aims. They had not perceived the situation as a stalemate.

The problem for the Communists, therefore, was to persuade U.S. leaders that a stalemate did indeed exist and that there was little the United States could do to break it. That, they concluded, would require intensifying the "coordinated struggle," bringing the war right into the enemy's most secure rear areas.[28]

NOTES

1. Philip Caputo, *A Rumor of War* (New York: Holt, 1977), p. xii.
2. James Lawton Collins, Jr., *The Development and Training of the South Vietnamese Army, 1950–1957* (Washington, D.C.: Department of the Army, 1975), pp. 47–48.
3. William C. Westmoreland, *A Soldier Reports* (New York: Doubleday, 1979), pp. 149–150; and Westmoreland, *Report on the War in Vietnam* (Washington, D.C.: GPO, 1968), passim.
4. For help in locating biographical information on Linh, Kiet, and Tra, I am indebted to Nayan Chanda and Paul Quinn-Judge.
5. *Quan doi nhan dan* [People's Army], May 26 and 28, 1964.
6. Van Tien Dung, *Dai thang mua xuan* [Great Spring Victory] (Hanoi: People's Army Publishing House, 1976).
7. "Nghi quyet quan uy mien Nam-I-1965" [Resolution of the Party Military Committee, Southern Region, January 1965]. In author's possession.
8. Statement of the party military committee, quoted in War Experiences Recapitulation Committee of the High-Level Military Institute, *The Anti-U.S. Resistance War for National Salvation 1954–1975: Military Events*, trans. by the Joint Publications Research Service, JPRS no. 80,968 (Washington, D.C.: GPO, June 3, 1982), p. 62. Text hereinafter cited as *The Anti-U.S. Resistance War.*
9. Ibid.

10. Quoted in Michael Maclear, *The Ten Thousand Day War* (London: Thames Methuen, 1981), pp. 127–128.

11. Westmoreland, *Report on the War,* p. 102.

12. Secret speech given in March 1966, in Department of State, *Working Paper on the North Vietnamese Role in South Vietnam: Captured Documents and Interrogation Reports* (Washington, D.C.: Department of State, May 1968), item 302.

13. "Status of Batangan," DCF III MAF/PSA, Quang Ngai, May 6, 1969. Uncatalogued document, Carlisle Barracks, Pennsylvania.

14. From notes of a cadre who attended the speech in Department of State, *Working Paper,* item 65.

15. The lively debate on this issue can be read in articles translated in Patrick J. McGarvey, ed. and trans., *Visions of Victory: Selected Vietnamese Communists Military Writings, 1964–1968* (Stanford: Hoover Institution Publications, 1969).

16. Department of State, *Working Paper,* item 65.

17. *The Anti-U.S. Resistance War,* p. 89.

18. Willard Pearson, *The War in the Northern Provinces, 1966–1968* (Washington, D.C.: Department of the Army, 1975), pp. 3–9.

19. From a letter written a year later to the Saigon–Gia Dinh party organization, quoted in *The Anti-U.S. Resistance War,* pp. 87–88.

20. Bernard William Rogers, *Cedar Falls–Junction City: A Turning Point* (Washington, D.C.: Department of the Army, 1974), pp. 11–12.

21. PLAF Tactical Operations Center, "Tay Ninh Campaign (3 November–30 December 1966)," February 1, 1967. Translated captured document in author's possession.

22. Jonathan Schell, *The Village of Ben Suc* (New York: Vintage, 1967).

23. William E. DePuy, quoted in Rogers, *Cedar Falls–Junction City,* p. 78.

24. PLAF Tactical Operations Center, "Tay Ninh Campaign."

25. Rogers, *Cedar Falls–Junction City,* p. 158.

26. Thomas C. Thayer, "We Could Not Win the War of Attrition We Tried to Fight," *The Lessons of Vietnam,* W. Scott Thompson and Donaldson D. Frizzell, eds. (London: MacDonald and Jane's, 1977), p. 86.

27. Laurence I. Hewes, Jr., "Foot-Dragging on Land Reform in South Vietnam," *Center Report* (June 1972), p. 19. Hewes was an

agricultural economist who advised the U.S. government on land reform problems.

28. See article by Truong Son (pseud.) in McGarvey, *Visions of Victory,* pp. 119–149; and Van Tien Dung, *May van de nghe thuat quan su Viet-nam* [Problems of Vietnamese Military Art] (Hanoi: People's Army Publishing House, 1968), pp. 127–193.

5

Air War

The stalemate in the South meanwhile was paralleled by a stalemate over the North in the form of the air war conducted by the U.S. Air Force and Navy. Begun ostensibly as reprisal, the air war quickly broadened into an attempt to force compromise on Hanoi and to interdict Northern logistical support of revolutionary forces all over Indochina.

On an area one-third larger than France, the United States dropped 7.8 million tons of bombs, an amount greater than the total dropped by all aircraft in all of World War II. One-third of the tonnage fell from B-52s, each equipped to carry 27,000 kilograms of bombs. From altitudes over 10,000 meters, a "cell" of three B-52s could carpet a "box" one kilometer wide and three kilometers long. More than 4 million tons of bombs fell on South Vietnam, principally in remote areas or in tactical support of ground combat. About 1.5 million tons fell similarly on Laos and over 500,000 tons on Cambodia. More than 1 million tons were dropped on North Vietnam in the most intensive campaign of strategic bombing in the history of warfare.

A STRATEGY IN SEARCH OF REASON

U.S. bombings outside the South began on December 14, 1964, with eight sorties a week against the Ho Chi Minh Trail in Laos. Communist attacks on U.S. installations at Pleiku and Qui

Nhon in February provided a pretext to strike the North directly. From "reprisal airstrikes," it was a short step to sustained bombing. By late March, Operation ROLLING THUNDER was sending aircraft against the North daily. From 25,000 in 1965, the number of sorties grew to 79,000 in 1966 and 108,000 in 1967.

In the beginning, the bombing concentrated on military targets in the panhandle south of Hanoi, largely for fear of provoking Chinese intervention. But as that fear waned and panhandle targets were destroyed, restrictions on bombing near major cities and in the Red River Delta were dropped. By 1966, U.S. airplanes were striking industrial, transportation, and petroleum facilities. A year later, they were attacking just about any object, military or economic, as far north as the Chinese border. Aside from supply vehicles and bridges (repaired many times over), very few such targets remained once they'd been bombed.

The initial rationale was to coerce Hanoi into suspending its support for the revolution in the South. U.S. leaders assumed that Hanoi could not be so deeply committed to reunification that it would jeopardize the economic progress of the North in order to achieve that goal. "Graduated pressures," or "phased escalation," they theorized, would demonstrate U.S. resolve and extract concessions in negotiations. U.S. assumptions quickly proved erroneous, however. Hanoi was willing to negotiate, but not over what it maintained were basic national rights that had been guaranteed by the Geneva Agreements.[1] Nor could the bombing curtail the flow of men and supplies over the Ho Chi Minh Trail into the South. The North, in fact, was able to *increase* the flow of men and supplies over the Ho Chi Minh Trail into the South. The U.S. strategic rationale therefore shifted in mid-1965 to limiting the flow's increase. But the North, unlike Germany in World War II, possessed neither munitions plants nor industries vital to its war effort, and political considerations forbade targeting population and ports. The bombs had to fall on roads, bridges, and transportation complexes. Such targets could be quickly repaired, moved, or circumvented and so had to be bombed again and again. It seemed to many that Washington had accepted Air Force General Curtis Lemay's advice,

"We should bomb them into the stone age."[2] Punishment was the most plausible rationale left.

Bombing advocates argued that the North could be pushed to some sort of psychological "breaking point." But just what that point was and exactly how the bombing was to push the North over it—something that conventional bombing had never done to any society before—were questions U.S. strategists never posed. Nothing more clearly revealed U.S. arrogance than the facile assumption that the North Vietnamese would succumb to pressures that the British and Germans had survived in World War II. Though "graduated" intensification of the bombing gave Hanoi time to brace for attack, the keys to the North's survival were a world view and a methodology that long ago had made it certain that the North would persevere.

RESURRECTING THE RESISTANCE

The society against which the United States threw its latest technology of war was one of the world's poorest. In a population of 19 million, three-quarters were peasants. Despite some recent improvements in farming techniques, agricultural methods were largely the same as they had been for a millennium. Agricultural production was increasing at an average annual rate of 4 percent and national income at 8 percent, but in the North food was still scarce, the Red River Delta was one of the world's most densely populated, and per capita income was among the world's lowest. However, nearly 90 percent of all peasant families belonged to cooperatives. Though some families had been reluctant to join the cooperatives when established in the late 1950s, the cooperatives were based on the communities to which almost all Vietnamese felt a primordial attachment. Furthermore, a large majority of these communities had given their support to the Viet Minh during the resistance against France. (Five thousand out of 7,000 in the Red River Delta alone had done so, according to French General Henri Navarre.) As the bombing began, only ten years since the first war's end, these communities were prepared to respond almost reflexively to a call for measures to assure, as their leaders put it, "national salvation."[3]

In December 1964, People's Army propaganda teams began fanning out across the Northern countryside to organize "civilian-military unity days" in every hamlet and village. With skits and storytelling, the teams evoked the powerful imagery of national resistance, then organized the people to repair roads, ferry troops across rivers, and assist the army in every way.[4] Work also was stepped up on "combat hamlets" modelled after the fortress communities of resistance-era liberated zones. Each such hamlet had its own arsenal, underground bunkers and storehouses, outlying defenses with connecting trenches, and well-trained militia, making each hamlet a self-sufficient "basis of lasting struggle."[5] Militia forces grew to 2 million, roughly 10 percent of the population. Though these measures were carried out most urgently below the 20th parallel, much of the countryside was organized to keep supplies moving to the "front," repair bomb damage, and build an impenetrable thicket of popular self-defense against ground attack.

Meanwhile, on February 29, 1965, just two days before ROLLING THUNDER began and a day after U.S. officials announced that "reprisal airstrikes" would be extended, the North Vietnamese government issued an order to evacuate children and old people from major population centers. Vinh, the assembly point for the Ho Chi Minh Trail, quickly emptied. About 50,000 of Hanoi's less-endangered residents left by fall. A second evacuation order in April 1966 extended to everyone who was not "truly indispensable." Government agencies relocated outside the city, factories were dismantled, and the ration cards of "nonessential personnel" were invalidated. People literally had to follow their meal tickets to the countryside. Hanoi's population dropped by half. When raids killed 200 around Hanoi in November 1967, the city's population fell to 250,000, one-quarter of its pre-bombing total. Except in the port of Haiphong, the evacuation of cities that lacked Hanoi's importance was even more thorough.[6]

Dispersal of the economy followed the evacuation of the people. One objective was to move industrial targets, such as they were, away from population centers and aerial detection; another was to increase local economic self-sufficiency. A plan devised in mid-1965 envisioned the development of every prov-

THE DEMOCRATIC REPUBLIC OF VIETNAM

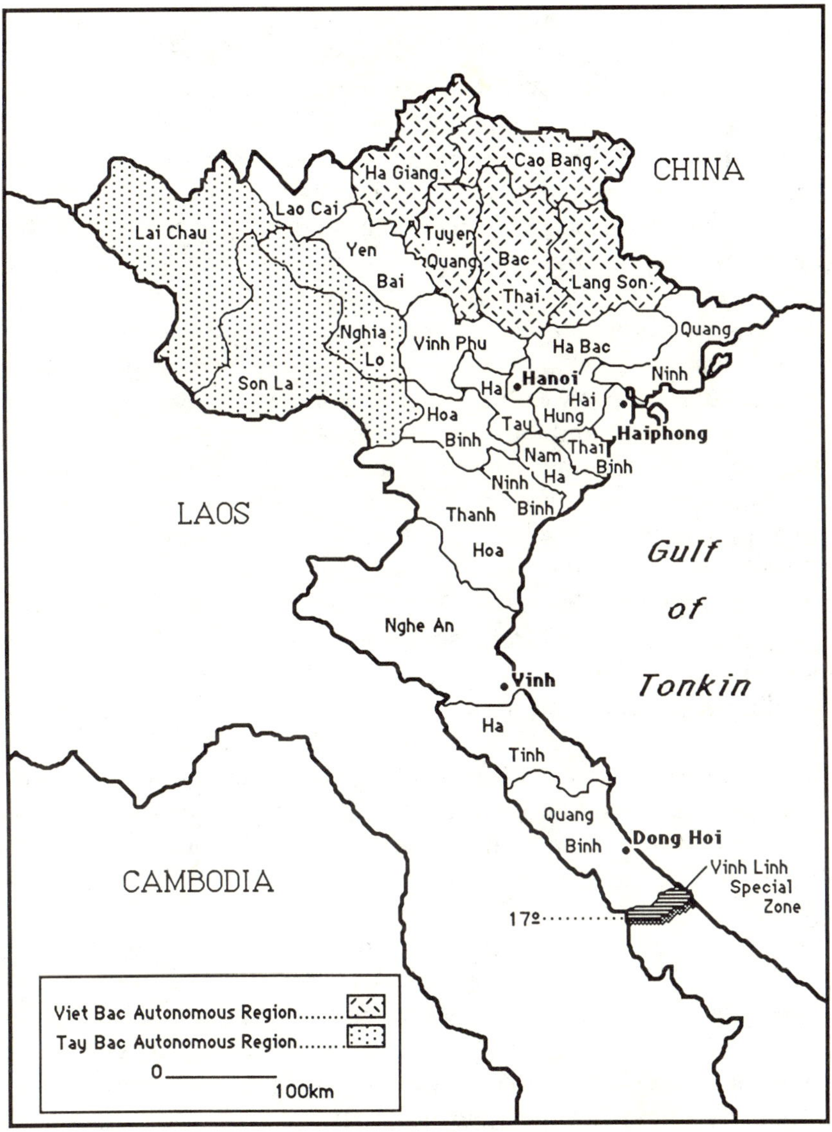

ince into an integrated, self-sustaining economic unit able to carry on resistance in the event of invasion or destruction of other provinces, just as revolutionary bases had struggled in isolation during the war against France.

The Thai Nguyen iron works and the Haiphong cement factory could not be moved. But pharmaceutical factories, machine shops, textile mills, and other enterprises were knocked down and carted off to the mountains, and in some cases were reconstructed in caves.[7] Some factories hid their machinery in huts scattered through a village; some had to relocate repeatedly to escape detection. Efficiency plummeted of course, and by 1967, many factories were producing less than half of their planned output. But home handicrafts and private production in tiny cottage industries sprang up to fill the gap in basic consumer needs. Finally, central planning gave way to local initiative. Local party cadres submitted to public criticism. Through decentralization and "direct democracy," the party sought to "recreate the resistance spirit of unity."

Nowhere were these measures more severely tested than in the panhandle provinces through which men and supplies funnelled toward the Ho Chi Minh Trail. Hit worst of all was the area just north of the demilitarized zone, which was just beginning to recover from some of the most savage typhoons on record when the bombing began. Yet people seemed more willing to sacrifice the more they were bombed. In Vinh Linh Special Zone, where even party members had shirked militia duty before the war, 42 percent of the entire population was enrolled in the militia by 1969.[8] In Quynh Luu district of Nghe An province, a dike that would have taken more than forty years to complete at prewar rates was said to have been built in six months.[9]

Such reports no doubt were colored by a desire to shore up confidence, but they also revealed a well-founded pride in the aptitude of Vietnamese villages for collective action when threatened. Northern (and central) Vietnamese society in particular had been formed in an unremitting struggle with nature. The annual cycle of drought and flood always had made individual security dependent on cooperation with others. To this, the two millennia of conflict with China had added a strong cultural identity marked by antipathy to foreign influence and deep pride in the nation's indomitability. On an almost yearly basis, the peasants had fallen back on village-based cooperation to survive natural calamity, and many times their rulers had done so to thwart a foreign invasion. So it was this time, even to the point of digging vast underground galleries in heavily bombed areas and preparing to fight entirely with local forces, as had been done in the Scholar's Revolt of the 1880s and more successfully in the war with France. Against this background, the bombing—like flood, drought, typhoon, or Chinese invasion—appeared as just one in the succession of disasters that it had been the region's lot to endure. Thus it is not surprising that the regime, which had come to power partly on the strength of village-based patriotism, was able to extract enormous sacrifices from people who made them, for the most part, without complaint.

Of course, the conditions of daily life were extremely hard, and not just in the worst-hit regions. Villages that escaped destruction of a road, bridge, or buildings nonetheless suffered from the loss of manpower, the disruption of markets, and the decline of essential supplies. Only large infusions of aid from China and the Soviet Union kept the people fed at a barely adequate level, as population growth outpaced production. Ingenious and strenuous measures maintained health care and education, but the quality of both declined. Yet the regime apparently had little difficulty persuading the people to blame their hardships on U.S. aggression and to fight back.[10] Partly to instill resolve, the regime distributed hand-held weapons to peasants and militia with instructions to set up "networks of fire" in which to ensnare low-flying planes.

The bombing actually appears to have helped the party promote some of its social objectives. Before the war, only 31 percent of all Catholic families in Nghe An province had joined cooperatives, but after just two years of bombing their 80 percent membership was near the national rate.[11] Ethnic minorities who made up 15 percent of the North's population and straddled sensitive borders found themselves the object of accelerated effort to secure their loyalty to Hanoi. Women, the second-class citizens of Confucian society, were catapulted into positions of responsibility and power.[12]

There were signs of discontent, to be sure. No less a figure than Truong Chinh grumbled openly about survival measures that had the effect of repealing socialism. Reporter Don Oberdorfer in his book *Tet!* claims on the basis of defector testimony that dissent led to the arrest of 200 officials in September 1967. A decree on punishment of "counterrevolutionary crimes" issued in November suggested, simply by its publication, that problems did exist. The state's centralized administrative control weakened. But despite all of the signs of stress, none suggested imminent collapse.

THE LIMITS OF BOMBING

President Johnson declared an end to the bombing on October 31, 1968. A response to fundamental shifts in U.S. perceptions of the war (see Chapter 6), the decision also reflected tacit acknowledgment that the United States could not go on pulverizing a society that was so much smaller, weaker, and poorer than itself without provoking moral outrage at home and abroad. U.S. strategists boasted that the campaign was "precise" and "discriminating," but they could not tell where bombs would fall when pilots jettisoned ordnance to evade attack or missed their targets. Fifteen months before the bombing ended, McNamara himself had guessed it was inflicting 1,000 civilian casualties a week and had found the spectacle disgusting.[13] Evidence that the bombing had influenced Hanoi's negotiating position was nil; evidence that it had staunched the southward flow of men and equipment was ambiguous. Besides, the United States had lost 918 aircraft, and 818 U.S. airmen had died, as a result of fire from the North's 6,000–7,000 anti-aircraft batteries and nearly 200 SA-2 missile sites. The bombing had indeed found a "breaking point," but it had turned out to be the limit of U.S. will to bomb for dubious gain.

The North was still in ruins when U.S. planes returned during 1972 to carry out the most devastating raids of the entire war.

Later, the party would reveal that the bombing had destroyed virtually all industrial, transportation, and communications facilities built since 1954, blotted out ten to fifteen years' potential economic growth, flattened three major cities and twelve of twenty-nine province capitals, and triggered a decline in per capita agricultural output.[14] Still, the North, as party leaders put it, had "defeated" the U.S. "air war of destruction" and so was able to go on serving as the "great rear" for the war in the South.

NOTES

1. Hanoi offered four points as bases for negotiations, which the United States summarily rejected. For discussion, see Paul M. Kattenburg, *The Vietnam Trauma in American Foreign Policy* (New Brunswick, N.J.: Transaction Books, 1980), pp. 131–133.
2. Quoted in David Halberstam, *The Best and the Brightest* (New York: Random House, 1969), p. 560.
3. An excellent study of the northern countryside in this period is Gerard Chaliand, *The Peasants of North Vietnam* (Baltimore: Penguin Books, 1969).
4. *Quan doi nhan dan* [People's Army], January 9, 1965, pp. 1, 2.
5. Ibid., November 14, 1964, p. 2.
6. See William S. Turley, "Urbanization in War: Hanoi, 1964–1973," *Pacific Affairs* (Fall 1975), pp. 370–397.
7. The only comprehensive survey in a western language of these measures is Jon M. Van Dyke, *North Vietnam's Strategy for Survival* (Palo Alto, Calif.: Pacific Books, 1972), pp. 189–215.
8. Article by Tran Dong, *Hoc Tap* [Study and Practice] (March 1969), p. 19.
9. Article by Ho Dinh Tu, *Hoc Tap* [Study and Practice] (August 1967), p. 30.
10. Chaliand, *The Peasants*, passim.
11. Article by Nguyen Si Que, *Hoc Tap* [Study and Practice] (March 1969), p. 49.
12. See William S. Turley, "Women in the Communist Revolution in Vietnam," *Asian Survey* (September 1972), pp. 703–805.

13. On McNamara's change of attitude see Halberstam, *The Best and the Brightest,* pp. 765–770.

14. Vietnam Communist Party, Central Committee Political Report, Fourth Party Congress, December 1976; and *Vietnam: Destruction, War Damage* (Hanoi: Foreign Languages Publishing House, 1977), p. 28.

6

Tet

At midnight on January 31, 1968, a million tiny explosions roared across the city. The bright flashes of firecrackers glowed and flickered against the buildings and rising smoke. It was Tet in Saigon, the beginning of the New Year, a sacred time of reunion and renewal. Two and one-half hours later, an old Renault taxi and a small truck crept through the now silent streets and stopped in front of the U.S. Embassy. Nineteen sappers piled out, blew a hole in the compound wall, and rushed in. Meanwhile, some 84,000 communist troops moved toward their targets in five municipalities, thirty-six province capitals, and sixty-four district seats. The Tet Offensive was under way.

For weeks the Communists had meticulously stocked weapons, ammunition, and food in the homes and businesses of urban sympathizers. Vegetable carts bound for market had carried rifles. A ship from Hong Kong had unloaded crates of ammunition marked "firecrackers" onto a dock in Saigon. Combatants and agitators had trickled into the cities one by one or in small groups aboard buses, bicycles, or on foot. Others had gathered at secret locations on the outskirts of the cities. Political cadres had made discreet contact with urban dissidents.

Not every movement went undetected, and by late January, it was apparent that something was about to happen. But the rumors had been heard before, and the evidence hinted at something too audacious to be believed. The attacks achieved almost complete surprise. Despite three years of massive U.S. involvement, the communist offensive was bigger and more complicated than ever before. It struck the very centers of previously inviolable cities. The bulk of the assault forces were indigenous Southern irregulars, and the preparations for the offensive required at least the passive collusion of many of its supposed victims. No matter how the fighting ended, U.S. claims of military victory would not be able to erase the impression that all the blood and expense had been, and always would be, for naught.

BIRTH OF AN URBAN-RURAL STRATEGY

The Tet strategy was hardly a new idea for the Vietnamese Communists. Its germ was the August Revolution, in which the Communists had provided a nucleus of armed force for the popular uprisings that had brought the party to power in 1945. Party doctrine subsequently held that surrounding the cities with rural revolution, as Maoists advocated, was insufficient in Vietnam. For if cut off from the countryside, the cities could still hold out with support from the "imperialist" hinterland. Moreover, given Vietnam's cramped geography, enemies that controlled the cities could launch powerful attacks into liberated areas if not distracted by turbulence in their own rear. The strategic solution, called "general offensive and general uprising," was to mount simultaneous armed attacks and popular uprisings at all geographical points. Even if this plan did not sweep the revolution to power, the Communists theorized, it would destroy the enemy's illusion of success.

The idea exercised a powerful hold on revolutionaries who saw themselves as ordained to lead a small, impoverished nation in resistance against more powerful foes. It was especially popular among party members whose revolutionary careers had begun amidst the patriotic fervor that had seized the cities in August 1945. Many believed that the proper stimulus could make the cities explode again. Party leaders had never neglected to consider the cities in their plans and had considered attack in the enemy's most secure areas, in coordination with region-wide popular uprisings, as their ultimate weapon. The Central Committee's resolution 9 in 1963 had foreseen the need for a "general offensive and general uprising," and in 1964, COSVN had drawn up tentative plans, selected targets, and subdivided Saigon into five "lines of attack."[1] Fairly detailed planning was under way by mid-1966.[2]

The Communists realized they could not simply replay the August Revolution, however. The United States and the "puppet" Saigon regime presented a much more formidable obstacle than the shaky Japanese-installed administration a few mobs had overwhelmed in 1945. Much more military power would have to be projected now into the cities to have great effect. But unlike the situation in 1945, power was now available and securely based in the North. The party also had a large organization in the South with which leaders believed they controlled nearly 4 million people.[3] If they bypassed U.S. positions, revolutionary forces stood a chance of destroying the "puppet."

In June 1967, Nguyen Chi Thanh travelled to Hanoi to present a draft plan for attacking the cities to the Political Bureau. Several considerations weighed in the Political Bureau's deliberations. U.S. bombing had taken such toll that communist leaders were impatient for it to end, if only so they could strengthen the North's capacity to support the war in the South. Yet U.S. leaders still appeared to believe in the possibility of military victory, and rural struggle alone seemed unlikely in the near future to make them believe differently. New difficulties would arise if the United States prolonged its involvement or invaded the North.[4] It was imperative to ward off such moves and tilt the United States toward negotiation, which the Communists believed could be done by destroying U.S. confidence. If that effort succeeded, it would be necessary also for the Communists to break up pacification and recover control in the countryside so that "fighting-while-negotiating" could be conducted from a position of strength. After heated discussion, the Political Bureau reached agreement that the time had come for the big blow.

Thanh's plan for an all-out effort apparently encountered resistance, however. General Giap, for one, doubted that Southern irregulars could do the job unaided but was loathe to place precious main forces at risk.[5] Differences over strategy stemmed partly from disagreement over the realism of seeking the immediate termination of U.S. involvement as opposed to preempting further U.S. escalation. Thanh's death on July 6, 1967, may have cleared the way for agreement on a scaled-down version of his plan.[6] In an article serialized in *Nhan dan* (The People) during September, Giap gave his grudging approval but warned against expecting quick victory. Orders went out to Southern command organs the same month. PLAF units and Southern irregulars, those orders made clear, were to bear the main burden of attacking the cities while the PAVN created diversions and stood in reserve.

What, then, did the Communists hope to achieve? Party leaders differed in expectations but agreed it should be possible to jolt the war into a new phase leading toward, if not immediately causing, U.S. withdrawal. The most optimistic hope was that the offensive would paralyze the Thieu regime's military and administrative apparatus, generate popular demand for Thieu to step aside, and end in coalition government. Thus deprived of the "puppet" on whom the United States depended to justify intervention, the United States would have no choice but to fix a date for its withdrawal. Somewhat less sanguine was the hope that the offensive would convince U.S. leaders of the futility of their "limited war" strategy. If, as the Communists surmised, the United States would be unable to escalate further, it would have to give up hope of military victory and seek a way out through negotiations.

ISLANDS OF PEACE

The cities up to this time had experienced a few terrorist incidents, but never had the fighting in the countryside pushed into their confines. A person born in Saigon, Hue, Danang, or Can Tho easily could have reached maturity without feeling any direct effect of the war. For many urbanites, U.S. intervention brought jobs and larger pay packets, not pain and suffering. The only sound of combat audible in Saigon was the low rumble of B-52 strikes thirty kilometers away. City youth also were more likely than rural youth to qualify for student draft deferment or to have families with the financial or political means to arrange avoidance of military service altogether. Urbanites were largely oblivious to the terror endured by peasants in "contested" areas and could, if they wished, regard the war as someone else's misfortune.

However, the combined effects of rural insecurity, the destructiveness of U.S. tactics, and economic distortions also had stimulated a cityward migration. The proportion of total population living in the countryside had dropped from 80 to about 70 percent, a trend that would continue and be largely irreversible.[7] This movement threatened to shrink the Communists' base of support in rural areas where they had their main strength. But it also gave them reason to hope that in the bidonvilles spreading in the outskirts and back streets of Saigon and in Danang, Qui Nhon, Cam Ranh, and a dozen lesser provincial capitals, they might find an enlarged pool of urban supporters.

Noteworthy, too, was the changing political scene in Saigon. The era of revolving-door juntas had ended, and Nguyen Van Thieu was safely ensconsed in Independence Palace. On the surface it seemed that a new elite—younger, more career-oriented, and more susceptible to U.S. influence by comparison with the mandarin Francophiles it displaced—had consolidated a firm hold on power. Thieu certainly typified the new group. Born a Buddhist in 1923, Thieu was from a modest, provincial background. Emerging from the first war a major in the French Army, he had transferred to the ARVN and in 1957 had gone for training in the United States. The next year, at the height of the Diem era, he had married into a wealthy Catholic family and converted. With his wife's connections, the right patrons, and a knack for clever maneuver, Thieu was admirably equipped to rise in the armed forces but not to provide inspiring leadership.

The consolidation of the Thieu regime had begun with elections for a Constituent Assembly in 1966 when Thieu as chief of state still shared power with Premier Nguyen Cao Ky. Elections for village councils and hamlet chiefs had followed in spring 1967, a genuine if fragile accomplishment that laid a basis for the rehabilitation of Saigon-sponsored local government.[8] At the top, however, Thieu and Ky had parted over which of them should run for the presidency provided in the new constitution. Leaders of opposing cliques, they threatened to split the military once again. Only when it became clear that the majority of senior officers as well as the United States supported Thieu had Ky agreed in June to run for vice president on Thieu's ticket.

Attention then shifted to culling the civilian candidacies, partly to reduce their exorbitant number but also to remove some genuine electoral threats. Maneuvers in the Constituent Assembly disqualified General Duong Van "Big" Minh, who had announced his intention of returning from exile on the tennis courts of Bangkok. The popular, former minister of economics, Au Truong Thanh, who revealed he once had withheld a gold sales distributorship from the chief of police, also was eliminated. Further manipulations pared down the number of slates to eleven. Of these, the best known of the civilian tickets was headed by Phan Khac Suu and Dr. Phan Quang Dan, both of whom had gained repute by spending time in Diem's jails. Another, headed by Tran Van Huong and Mai Tho Truyen, could count on the aging Huong's prominence as a lay leader of the Southern Buddhist Association to win support among Buddhists in the deep south. A third slate consisting of Truong Dinh Dzu and Tran Van Chieu lacked personal distinction but captured attention by calling for negotiations to end the war. The Dzu-Chieu slate was promptly dubbed the peace ticket.

The campaign was to have begun with a tour of the provinces by all eleven slates of candidates. But Thieu and Ky refused to join, and the air force C-47 that was to carry the other candidates to their first destination delivered them to the wrong airport. Huong claimed that "the government purposely arranged the trip to humiliate us and make clowns out of us."[9] The tour fell apart, and though a second was arranged, the civilians held the military responsible for irregularities that continued down to the end of the campaign. Thieu and his associates, however, were constrained from blatantly rigging the election by the realization that this would create insurmountable problems in Washington and that the election would take place under the scrutiny of a huge foreign press corps and other observers. On September 3, according to the published results, 83.8 percent of the South's registered voters cast ballots. The Thieu-Ky ticket won, but with only 34.8 percent of the votes. The pattern of local results suggested that Thieu and Ky did best where the military felt most free to help; they lost in Hue, Danang, and Saigon. If the results were at all accurate, it was clear that not one of the slates was the first choice of any significant segment of the electorate.

U.S. officials naturally pointed to the turnout as evidence that most South Vietnamese preferred a noncommunist government. But the election did little to confirm the stature of Thieu as the man to head it. Moreover, it had taken U.S. pressure to assure that elections were held and to unify the military. It was also obvious that civilian elites, once united in opposition to Diem, were now antagonistic to the military government, and the elections had helped to sharpen that antagonism. These elites were also deeply divided among themselves. The threat of collective defeat by the revolution was no more sufficient in 1967 than in 1964 to restrain personal ambition or vanity. Although the city scene was changing, none of this change suggested any worsening of prospects for the Communists.

KHE SANH

Communist strategy called for luring U.S. forces away from population centers, and so the Tet Offensive began neither at Tet nor in the cities. It began at Khe Sanh, the remote outpost of a U.S. Marine rifle company near the western end of Route 9. Located on an open plateau, the marine camp and nearby Khe Sanh village faced peaks over 850 meters high, behind which forested hills rolled into Laos and the demilitarized zone. There the marines found the PAVN 325c division digging into the peaks during spring 1967.[10]

The small marine camp was highly vulnerable. Though supported by artillery at the Rock Pile and Camp Carroll, it was just fourteen kilometers from the terminus of an improved road over which the PAVN could move heavy equipment. The marines therefore sent in two battalions of reinforcements. After a few sharp engagements the PAVN division shifted eastward to join other units in feints and jabs along Route 9. Infantry assaults on strongpoints, then artillery barrages, made northern Quang Tri province once again a major focus of U.S. attention.

The 325c was accompanied by the 304th division when it returned to the Khe Sanh area in December 1967. More marine reinforcements plus an ARVN battalion brought the number of base defenders up to 6,000. Finally, on January 21, the two PAVN divisions broke the suspense with attacks on hilltop outposts and a massive artillery barrage that destroyed the base's largest ammunition dump, cratered the runway, and damaged a dozen helicopters. The "siege" of Khe Sanh had begun.

Reports of PAVN divisions maneuvering in the hills around Khe Sanh conjured up the spectre of Dien Bien Phu. The U.S. command pulled 15,000 elite troops from all over the South's five northern provinces to reinforce the Route 9 combat bases, and soon a total of 50,000 U.S. troops were tied down at Khe Sanh or in its support. By the end of January, as communist assault forces assembled on city outskirts, attention in Saigon and Washington was riveted on the mountains. For days after the Tet attacks in the cities, Westmoreland and Thieu believed Khe Sanh was the "real" target and the city attacks the diversion, such a hold did Dien Bien Phu have on their thoughts.

PAVN commanders surely would have been happy to overrun Khe Sanh if given the opportunity. But the victors of Dien Bien Phu could not have been less aware than Westmoreland of the differences between the two battlefields. In the first place, Khe Sanh was not really remote, as Dien Bien Phu had been. It was barely 50 kilometers from the sea and half an hour by air from the huge airbase at Danang. The French, by contrast, had bottled themselves up in rugged mountains over 300 kilometers from their support in Hanoi. Compared to the 325 assorted aircraft available to the French Union force, the United States could draw from 2,000 aircraft including big C-123 and KC-130 transports to supply Khe Sanh with almost constant aerial cover and supplies in excess of need. Second, Khe Sanh was not a valley ringed by mountains but a plateau facing hills on one side only, and the marines held several of the peaks. The possibility of encircling the base from high ground did not exist as it had at Dien Bien Phu. Finally, although the PAVN used more firepower at Khe Sanh (122-mm artillery, 122-mm rockets, 120-mm mortars, Soviet-built PT-76 light amphibious tanks) than in any single engagement up to that time, it faced, aside from the base's own ample artillery, the 175-mm guns of Camp Carroll and massive, all-weather aerial bombardment. By the time the siege eased in mid-April, U.S. aircraft had dropped more than 100,000 tons of bombs (including 60,000 tons of napalm) on a battlefield of a dozen square kilometers.

The 20,000 PAVN troops deployed at Khe Sanh were less than one-half the number used at Dien Bien Phu (a deployment indicative of PAVN strategists' true objectives), though the PAVN had tripled in size since 1954. U.S. estimates of PAVN casualties were less than one-half the 23,000 suffered in the earlier battle. The PAVN attempted to dig siege trenches, but it was a belated effort. The PAVN never tunnelled beneath marine positions as required for an all-out assault. The level of effort was sufficient to sustain a credible diversion, but not to mount a realistic attempt to overrun the base so long as the United States was determined to hold it.

The deputy editor of *Quan doi nhan dan* (People's Army) newspaper, interviewed in Hanoi in 1984, affirmed that Khe Sanh was never intended to be another Dien Bien Phu. The earlier battle took place after seven years of war had worn down the French, whereas the United States in 1968 was at the peak of its military power. Another Dien Bien Phu at Khe Sanh, this officer said, would have been "impossible." Rather, he went on, the Khe Sanh battle, aside from providing a strategic diversion, was a test of the U.S. reaction to the PAVN's use of the demilitarized zone (DMZ). The PAVN command wanted to determine how the United States would respond if the PAVN staged attacks from the zone, specifically whether the United States would sent troops into the North.[11]

Hanoi derided the Western preoccupation with the Dien Bien Phu analogy as it applied to Khe Sanh. Communist commentators pointed instead to Lang Vei, a Special Forces/Civil Indigenous Defense Group (CIDG) camp eight kilometers east of the besieged marines. Led by eleven PT-76s, PAVN forces on February 7 completely overran the camp, killing 250 montagnard and 24 U.S. defenders.

THE ATTACK ON THE CITIES

As the PAVN hit Khe Sanh and several other highland targets, assault forces slipped around lowland outposts to penetrate the cities. Some struck prematurely at Qui Nhon, Kontum, Pleiku, Darlac, and Nha Trang on January 29, but U.S. and ARVN intelligence missed the attacks' significance. More than one-half the ARVN was on leave for Tet. If a skittish commander had not pulled several U.S. battalions closer to Saigon in early January, the city would have been almost completely devoid of reaction forces. General Westmoreland's intelligence officer later admitted that communist plans seemed so "preposterous" that no one would have believed what was about to happen had anyone known them in detail.[12] The U.S. and ARVN commands so poorly understood the strategy of their enemy that they could not take seriously the evidence of its intentions. So in the wee hours of Tet the cities lay open.

The estimated 67,000 maneuver forces and 17,000 hastily recruited guerrillas that attacked the cities had been led to believe final victory was at hand. Instructions to local party cadres spoke of annihilating Saigon's administrative apparatus and organizing the masses to help consolidate revolutionary power.[13] At higher levels, however, it was understood that these were maximum objectives. During an interview with the author in 1973, a former PLAF colonel who helped plan the attack on Saigon-Cholon remarked that "the party did not say certain places had to be held for so long, but that what could be occupied should be held as long as possible, the longer the better. Any occupation for some length of time was in some measure a success, a victory."[14]

The wave of attacks that broke on January 31 was the first of three violent surges planned for 1968. The assault on the U.S. Embassy was but the tiny if symbolically devastating kickoff. An estimated 4,000 troops joined in the attacks on Saigon, hitting Tan Son Nhut airfield, the ARVN general staff compound, government ministries, and Independence Palace. Battalion-sized forces invested several neighborhoods in Cholon. Tanks and helicopter gunships, sent to evict them, reduced entire city blocks to rubble. Forces that seized large portions of several delta towns were destroyed along with the buildings they occupied. In the large majority of cases, the attacks were beaten back in a few days.

Only in Hue did attacking forces hold out longer. The estimated 7,500-man assault force, one of the few consisting largely of uniformed PAVN regulars, entrenched itself behind the walls of the old city and fought until February 24. Roughly two-thirds of the attackers and nearly 500 ARVN and U.S. troops died in bitter door-to-door fighting, artillery shelling, and aerial bombardment that left 100,000 civilian refugees. In the aftermath, 2,800 bodies were found in mass graves, and another 2,000 people were missing, leaving behind them questions that are hotly disputed to this day (that is, who or what killed them and why).[15]

The first wave of attacks spluttered to an end with mortar and rocket barrages against several cities. Though U.S. and ARVN forces held the streets, half of all U.S. maneuver battalions were tied down in I Corps, and the ARVN had pulled back into defensive positions, leaving the countryside undefended. On April 20, a handful of dissident intellectuals presented themselves as the Vietnam Alliance of National Democratic and Peace Forces and declared adherence to the NLF in a move to broaden the revolution's appeal. A second wave of attacks in early May attempted to build on the momentum of the first, but, lacking surprise, the attacks were quickly beaten back. A third still weaker wave brought the offensive to a close in August.

Despite initial panic, neither the ARVN nor the Saigon government had collapsed. Students and sympathizers had helped to form a "revolutionary administration" in Hue and Tra Vinh, but the population mostly had taken to shelter when banner-waving activists appeared in the streets. Cadres who had freely entered rural communities as ARVN and U.S. forces withdrew to defend the cities found themselves exposed when those forces pushed back out into the countryside to resume pacification.

The U.S. estimate of 40,000 communist troops killed in the first wave of attacks was inflated, but the losses were cripplingly high. Communist battalion-sized attacks tapered off, and Washington and Saigon claimed a military victory.

THE AMBIGUITIES OF DEFEAT

But the military balance hardly mattered. As the fighting subsided in Hue, General Westmoreland claimed the Communists had used up all of their "military chips" in one last "throw of the dice." Now weakened and overextended, he said, they were vulnerable as never before, and their vulnerability presented a "great opportunity" to go for the kill. With the agreement of the Joint Chiefs, Westmoreland proposed an "amphibious hook" around the demilitarized zone to destroy bases and staging areas, attacks on sanctuaries in Laos and Cambodia, and intensified bombing of the North. Westmoreland's proposal required 206,000 more troops, an increase that would require mobilization of the reserves.[16]

Westmoreland's request was submitted in a report by General Earle G. Wheeler, chairman of the Joint Chiefs, which presented a bleak prospect if the request were not granted. Though crafted to win approval, the report, dated February 27, 1968, was more realistic than many that had preceded it. Reproduced in *The Pentagon Papers,* it made the following points:

- The current situation in Vietnam is still developing and fraught with opportunities as well as dangers.
- There is no question in the mind of MACV that the enemy went all out for a general offensive and general uprising and apparently believed that he would succeed in bringing the war to an early successful conclusion.
- The enemy failed to achieve this initial objective but is continuing his effort. Although many of his units were badly hurt, the judgement is that he has the will and the capability to continue.
- Enemy losses have been heavy; he has failed to achieve his prime objectives of mass uprisings and capture of a

large number of the capital cities and towns. However, with replacements, his indoctrination system would seem capable of maintaining morale at a generally adequate level. His determination appears to be unshaken.

- The enemy is operating with relative freedom in the countryside, probably recruiting heavily. . . . His recovery is likely to be rapid; his supplies are adequate; and he is trying to maintain the momentum of his winter-spring offensive.
- The structure of the GVN [Government of Vietnam, i.e., Saigon] has held up but its effectiveness has suffered.
- The [ARVN] held up against the initial assault. . . . However, ARVN is now in a defensive posture around towns and cities and there is concern about how well they will bear up under sustained pressure.
- The initial attack nearly succeeded in a dozen places, and defeat in those places was only averted by the timely reaction of U.S. forces. In short, it was a very near thing.

The report then came to its sober conclusion:

- MACV has three principal problems. First, logistic support north of Danang is marginal owing to weather, enemy interdiction and harassment and the massive deployment of U.S. forces into the DMZ/Hue area. Opening Route 1 will alleviate this problem but takes a substantial troop commitment. Second, the defensive posture of ARVN is permitting the VC to make rapid inroads in the formerly pacified countryside. ARVN, in its own words, is in a dilemma as it cannot afford another enemy thrust into the cities and towns and yet if it remains in a defensive posture against this contingency, the countryside goes by default. MACV is forced to devote much of its troop strength to this problem. Third, MACV has been forced to deploy 50 percent of all U.S. maneuver battalions into I Corps, to meet the threat there, while stripping the rest of the country of adequate reserves. If the enemy synchronizes an attack against Khe Sanh/Hue-Quang Tri

> with an offensive in the Highlands and around Saigon while keeping the pressure on through-out the remainder of the country, MACV will be hard pressed to meet adequately all threats. Under these circumstances, we must be prepared to accept some reverses.[17]

The report was partly a political ploy to alarm the president into expanding the war. But coming less than three months after Westmoreland had said the end of the war was in sight, it only confirmed the pessimism of the new secretary of defense, Clark Clifford, and caused the president to turn to dovish civilians for advice.[18] Disclosure of the troop request on March 10 in the *New York Times* provoked a public uproar. The official optimism of years past suddenly seemed proof of incompetence or deception. Moreover, no one could be certain that even with 206,000 additional troops the United States could impose a military solution or intimidate Hanoi into submission. Something messier seemed just as likely.

The Senate Foreign Relations Committee meanwhile had held hearings on the Tonkin Gulf Incident that cast doubt on Johnson's version of that pivotal event. Hitherto solid congressional support for the war began to ebb away. In mid-March, Senator Eugene McCarthy, the "peace candidate" for the Democratic party's presidential nomination, took 45 percent of the vote in the New Hampshire primary, inspiring Senator Robert Kennedy to join the race on an anti-war platform. Though Johnson won the primary, he sensed impending defeat. If he stood for reelection, the campaign would divide the nation; if he won, his presidency would be ineffectual. So on March 31, Johnson announced he would not seek nomination for another term, declared a bombing halt over the North except for a narrow strip above the demilitarized zone, and called on Hanoi to agree to peace talks. Hanoi accepted on condition that the talks begin by discussing a halt to the bombing altogether, and formal talks opened in Paris in May.

The Tet Offensive demolished the credibility of officials who had claimed progress, improvement, and "light at the end of the tunnel." Dovish opinion gained respectability within the

FIGURE 6.1 U.S. public support for the war

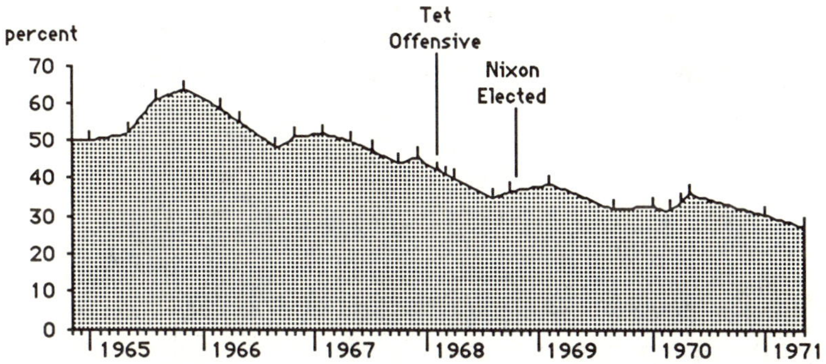

Based on Gallup Poll figures in John E. Mueller, "Trends in Popular Support for the Wars in Korea and Vietnam," The American Political Science Review, vol. 65, no. 2 (June 1971), p. 363, and The Gallup Opinion Index, no. 69 (March 1971), p. 12, and no. 73 (July 1971), p. 3. The three different questions used at various times to measure support all asked for opinion on the initial decision to involve U.S. forces in the fighting (e.g., was it a "mistake" or "the right thing?"). The months in which polling took place are indicated by points (ˈ) on top line.

administration itself. But in large measure, it was Lyndon Johnson who had defeated both himself and his policies by refusing to make hard choices. A consensus-seeking, centrist politician, he had sought to hoard the capital of his 1964 landslide victory by antagonizing no one. Fearful of the right, he had refused to "sell out" Saigon and withdraw. Reluctant to antagonize the left, he had given the Joint Chiefs less than what they asked. Needing support for domestic reforms, he had abhorred becoming the first U.S. president to lose a war. At each moment that called for decision, Johnson had chosen only to stave off defeat. But absence of defeat was a recipe for stalemate, and endless war was acceptable to no one.

Public support in the United States for the Vietnam War was about what it had been for the Korean War, though less than for World War II and a good deal more than for World War I. Support fell in response mainly to the rise in casualties and apparent inconclusiveness of the fighting (see Fig. 6.1). Vocal opposition was largely confined to the intellectual, nonunion left. As for the anti-war protest movement, it is credited by a student of U.S. wartime opinion with electing Richard Nixon twice: once in 1968 by withholding votes that would have given victory to Hubert Humphrey, and once in 1972 by capturing control of the Democratic party and nominating George McGovern, "the worst presidential candidate any party has put forward in modern times."[19]

THE COMMUNIST VICTORY

How did the Communists view Tet and its aftermath? The first COSVN assessment on January 31 claimed success in "paralyzing" the Saigon administration, confusing the U.S. command, and inflicting heavy damage. But efforts to seize "primary objectives" and to "motivate the people to stage uprisings and break the enemy's oppressive control" were disappointing.[20] The Communists realized from the start that they were unlikely to achieve their maximum aims.

In March, a fuller COSVN assessment directed attention to the successful disruption of the enemy's "two-prong tactic" of military action and rural pacification. U.S. and ARVN forces, the assessment observed, had been forced to disperse in order to defend the towns, cities, and lines of communication. In consequence, "additional wide areas in the countryside containing a population of 1.5 million inhabitants" had been liberated. The revolution had gained access to "immense resources of manpower and material." But the offensive had failed to eliminate much of the enemy armed force, the urban attacks had "not created favorable conditions for motivating the masses to arise," and recruitment was insufficient to sustain "continuous offensives and uprisings." Only in a fleeting reference to "internal contradictions" that "weakened the U.S. will of aggression" did the assessment include the Tet Offensive's U.S. domestic scene.[21] Some kind of victory was still sought in altering the actual balance of military and political forces inside South Vietnam.

The Communists barely acknowledged the opening of the Paris talks as they proceeded in May with their second wave of planned attacks. "The Americans," *Quan doi nhan dan* editorialized, "have not given up, so our people will have to suffer more before we can win final victory." In fact, Southern cadres had begun to question whether they should do all of the suffering to obtain relief for the North alone; others wondered why, if negotiations had begun, they had to go on fighting. General Van Tien Dung, the PAVN chief of staff, felt constrained to point out that a bombing halt was essential if the North were to strengthen its role as the "great rear area" for the Southern revolution,[22] and a COSVN directive dated January 10 castigated cadres who had thought the campaign would be a "one-blow affair."[23]

The U.S. agreement to an unconditional bombing halt and to NLF participation in four-party talks allowed the Communist party to claim a satisfactory outcome. The United States, cadres were told, had been forced to deescalate, cease bombing of the North, and join Hanoi at the conference table.[24] Final victory was conceded to lie in an indeterminate future, but the "limited war" strategy had been discredited. U.S. plans to escalate had been preempted, and the war had entered the penultimate phase of "fighting-while-negotiating."[25]

The party's official history describes the Tet Offensive as a great victory, and in the only sense that mattered—the strategic outcome—it was. But many cadres had hoped to turn the tide of battle *inside South Vietnam* and regretted the cost they had had to pay just for psychological impact inside the United States. Former PLAF leader Madame Nguyen Thi Dinh described the post-Tet period to the author as an "especially difficult time" for the Southern revolution. Just why it was difficult has been explained in bitter detail by one of the offensive's chief planners, General Tran Van Tra:

> In Tet 1968, we did not correctly assess the concrete balance of forces between ourselves and the enemy. Nor did we fully realize that the enemy still had considerable capabilities while ours were limited. Consequently, we set requirements that exceeded our actual strength. That is, we based our action not on scientific calculations or careful weighing of all factors but, in part, on an illusion which arose from subjective desire. Although the decision was wise, ingenious and timely . . . and created a significant strategic turning point in Vietnam and Indochina, we suffered heavy losses of manpower and material,

> especially of cadres at various echelons, which caused a distinct decline in our strength. Subsequently, we not only were unable to preserve all the gains we had made but also had to endure myriad difficulties in 1969-70 so that the revolution could stand firm in the storm. While it is obvious that the road to revolution is never a primrose path, . . . in Tet, 1968, had we considered things more carefully and set forth correct requirements in conformity with the balance of forces between the two sides, our victory would have been even greater, our cadres, troops and people would have spilled less blood, and the subsequent development of the revolution would have been much different.[26]

Whether Tra blamed himself or others is not clear. But Southern cadres tended to believe that things would have been different if Nguyen Chi Thanh had lived. He, many believed, would have kept the more cautious high command in Hanoi from scaling down his plan, and his genius for mass organization would have guaranteed a better popular response in the cities. The first wave of attacks would have been more powerful, touching off uprisings that would have made the second wave more powerful still. Each successive surge of violence would have been stronger than the last. As it was, complained one former regroupee captain, the campaign had "an elephant's trunk and a snake's tail": It started small and ended smaller.[27] Behind such views lay the firm conviction, held even by defectors, that what had prevented the masses from rising to support the revolution was fear of reprisal. If the enemy's "oppressive apparatus" had been broken, the people would have flocked to the revolution's banner. A short leap of faith sustained Southern cadres' confidence that more force and better organization would inspire greater uprisings next time. As General Tra wrote, "Tet 1968 was an extremely valuable practical experience."[28]

NOTES

1. Tran Van Tra, *Nhung chang duong cua "B2-Thanh dong": tap V, Ket thuc cuoc chien tranh 30 nam* [Stages on the Road of the B2-Bulwark, vol. V, Concluding the 30 Years War] (Ho Chi Minh City: Van Nghe Publishing House, 1982), p. 144.

2. See the letter from comrade Ba (Le Duan) to the Saigon regional party committee, *Viet-Nam Documents and Research Notes* [hereinafter cited as *VNDRNs*], no. 102, part I (Saigon: U.S. Mission, February 1972).

3. Tra, *Ket thuc cuoc chien tranh 30 nam,* p. 128.

4. See planning documents for attacks on Saigon-Cholon, *VNDRNs,* no. 45 (October 1968), especially p. 10.

5. Vo Nguyen Giap, *May van de ve duong loi quan su cua Dang ta* [Some Problems of Our Party's Military Line] (Hanoi: Truth Publishing House, 1970), pp. 325–384.

6. Thanh's official obituary, corroborated by defectors, said he died of heart failure in Hanoi. U.S. intelligence claimed he died in a B-52 strike in Binh Duong province (or in Hanoi from wounds suffered in such a strike).

7. See Allen E. Goodman and Lawrence M. Franks, "Dynamics of Migration to Saigon, 1964–1972," *Pacific Affairs,* 48, no. 2 (Summer 1975), pp. 199–214.

8. For a hopeful assessment of prospects for creating "political community" through elections, see Allen E. Goodman, *Politics in War: The Bases of Political Community in South Vietnam* (Cambridge, Mass.: Harvard University Press, 1973).

9. *Saigon Post* (August 8, 1967), cited in Charles A. Joiner, *The Politics of Massacre: Political Processes in South Vietnam* (Philadelphia: Temple University Press, 1974), p. 126; also see pp. 97–171 for detailed analysis of this election.

10. Background on Khe Sanh found in Willard Pearson, *The War in the Northern Provinces, 1966–1968* (Washington, D.C.: Department of the Army, 1975), pp. 29–80; and in Bernard C. Nalty, *Air Power and the Fight for Khe Sanh* (Washington, D.C.: United States Air Force History, 1973).

11. Interview with Colonel Nghiem Tuc by the author in Hanoi, April 23, 1984.

12. Westmoreland, *A Soldier Reports* (New York: Doubleday, 1979), p. 321.

13. See the directive of November 1, 1967, from the party's southern provincial-level standing committee in Gareth Porter, ed., *Vietnam: The Definitive Documentation of Human Decisions* (Stanfordville, N.Y.: Earl M. Coleman Enterprises, 1979), pp. 477–480.

14. Interview with the author.

15. Saigon and U.S. propaganda blamed communist terrorism for the civilians found dead in mass graves and for the civilians considered missing. A former PAVN senior captain who had commanded a

battalion just north of Hue, interviewed by the author in 1973, blamed U.S. bombardment. Other reports blamed a combination of deliberate communist executions, poorly supervised cadres, personal vendettas, and the crossfire. See Dan Oberdorfer, *Tet!* (Garden City, N.Y.: Doubleday, 1971); Steve Hosmer, *Viet Cong Repression and Its Implications for the Future* (Lexington, Mass.: Heath, 1970), p. 28; and Gareth Porter, "U.S. Political Warfare in Vietnam—The 1968 'Hue massacre,'" *Indochina Chronicle* (June 1974).

16. John B. Henry, "February 1968," *Foreign Policy* (Fall 1971), pp. 17, 21.

17. *The Pentagon Papers,* Senator Mike Gravel edition (Boston: Beacon, 1971), vol. 2, pp. 546–547.

18. See Clark Clifford, "A Viet Nam Reappraisal," *Foreign Affairs* (July 1969), pp. 601–622.

19. John Mueller, "Reflections on the Vietnam Antiwar Movement and on the Curious Calm at the War's End," in Peter Braestrup, ed., *Vietnam as History* (Washington, D.C.: University Press of America, 1984), p. 153.

20. "Circular from Central Office of South Vietnam," in Patrick J. McGarvey, ed. and trans., *Visions of Victory: Selected Vietnamese Communists Military Writings, 1964–1968* (Stanford: Hoover Institution Publications, 1969), pp. 252–256.

21. "Requirement and Purpose of Study of the Sixth Revolution of Nam Truong," notes of a cadre, *VNDRNs,* no. 38 (July 1968).

22. *Quan doi nhan dan* [People's Army], June 17, 1968, pp. 1–3.

23. Captured document released to the press by the U.S. Mission, Saigon, August 21, 1968, in Porter, *Vietnam: The Definitive Documentation,* pp. 512–516.

24. Captured document released to the press by the U.S. Mission, Saigon, November 8, 1968, in Porter, *Vietnam: The Definitive Documentation,* pp. 517–519.

25. Cuu Long (pseud.), in *Quan doi nhan dan* [People's Army], January 15, 1969, pp. 2–3.

26. Tra, *Ket thuc cuoc chien tranh 30 nam,* pp. 57–58.

27. Interviewed in Saigon in 1973.

28. Tra, *Ket thuc cuoc chien tranh 30 nam,* pp. 57–58.

7

The Road to Paris

On Sunday afternoon October 8, 1972, Henry Kissinger had his "most thrilling moment in public service." The venue, no. 108 avenue de General Leclerc in Gif-sur-Yvette, was the one-story cottage that cubist painter Fernand Léger had bequeathed to the French Communist party. Seated across the green baize table, Political Bureau member Le Duc Tho was repeating over and over: "This is what you yourself have proposed. . . . It is the same proposal made by President Nixon himself—ceasefire, release of prisoners, and troop withdrawal. . . . As to the internal political and military questions of South Vietnam we agree on principles. . . . This new proposal is exactly what President Nixon himself proposed." Kissinger, President Nixon's national security adviser, instantly recognized Tho's words as the breakthrough he had long desired. Eighteen days later, Radio Hanoi unveiled what four years of secret negotiations had wrought, and Kissinger announced that "peace is at hand."[1]

But peace was still three months away. The war continued as it had during the four years of talks, bloody as ever. From beginning to end, getting out of the war proved to be more difficult than getting in. For Nixon and Kissinger were determined to withdraw at no cost to U.S. prestige, and the Communists demanded withdrawal on terms the United States had vowed never to accept. Groping for "peace with honor," the only options the United States had were to impose a solution by some massive spasm of violence or to shift the burden to their South Vietnamese allies. In the end the United States exercised both options, obtained peace for itself, and left the Vietnamese to continue the fighting.

With thrusts into Cambodia and Laos and resumed bombing of the North, Lyndon Johnson's successors sought to wring concessions from Hanoi as they turned over vast amounts of equipment to a growing, improving ARVN. But the inevitability of U.S. disengagement, declared by U.S. leaders themselves, gave the Communists reason to hold out for their maximum terms. "Fighting while negotiating," the Communists coordinated military with diplomatic struggles in an effort to deepen the "contradictions" in the enemy camp. Thus protracting the conflict, they sought to corrode U.S. will to the point where Washington would beg permission to leave.

THE NIXON-KISSINGER STRATEGY

Richard Nixon was an unlikely peacemaker, especially where Indochina was concerned. As a junior congressman in the 1940s, he had built a reputation battling the spectre of domestic communism. As vice president in the Eisenhower administration, he had recommended that the United States intervene to rescue the French at Dien Bien Phu, and Lyndon Johnson, then leader of the Democratic party majority in the Senate, had denounced "Nixon's war." In 1967, Nixon had vigorously defended the U.S. involvement in Vietnam on the grounds that it had contained China and bought time for "free" Asian nations to build themselves.[2] But on taking office as president in January 1969, he declared a "war for peace." To an aide, he said: "I'm not going to end up like LBJ [Johnson], holed up in the White House afraid to show my face in the street. I'm going to stop that war. Fast."[3]

In Henry Kissinger, the German-born Harvard professor and strategist of global power, Nixon found an improbable ally. Nixon was often thought of as vindictive, aloof, and insecure; Kissinger loved to charm and jest. Prior to his appointment by moderate conservative Nixon, Kissinger had associated with Republican liberals and run diplomatic errands for Democrat Johnson. But, like Nixon, Kissinger disdained bureaucracy and savored intrigue. Although Kissinger had equivocated about U.S. involvement in Vietnam at the beginning, he had come to see the commitment as important because it had been made. Consummate courtier and cunning bureaucratic infighter, Kissinger was abundantly willing and superbly qualified to supply the shape for Nixon's wish. On taking office, the two men were optimistic that a fresh start and new approaches could break the negotiating deadlock.

But huge gaps in perception and principle still divided the two sides. Hanoi's terms had not changed since April 8, 1965, when Premier Pham Van Dong had enunciated "four points" based on the 1954 Geneva Agreements. The four points called for (1) recognition of Vietnam's national right to peace, independence, sovereignty, unity, and territorial integrity, and cessation of all U.S. military activity in both the North and South; (2) strict implementation of the 1954 proscription against military alliances with foreign countries and foreign military bases "while Vietnam is still temporarily divided into two zones"; (3) settlement of South Vietnam's internal affairs "in accordance with the program of the South Vietnam National Front for Liberation"; and (4) peaceful reunification by the Vietnamese people in both zones without foreign interference.[4] The third point required establishment of a coalition government that would have to include the NLF.

The United States, ironically, had been no less enthusiastic than Hanoi in professing fidelity to the Geneva Agreements. Washington's "fourteen points" of January 7, 1966, had listed the Geneva Agreements in the first place as "an adequate basis for peace in Southeast Asia." But Lyndon Johnson also had said in 1965, in a speech at Johns Hopkins University on April 7, that the United States was committed "to help South Vietnam defend its independence." This implied that South Vietnam was a sovereign independent state with the sole right to fix the terms on which it would consider reunification with the North, if at all.

Accordingly, the Johnson administration had insisted on withdrawal of North Vietnamese troops in advance of U.S. withdrawal and had refused to discuss political arrangements except in terms of the South's "self-determination." Nixon and Kissinger supported these positions. To get talks moving, Kissinger persuaded Nixon to propose a mutual troop withdrawal and "restoration" of the demilitarized zone as a boundary. But this proposal, by implying that North Vietnamese as well as U.S. troops were "foreign" to South Vietnam and that Vietnam was two countries, ran directly counter to Hanoi's nonnegotiable position that Geneva had affirmed Vietnam's juridical unity.

The Nixon-Kissinger proposal was tantamount to a demand for an independent and noncommunist South Vietnam as a prerequisite of U.S. withdrawal; what happened later was for the Vietnamese to decide. The United States also insisted that withdrawal had to occur under circumstances that could not be construed as defeat. U.S. credibility among wavering allies in Europe and its value as a counterweight to Soviet power in Asia were now at stake. To those who urged Nixon to imitate De Gaulle's pullout from North Africa, Kissinger pointed out that the general had taken four years to extricate France from Algeria precisely because it had been crucial to keep his nation's "cohesion and international stature intact." This had required De Gaulle to withdraw "as an act of policy, not as a collapse, in a manner reflecting a national decision and not a rout."[5] Nixon and Kissinger intended to do the same.

As for means, Kissinger had conceded before his appointment that military strategy was incapable of producing victory. Therefore, he had written, military operations should be geared solely to negotiating objectives, and the responsibility for conduct of the war should be turned back to the South Vietnamese. The United States should negotiate only over military issues, leaving political questions to the Vietnamese. If Hanoi proved intransigent and the war dragged on, Kissinger concluded, "we should seek to achieve as many of our objectives as possible unilaterally."[6] The final element in the U.S. strategy was supplied by Nixon's "madman theory of war." "'They'll believe any threat of force Nixon makes because it's Nixon,' the president explained to an aide. 'We'll just slip the word to them that, for God's sake, you know Nixon's obsessed about Communism . . . and he has his hand on the nuclear button.'"[7] Fearful of that "madman Nixon," Nixon calculated, Hanoi would gladly negotiate with the good Dr. Kissinger. Such, then, was the Nixon-Kissinger plan for "peace with honor." To the Communists, however, a plan for withdrawal that left the South firmly in the hands of an anticommunist government looked like a plan for peace through U.S. victory. This they were bound to resist.

WIDENING THE WAR

Nixon and Kissinger soon had a chance to test their ideas. Although Johnson had stopped the bombing unconditionally, the United States believed it had Hanoi's promise that communist forces would cease attacks on major cities and across the demilitarized zone. A pullout from the South by a few PAVN units in summer and fall 1968 seemed to confirm Hanoi's assent to the "understanding." But Nixon had no sooner settled into office than he received evidence that Hanoi had begun to infiltrate more troops and to prepare for a new offensive. Rather than resume the bombing of the North, which was sure to provoke a public outcry, the president turned his attention to the communist sanctuaries in Cambodia.

Thirteen in number, the sanctuaries were a string of staging areas, supply dumps, and rear-echelon headquarters scattered from Laos to the Gulf of Thailand just inside or straddling Cambodia's border with Vietnam. Since the massive "search and destroy" operations near the border in 1966, the Communists had relied increasingly on the sanctuaries, with the reluctant consent of Cambodia's Prince Norodom Sihanouk. Sihanouk also had given the Vietnamese access to the port of Sihanoukville. With the connivance of the Royal Cambodian Army, supplies destined for the sanctuaries were hauled by the Hak Ly Trucking Company to the Parrot's Beak, a salient of Cambodian territory that jutted toward Saigon.

Resigned to a communist victory in Vietnam, Sihanouk had sought to salvage some benefit from what he could not prevent. In return for his cooperation, he demanded firm recognition of the existing Vietnam-Cambodia border; that recognition was given by the NLF (not Hanoi). The Vietnamese also limited the support they almost certainly otherwise would have given to the Cambodian Communists, or Khmer Rouge, and the number of Khmer Rouge combatants remained stable at about 1,500 to 3,000 throughout the late 1960s.[8] Meanwhile, the Vietnamese had kept to themselves in bases located hard on the border in thinly populated areas.

Though the U.S. military command in Saigon considered the sanctuaries a menace, recommendations to attack them had clashed with Washington's political scruples. Cross-border operations had been limited to sporadic ARVN intrusions in "hot pursuit" and highly clandestine forays by montagnard mercenaries under Green Beret officers.[9] But Nixon wanted to preempt communist offensives, and in the absence of more attractive alternatives, bombing the sanctuaries gained appeal. So did the idea of signalling Hanoi that Nixon was prepared to take unprecedented steps to break the negotiating deadlock.

Into this receptive environment, General Creighton Abrams, General Westmoreland's replacement since mid-1968, sent a cable on February 9 claiming to have located COSVN headquarters in Base 353, five kilometers inside Cambodia, and requested authority to attack with B-52s. On the 23rd, Nixon approved.

Thus began the secret bombing of Cambodia. On March 18, following procedures that had been carefully contrived to conceal their destination, forty-eight B-52s dropped their long strings of bombs into a patch of Cambodian territory covering twenty-five square kilometers. The mission, code-named Operation BREAKFAST, went unnoticed and unprotested. After BREAKFAST came LUNCH, SNACK, and DINNER, until over a period of fourteen months 3,630 B-52 sorties had dropped bombs on all but two of the sanctuaries in operations known collectively as MENU.

The secret, revealed in the *New York Times* on May 9, aroused no public interest. Nixon, however, rushed to plug the leak with taps on the telephones of key officials. Lacking judicial warrant, this action violated U.S. law—the first such abuse of power that would lead to Watergate. What did the administration want so desperately to keep secret? Given that the Communists had been the first to compromise Cambodia's neutrality, Washington might have seen benefit in making its riposte public. Moreover, the United States had interpreted signs from Sihanouk the year before as indications he would acquiesce to this action,[10] and, indeed, Sihanouk denied knowing about the bombing for months after it began. The ostensible reason for secrecy was, as Kissinger put it, "to avoid *forcing* the North Vietnamese, Prince Sihanouk . . . and the Soviets and Chinese into public reactions they might not be eager to make."[11] But the administration also did not seek congressional approval for what was, regardless of the justification, an act of war that expanded the fighting just as sentiment in Congress was building to end it. Not until June was a full briefing given to congressional leaders, and the briefing was limited to figures who could be counted on to support military action. Secrecy helped to avoid a confrontation with Congress, but it also assured that when the discovery was made, the confrontation would be sharp.

In Cambodia, elements within Sihanouk's government were emboldened by the bombing to press for closure of the sanctuaries. In April 1969, war goods ceased to pass through Sihanoukville or were held up in Royal Cambodian Army depots.[12] Diplomatic relations with the United States, suspended since 1965, were resumed in June. Of these developments, a PLAF headquarters cadre wrote in early fall that "due to the confusing political situation in Cambodia, . . . we have met many difficulties in our diplomatic relations with Cambodia from the Central down to the local levels." The United States, he predicted, "will attack deep in the border areas to pressure Cambodia. They will try to sow division among Cambodian ranks and undermine the solidarity of Cambodia and our country. As for Cambodia, insurmountable difficulties will arise if she demands aid from the U.S."[13]

It was a prediction the Vietnamese Communists knew they could make come true. In January 1970, the Central Committee's 19th Plenum foresaw disruption of supply routes to the Mekong Delta and ordered work to begin on a pipeline network and upgrading of land routes. "Special attention," the plenum added, should be paid to coordination with "Laotian soldiers and people in central and southern Laos" as well.[14] The whole delicate arrangement by which Sihanouk had kept his country out of the war, and the Khmer Rouge at bay, was about to unravel.

Meanwhile, if the bombing of Cambodia damaged the Communists' rear bases, it did nothing to modify their stand in negotiations. The NLF unveiled "ten points" on May 8 that reiterated demands for unconditional U.S. withdrawal and a coalition government excluding Thieu. This was followed a month later by the creation of a Provisional Revolutionary Government of the Republic of South Vietnam (PRG) headed by Huynh Tan Phat, chief of the People's Revolutionary party, actually the Communist party's Southern branch. NLF President Nguyen Huu Tho, a party member since 1963, became chairman of the PRG's council of advisers. The DRV National Assembly recognized the new structure as the "legal government and true representative of the people of South Vietnam."[15]

Perceiving no basis for compromise yet under pressure in the United States to end the war, Nixon and Kissinger proceeded unilaterally with gradual troop withdrawals and accelerated strengthening of the ARVN. The first step, they calculated, would silence domestic criticism and deprive Hanoi of hope that the U.S. people would press for peace on communist terms; the second would lay a basis for eventual total withdrawal in circumstances acceptable to the United States, whether Hanoi agreed or not. Nixon announced the first withdrawal of 25,000 troops in June, and a month later, in what came to be known as the Nixon Doctrine, he expressed the opinion that the United States in future should not involve U.S. manpower in limited wars between Asian states.

But Nixon, afraid of losing public support if he did not soon break the negotiating logjam, also ordered the National Security Council to draw up plans for "savage, punishing blows"—an order that was deliberately leaked to the press in the hope of softening Hanoi's stance. He also made known his desire to improve his relations with Moscow—if Moscow would help wring concessions from Hanoi. Kissinger then sought a secret meeting with DRV plenipotentiary Xuan Thuy, through the assistance of Jean Sainteny, the former French delegate-general in Hanoi. Meeting with Thuy in Sainteny's Paris apartment on August 4, Kissinger suggested compromise.

This was not the first time that Hanoi and Washington had made surreptitious contact. Indirect contact had been made through representatives of the Canadian, French, British, Italian, Polish, Romanian, Norwegian, Soviet, and Chinese governments at various times, beginning as early as June 1964. The first official direct contact had taken place between the U.S. ambassador and the DRV consul general in Rangoon, Burma, in December 1965; another such channel had opened briefly between the U.S. and DRV embassies in Moscow in January 1967. Kissinger himself, while still professor of government at Harvard, had joined with two Frenchmen, Herbert Marcovich and Raymond Aubrac, the latter a personal friend of Ho Chi Minh, to convey messages between Washington and Hanoi. Marcovich and Aubrac had made a trip to Hanoi in July 1967 with the blessing of both the French and U.S. governments, and from then until October, they and Kissinger had served as conduits for a spate of exchanges. But these contacts had been only preliminaries, not negotiations of substance, and they had come to naught. So too had the secret meetings that took place, once the Paris talks had opened, between the heads of the DRV and U.S. delegations. In meeting Thuy, Kissinger could only hope that a new mix of carrot-and-stick strategies, spelled out in a new context, might lead eventually to an exchange of concessions. But Thuy, though he consented to continue secret discussions at a higher level, was impervious to Kissinger's pleas for compromise.

In fact, Hanoi was calling the U.S. bluff, and it was the United States that backed down. The National Security Council reported that airstrikes and blockades of Northern ports would be insufficient to extract concessions. Key presidential advisers recommended against action that might provoke a domestic backlash. The anti-war movement displayed undiminished vigor in demonstrations on October 15. Troop withdrawals, it was found, did not win back support for the troops that remained but rather fueled demand for more withdrawals. By November, Nixon, abandoning plans for "savage, punishing blows," had no policy save the rather vague idea of turning the war over to the South Vietnamese.

But the disappointment also made Nixon combative. In a speech on November 3, he conjured up a spectre of the bloodbath that would follow "precipitate withdrawal," pinned the blame on the protesters, and appealed for support from the patriotic "silent majority." Opinion polls showed that the majority of the U.S. population believed the initial decision to enter the war had been a mistake, but approval of Nixon's handling of it shot up dramatically (to 65 percent in January 1970). The U.S. public wanted out of the war, the polls said, but on Nixon's terms. Nixon was pleased. "We've got those liberal bastards on the run now," he told an aide.[16] But all he really had done was to buy a little time to consider his options, among which "savage, punishing blows" remained very much alive.

THE LULL

The temptation to strike was irresistible, partly because Nixon's own program of withdrawals had set a limit on how long U.S. power would be available for that purpose. Moreover, the Communists had suffered setbacks and seemed vulnerable. Under the combined pressure of 500,000 U.S. troops, a growing ARVN, and accelerated pacification, the Communists had been unable to recover from losses suffered in the 1968 offensive. A revolution that once had promised rural youths adventure and advancement was now known to be filled with hardship and death. There was "no point in drafting more people," one local party organ reported, "because they will desert anyway."[17] Northern regulars increasingly filled in PLAF units and sometimes found themselves sharing even their food with local guerrillas who were supposed to be self-sufficient.[18]

U.S. intelligence estimates showed communist armed forces in the South declining from 250,300 in 1968 to 197,700 in 1971.[19] With the number of PAVN troops in the South during those years fairly stable at 80,000 to 90,000,[20] the decline in the communist armed forces had come largely from the depletion of Southern ranks. General Abrams, charged with fighting a rearguard action anyway, abandoned Westmoreland's big unit "search and destroy" strategy of attrition. In its place the former tank commander and Patton protégé ordered his officers to place less emphasis on "body count," more emphasis on small-unit patrolling and territorial security, and to integrate combat operations with pacification.

The Communists felt the pressure. General Tran Van Tra recalled bitterly that in this period many local party organs and cadres were "lost." In heavily populated Long An province, the independent main force 320th regiment, sent to obstruct pacification, had to disperse into platoons and squads and take over the work of defunct political organizations. "Sending a concentrated main force unit to operate in such a dispersed manner," wrote Tra, "so that it could be said no longer to be a main force unit, was something we did most reluctantly, but there was no alternative under the circumstances at that time."[21] Lengthy articles by the PAVN's top brass in December 1969 obliquely acknowledged that the Southern revolution was "temporarily" in a defensive posture.

The revolution was not disintegrating, however. Though U.S. officials pointed proudly to TV antennas sprouting from thatched roofs as proof that the "other war" was being won, popular attitudes changed very slowly. Military power could increase the risk of supporting the revolution and force the Communists to revert to small unit warfare, but it could not impose a new set of loyalties. Communist cadres did not all die or defect; some went into hiding. James Trullinger, in *Village at War,* has described how one community, literally in the shadow of the U.S. Army 101st airborne division encampment, remained sympathetic to the revolution behind a "pacified" exterior. What is perhaps most revealing is that although U.S. combat deaths were declining, those of the ARVN were running at twice their pre-1968 levels and rising. The "lull," as it was called by the United States, referred only to the big unit warfare. Down in the villages and hamlets, the Communists still initiated most of the combat contacts and were exacting a fearful toll among their fellow Vietnamese (see Figure 7.1). But there was no denying that both the communist political "infrastructure" and armed forces in the South had been weakened, and in some

FIGURE 7.1 U.S. and ARVN combat deaths

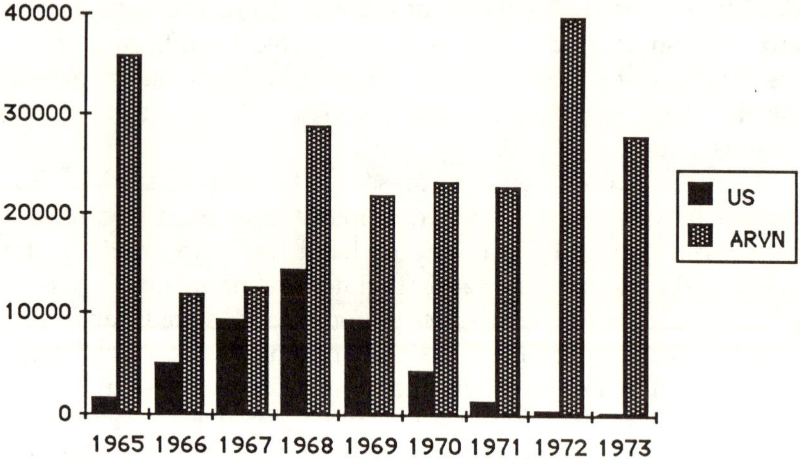

Figures cumulative to 1965. Based on figures in Peter Braestrup (ed.), Vietnam as History (Washington, D.C.: University Press of America, 1984), appendix I.

areas they were growing weaker. During what was a respite mainly for U.S. forces, the United States sought to back out, leaving South Vietnamese to carry on the war.

VIETNAMIZATION

In March 1969, MACV reported to the National Security Council that the situation in Vietnam had improved to the point where the United States could soon begin to "de-Americanize" the war. "'I agree,' Defense Secretary Melvin Laird replied, 'but not with your term 'de-Americanizing.' What we need is a term like 'Vietnamizing' to put the emphasis on the right issues.'"[22] Once named, necessity took on the aura of strategy.

In a sense, Vietnamization had begun in 1968 with a general mobilization that had raised the total of armed forces under Saigon's command to over 800,000, of which 380,000 were in the regular army. By 1970, the total was near 1 million; over half those troops were irregular territorial defense forces (see Table 7.1).

Table 7.1
Republic of Vietnam armed forces strength[a]

	Army	Air Force	Navy	Marine Corps	Total Regular	Regional Forces	Popular Forces	Total Territorial	Grand Total
1954–55	170,000	3,500	2,200	1,500	177,200	54,000[b]	48,000[b]	102,000	279,200
1959–60	136,000[c]	4,600	4,300	2,000	146,000	49,000[c]	48,000	97,000	243,000
1964	220,000	11,000	12,000	7,000	250,000	96,000	168,000	264,000	514,000
1967	303,000	16,000	16,000	8,000	343,000	151,000	149,000[c]	300,000	643,000
1968	380,000	19,000	19,000	9,000	427,000	220,000	173,000	393,000	820,000
1969	416,000	36,000	30,000	11,000	493,000	190,000	214,000	404,000	897,000
1970	416,000	46,000	40,000	13,000	515,000	207,000	246,000	453,000	968,000
1971–72	410,000[c]	50,000	42,000	14,000	516,000	284,000	248,000	532,000	1,048,000

[a]All figures are approximate.
[b]Civil Guard (later Regional Forces) and Self-Defense Corps (later Popular Forces) were officially authorized only in 1956.
[c]Decline due to increased desertions and recruiting shortfalls.

Source: James Lawton Collins, Jr., *The Development and Training of the South Vietnamese Army, 1950–1972* (Washington, D.C.: Department of the Army, 1975), appendix D, p. 151.

ARVN firepower also increased as departing U.S. units left behind their arms and equipment. By 1970, the ARVN was amply equipped with the latest U.S. small arms and was beginning to acquire sophisticated heavy artillery (e.g., 175-mm self-propelled guns), tanks, trucks, aircraft, and communications equipment. The value of U.S. arms transfers to Saigon rose from $725 million in 1968 to $925 million in each year of 1969 and 1970. (PAVN receipts from communist countries fell from $525 million in 1968 to $200 million in 1970.)[23] U.S. units began cutting back on offensive patrols, leaving them to the ARVN. Figures on III Corps near Saigon showed the ARVN accounting for only 20 percent of enemy killed-in-action in fall 1969, but by spring 1970 that figure was 32 percent and rising.[24] The Communists' charge that the aim of Vietnamization was to "change the color of the corpses" was crude but accurate.

Pacification received a boost, too. Realizing the inevitability of U.S. withdrawal, and seeing an opportunity in the Communists' post-Tet fallback, the United States had launched a three-month accelerated pacification program in November 1968 and then prolonged it as fixed policy. The "other war" finally got its chance.

"Accelerated pacification," i.e., a rush to "clear and hold" territory as communist strength declined, coordinated and updated programs that previously had functioned separately and been given low priority. One program, financed by the CIA and headed by former Viet Minh officer Nguyen Be, trained 59-man teams to spearhead "rural construction." Rural development, or RD, teams were sent out to help reorganize village administration, start construction projects, and train villagers to defend themselves. Another, the Chieu Hoi, or Open Arms, amnesty program, offered defectors (euphemistically called ralliers) a new life on the government side. Perhaps most controversial because easily abused was the Phoenix Program, which was supposed to upgrade Saigon's police and, through special "provincial reconnaissance units," to root out the Communists' political organization.

The hitherto missing political element was supplied when President Thieu, realizing his survival depended on enlarging his political base before the United States withdrew, agreed to village elections and administrative decentralization in 1969. A year later, he issued a sweeping decree under the slogan Land to the Tiller that recognized peasants' title to land given them by the Communists, and he set up a scheme to liquidate remaining tenancy. In theory, the reforms were to give the peasants a stake in defending their villages. Not incidentally, Thieu hoped the reforms would make the peasants grateful to him. In effect, however, the reforms only repealed his predecessors' most egregious sins, and they were little more attractive than the reforms the Communists had been offering for years. But, combined with the pacification programs, Thieu's reforms constituted Saigon's first serious attempt at a comprehensive political strategy.

The effort came late in the day. The 59-man RD teams had to recruit outside the villages they were supposed to help. Staffed heavily with urban youth fleeing the draft, the teams remained outsiders to the villages they were sent to rescue. When the teams moved on, the Communists moved back in. The Chieu Hoi program claimed over 47,000 "ralliers" in 1969 alone, but many were in fact pro-Saigon civilians who "rallied" at the instigation of Chieu Hoi officials for a share of the reward.[25] William Colby, the U.S. pacification chief (later head of the CIA), estimated that of the 79,000 guerrilla defectors reported in 1969 and 1970, only 17,000 were genuine.[26] The Communists, moreover, used the program to recycle their own cadres into a legal existence and into Saigon's territorial forces. (No figure on communist desertions or Saigon defections are available. However, figures on desertions from Saigon's side showed these continuing at an annual net rate of over 10 percent for all forces and about 30 percent for regular ARVN combat units.)[27]

As for Phoenix, the sharpening of Saigon's police force also enhanced its means of reprisal. CIA agents have described the provincial reconnaissance units that they had helped to create as "hit teams."[28] These did chase down communist cadres, mostly low ranking ones, but they also attacked cadres' relatives and sometimes were used by Saigon officials in personal political vendettas. Thieu's land reform halved tenancy rates in the Mekong Delta, and elected village councils gained a measure of control over local affairs, but profiteering and abuse increased in both programs when U.S. interest declined.[29] A computerized measure of security, the Hamlet Evaluation Survey, fixed the "contested portion" of the poulation (that portion not under the control of one side or the other) at just 5 percent in 1970, but the figures, biased to show "progress" in any case, could not measure depth or direction of popular commitment. Much of the increase in "secure" population was the result of movement from the countryside to the cities, not the extension of government "control" into the hamlets.[30]

Still, the situation was improving from Saigon's point of view. Whether this was simply the fallout from communist overexertion in 1968 or the result of pacification is difficult to tell. General Tra's comments suggest the Communists mainly blamed themselves. But the United States and its allies began to think that they, not the Communists, now held the keys to victory.

UNIFYING THE INDOCHINA BATTLEFIELD

Believing things were going well, Nixon and Kissinger in late 1969 requested another round of secret negotiations with Hanoi. On February 21, 1970, Kissinger had the first in a series of clandestine meetings with Le Duc Tho. Seconded to Hanoi's Paris delegation as "special adviser," Tho was in fact the fifth-ranked member of the Political Bureau, the sole civilian member of the Central Military Party Committee, and, after Le Duan, the party's chief strategist on Southern affairs. Reunification had been his specialty since serving as COSVN deputy secretary under Le Duan from 1951 to 1954. To Kissinger, Tho epitomized the stony graduate of colonial prisons: a rigid Leninist catechist, a Vietnamese chauvinist, and a xenophobe.[31] What Tho thought of Kissinger must be left to the imagination.

Kissinger tried to put Tho on the defensive with evidence of U.S. public support for Nixon and of communist reversals on the ground. Tho retorted: "Before, there were over a million U.S. and puppet troops, and you failed. How can you succeed when you let the puppet troops do the fighting? Now, with only U.S. support, how can you win?" Kissinger had to admit that the question already had begun to torment him.[32] Additional meetings in March and April ended inconclusively. Neither side felt compelled to make major concessions; each counted on further fighting to sway the other.

In fact, the Political Bureau had decided, over a month before the two men first met, to prepare for a widening of the war by coordinating advances all over Indochina.[33] The United States had enjoyed some success raising a mercenary army in Laos under H'mong tribal leader "Marshall" Vang Pao, and along with Thai "volunteers" (up to 25 battalions supplied by the Royal Thai Army), these forces had begun in 1969 to menace PAVN supply lines deep inside Laos. In February 1970, the Vietnamese and Pathet Lao struck back, pushing Royal Lao-Thai-H'mong forces out of the Plaine des Jarres and off the Xieng Khoang airfield. The PAVN went on to seize Attopeu and Saravane provinces for the Pathet Lao. But the real objective was to consolidate the logistical corridor running through southern Laos, as the "complicated" situation in Cambodia was expected to result in disruption of supply to the South.

The final collapse of Cambodia's tattered neutrality was now just days away. On March 12, with Prince Sihanouk out of the country, the Cambodian government demanded the immediate withdrawal of Vietnamese troops from Cambodian territory. The Vietnamese did not budge, and the Cambodian army attacked, with support from Saigon army artillery. Finally, on the 18th, after a coup d'état, the National Assembly deposed Prince Sihanouk and designated Lieutenant General Lon Nol chief of state. The Saigon government promptly pledged to help Lon Nol stamp out communist activity on the border, while in Beijing, Sihanouk declared the formation of a "national union government" that included his erstwhile enemies, the Khmer Rouge.

The United States did not plot Sihanouk's ouster, but Washington almost certainly anticipated it, and Nixon apparently welcomed it.[34] The MENU bombing had failed to break up the Communists' sanctuaries, and Sihanouk's ambivalent diplomacy seemed an obstacle to doing more. Though U.S. officials quickly realized that the coup was a mixed blessing, as a new war might shape up in Cambodia just as the United States was trying to extricate itself from Vietnam, it was also clear that the conservative figures now heading the Cambodian government would not be able to survive without U.S. support. If Sihanouk returned to power on communist shoulders, all of Cambodia would be enemy territory, outflanking South Vietnam. At the same time, the coup strengthened the temptation to clean out the sanctuaries and, for Nixon, as he confided to aides, to "show who's really tough."

With the ARVN champing at the bit, the United States decided in late March to support South Vietnamese "incursions" into Cambodia. Battalion-sized forces backed by U.S. helicopters crossed the border on March 27 and 28. The Communists countered on April 3 by spreading out from their sanctuaries and pushing westward, turning weapons and equipment over to the Khmer Rouge as they went. Ostensibly to "save" Phnom Penh and defend U.S. citizens remaining in South Vietnam, Nixon ordered what was in fact an attempt to crack the spine of the communist armies—without consulting Lon Nol.

On April 28, U.S. advisers and air support followed an ARVN force into the Parrot's Beak, and on the 29th, a joint U.S.-ARVN force of 20,000 men pushed into the Fishhook (another salient, north of Parrot's Beak). Meeting only rearguard resistance, U.S. and South Vietnamese forces uncovered sprawling complexes of living quarters, mess halls, training sites, and storage depots. Thousands of weapons, millions of rounds of ammunition, tons of rice, and hundreds of vehicles were seized. But the PAVN already had trucked much greater quantities of equipment deeper into Cambodia. The bases, it was found, did not hug the border but "extended far into Cambodia, often serviced by unknown roads and trails built specifically for the purpose."[35]

Military logic suggested pursuit, but Nixon limited U.S. intervention to sixty days and thirty-five kilometers into Cambodia to deflect domestic criticism. The gesture was futile, however. For the most violent demonstrations of the entire war broke out in the United States, and Congress proceeded to repeal the Tonkin Gulf Resolution and prohibit U.S. combat or advisory activity in Cambodia. After leveling the Fishhook towns of Snoul and Mimot, U.S. troops pulled out on June 29. To finish the job, they left behind 34,000 ARVN troops who were constrained by neither military nor political logic.

One of the Lon Nol regime's first acts had been to unleash a program against Vietnamese residents in Cambodia; their bloated bodies had floated down the Mekong River into South Vietnam. Ordered to attack the sanctuaries, the ARVN went on a vengeful spree, and ARVN commander General Dang Van Quang organized the theft of everything from civilian valuables to the equipment of the Royal Cambodian Army for distribution among his fellow officers.[36]

The ARVN's revenge was oil on the Cambodian fire. Once content to protect its sanctuaries and supply lines, the PAVN evicted the Royal Cambodian Army from much of the northern and eastern interior. As the ARVN rampaged through the countryside, the Communists placed their own troops under strict orders to avoid contact with the civilian population.[37] Specially trained teams then set to work with Khmer Rouge cadres to build an indigenous revolutionary movement. With the charismatic prince on their side and the ARVN crashing about on the other, this was not hard to do. Under the banner of Sihanouk's Front Unifié National Kampuchean (FUNK), the teams exhorted the Khmer to defend themselves against the U.S.–South Vietnamese "invaders." Hamlet-level FUNK committees began recruiting troops for the Khmer Rouge guerrilla army. By June, Hanoi's Political Bureau could declare that North Vietnam had become "not only the common rear area for the great front line in the South, but . . . also the common rear area of the Laotian and Kampuchean revolutions."[38] In late September, PAVN-supported Khmer Rouge closed several of the highways leading into Phnom Penh.

The Vietnamese Communists for decades had considered Indochina a "strategic unity, a single battlefield."[39] Geostrategic realities had forced the Communists to seek unrestricted use of the mountains for bases and access to the South and had invited their enemies to exploit opportunities in Laos and Cambodia to strike from the rear. To have a buffer against intervention on their flank, the Vietnamese had nurtured separate Communist parties for Laos and Cambodia since 1951. Revolutionary movements in Laos and Cambodia served not only to cloak Vietnamese activities on Laotian and Cambodian soil but also to deny the use of these countries by hostile outside powers. Against this background, the secret bombing, the Lon Nol coup, and the "incursions" could not but drag Cambodia deeper into war, setting the scene for the Khmer Rouge victory in 1975.

In one sense, however, the Vietnamese decided too late to match the challenge of Lon Nol and the United States in Cambodia by unleashing the Khmer Rouge. By 1970, the ultranationalist, chauvinistic faction led by Pol Pot had achieved ascendancy within the Cambodian Communist party. This faction had struggled in the bush for years while the Vietnamese dallied with Sihanouk and was deeply suspicious of Vietnamese long-range intentions. In a bitterly worded *Black Book* published in 1978, the Khmer Rouge accused the Vietnamese of having deliberately held back the Cambodian revolution during the 1960s, manipulating the internal affairs of the Cambodian party, attempting to poison Pol Pot, urging the Cambodians to seek a negotiated settlement, and plotting to annex Cambodia through control of Hanoi-trained Khmer cadres. Other evidence indicates that Pol Pot began to purge "pro-Hanoi" cadres from his ranks and to engage in skirmishes with PAVN units on Cambodian soil as early as 1973.[40] Thus even before the Second Indochina War had come to an end, the foundations of the Third Indochina War had been laid.

LAM SON 719

Still, in 1970, President Thieu was unperturbed by the sprawl of war around him. Encouraged by the ARVN's performance in Cambodia, he suggested invading North Vietnam. Though the United States was in no mood to accompany the ARVN on a northward march, it shared Thieu's belief that the ARVN was ready to take on the PAVN. With restraint lowered by the Cambodian incursion and attention habitually focused on logistical lines, the MACV and ARVN staffs zeroed in on the Ho Chi Minh Trail in southern Laos.

The trail complex was certainly an enticing target. B-52 bombardment had only slowed the crawl of men and equipment through the jungled hills, yet PAVN dependence on the trail had grown. In late 1970, U.S. intelligence detected a twofold increase in the rate of PAVN infiltration and an accumulation of supplies in one of the trail's key hubs near the Laotian town of Sepone. A drive from the Vietnamese border to Sepone during the Communists' peak resupply effort, the MACV/ARVN command calculated, would blunt PAVN initiatives for a year to come. Such was to be the objective of Operation LAM SON 719.

Overconfident, the U.S. and South Vietnamese commands failed to notice that Laos was not Cambodia. The PAVN's Laotian installations were not remote sanctuaries but the core of its logistical lifeline. The Sepone area bristled with nineteen PAVN anti-aircraft battalions, twelve infantry regiments, a tank regiment, an artillery regiment, and elements of five divisions. Reinforcements were only a few days' march away in nearby North Vietnam and other parts of Laos. Here, unlike in Cambodia, the PAVN was close to home, in absolute control of terrain it could not afford to lose, and in a country where U.S. troops were prohibited by Congress from going. The ARVN would have to attack alone.

Oblivious to these distinctions, 5,000 ARVN troops set out on February 8, 1971, to march down Route 9 into Laos. The United States provided logistical support from Khe Sanh. Ten kilometers into Laos, the attack stalled until reinforcements brought the force up to 21,000. Behind a shield of B-52 bombardment, the ARVN pushed forward, reaching the outskirts of Sepone on March 6 and destroying PAVN supply dumps. But by then ARVN units were strung like threaded beads across forty kilometers of PAVN-infested jungle. Heavily reinforced, the PAVN struck back at the ARVN "tail" on Route 9, assaulted outlying firebases, shelled Khe Sanh, and set up a network of anti-aircraft fire. As bad weather closed in, withdrawal turned into a rout. What MACV/ARVN spokesmen called an "orderly retreat," newsmen captured in images of terrified ARVN troops dropping from the skids of overloaded helicopters. On March 24, a day ahead of schedule, the ARVN pulled its last troops out of Laos, admitting to 1,200 dead, over 4,200 wounded, and

107 helicopters shot down. Whether the ARVN would soon be able to fight alone was suddenly in doubt.

The Communists suffered heavily too. It appears moreover that they had to revise their timetable for recovering the "strategic offensive position," that is, resuming the major main force offensive action, and entering the "decisive period" in 1971.[41] But the Sepone base was back in service only days after LAM SON 719 ended, and the southward flow quickly resumed over alternate routes. More important, the battle was interpreted by the Communists as opening up a new situation. "It was proof," a PAVN military historian told the author, "that the PAVN could defeat the best ARVN units. We had not been certain we could do this before. 'Vietnamization' did create a strong ARVN, and in the battles of 1969–1970 we did not defeat the ARVN, which left us doubtful and apprehensive. Our army had to learn how to organize large-scale battles. So 1971 was a big test."[42] The geographical expansion of the battlefield also played into the Communists' hands. For as the United States withdrew, Saigon was left, in effect, to do more with less. The United States could help Saigon forces "unify the Indochina battlefield," as communist strategists put it, but they were leaving the ARVN to fight on it alone.

SPRING OFFENSIVE

In May 1971, the Political Bureau resolved to make 1972 the year of "decisive victory."[43] Hanoi's need for a showdown was now urgent. The Communists could not be sure just how the emerging U.S. détente with the Soviet Union and China would affect them. For years Hanoi had sought to mediate the Sino-Soviet dispute in the belief that bloc unity was preferable to division, but the dispute had prevented united action, and as time passed it had made both Moscow and Beijing anxious to improve relations with the United States. Though neither of the communist Great Powers could afford openly to sell out the Vietnamese, Hanoi had reason to fear their support might slacken if the war went on much longer. China in particular was beginning to see the United States as a counterweight to a

Soviet threat. China's aid had declined after 1968, and Chinese leaders had suggested that perhaps Vietnam's reunification should be a long drawn out affair, a suggestion apparently made in response to Nixon and Kissinger's aggressive wooing.[44] Furthermore, the approaching U.S. election year and scheduled withdrawal of U.S. forces from ground combat presented a moment of opportunity. "Decisive victory," said the bureau, meant forcing the United States "to end the war by negotiating from a position of defeat."[45]

The 1972 U.S. presidential elections counted in communist calculations only as a check on Nixon's bellicose instincts, however. Hanoi's main objective was to demonstrate that Vietnamization would never enable the ARVN to stand on its own. Unable to return in force and faced with Saigon's inevitable collapse, the Communists reasoned, the United States' only recourse would be to end its involvement on terms dictated by Hanoi. The Communists also needed to reverse the deterioration of revolutionary strength at the local level inside South Vietnam to establish a position of strength for whatever was to follow, whether a negotiated settlement or more war. Behind an onslaught of conventional force, the Communists aimed to roll back pacification and revitalize the guerrilla movement. At the least, they wanted to make sure that when the United States had finally withdrawn, the situation would be no worse than it had been before the United States intervened—when communist forces had pushed Saigon nearly to the point of collapse.[46] At the most, the Communists aimed to cause the ARVN's disintegration, which they expected would lead to Thieu's removal, the creation of a "transitional government at the upper level," and formation of a "three-segment coalition government."[47]

Shades of 1968, but with a difference: This time Hanoi had taken care to obtain a threefold increase in Soviet arms, including T-54 medium tanks, armed personnel carriers, 57-mm antiaircraft batteries, SA-7 hand-held missiles, and a vast array of artillery from 76-mm through 130-mm field guns. Supplies were pre-positioned near targets in sufficient quantities to sustain combat for weeks. Though still much inferior in firepower to the ARVN (which enjoyed a 20-to-1 advantage in artillery shells and could call on U.S. airpower in emergency), the PAVN would not again pull its punches. With the U.S. force level down to 95,000 (of which only 6,000 were combat troops and the rest were support troops), communist strategists assumed they had only to contend with the ARVN.

In early 1972, while Washington and Hanoi dithered over revisions of their negotiating proposals, all but three of the PAVN's thirteen combat divisions moved toward targets in the South. With PLAF units (heavily reinforced by Northern troops), the force numbered up to 200,000 men. Their assignment was to attack on widely separated fronts, draw the ARVN away from populated areas, break up Saigon's outermost ring of defense, and help local lowland forces carry the attack into the enemy's "secure rear areas."

In the dawn of March 30, 1972, under cover of clouds and rain, three divisions supported by several artillery regiments crossed the demilitarized zone.[48] It took them just two days to overrun all twelve of the bases and outposts that U.S. Marines had turned over to the ARVN 3rd division. The 3rd division's 56th regiment defected, the rest of the division began to disintegrate, and the entire northern half of Quang Tri province fell under PAVN control. Further south, in Thua Thien province, PAVN and local regional forces seized the approaches to Hue.

The PAVN 320th division opened a second front in the western highlands. Behind tanks and anti-aircraft weapons that had just moved down newly constructed roads, the division attacked more than a dozen ARVN outposts southwest of Kontum and blocked Routes 14 and 19.

A third front, opened on April 2 in northern Tay Ninh province, quickly forced the ARVN to withdraw from outlying positions in order to defend the province capital. On the 5th, two regiments of the PLAF 5th division fell on Loc Ninh, where they were joined by twenty-five tanks the next day. Radio contact with Loc Ninh ceased on the 7th. Even as Loc Ninh's survivors fled toward An Loc, nineteen kilometers in the direction of Saigon, An Loc was being probed by the PLAF 9th division. Suddenly, the PLAF 7th division blocked Route 13 about twenty-five kilometers south of An Loc, and the town's five ARVN regiments and 10,000 civilians found themselves under a siege that would last until June 18.

The fourth front was the Mekong Delta. Here pacification had made the deepest inroads, and the Communists desperately needed to recover access to rice and manpower. Waiting until the ARVN 21st division had departed to join the relief of An Loc, a PAVN infantry regiment moved out of Cambodia into Kien Tuong province where it linked up with two other infantry regiments and a sapper regiment to attack lightly defended ARVN and regional force outposts. Masked by over 100 guerrilla-style attacks, more PAVN units infiltrated the delta (particularly Dinh Tuong province) and forced suspension of the pacification program.

The rapidly deteriorating military situation placed the United States in a difficult position. The United States could not stand aside while everything it had worked twenty years to accomplish came unstuck. But neither did Nixon and Kissinger, on the brink of major breakthroughs in détente with the Soviet Union, wish to jeopardize the Moscow summit planned for May 22. Would the Soviets cancel the summit if the United States retaliated against Hanoi? What would happen to relations with China, relations just reestablished after twenty years' suspension by Nixon's dramatic visit to Beijing in February? Nixon and Kissinger had counted on détente with Moscow and Beijing to isolate Hanoi, but now their own hopes restrained them.

Hanoi's leaders had calculated correctly that Nixon would not return U.S. ground forces to combat. They professed not to fear tactical use of U.S. airpower in the South. But they underestimated the lengths to which Nixon was prepared to go, election year or not, to prevent an outright defeat while the U.S. reputation was still at stake. On April 6, U.S. fighter bombers raided military targets 100 kilometers north of the demilitarized zone. Meanwhile, a massive strike force of B-52s and other aircraft was readied at Utapao in Thailand, at Danang in South Vietnam, on Guam, and aboard six aircraft carriers at sea. Uncertainty about Moscow's reaction stayed Nixon's hand, but evidence that Hanoi had committed its forces to the complete destruction of the Saigon regime—and was succeeding—overcame Nixon's hesitation. On the 15th, and for the next two days, Nixon sent B-52s over the North for the first time since 1969. Aimed at military targets in Hanoi and Haiphong, the raids damaged four Soviet vessels. The protest over the bombing, however, was greater in the U.S. Congress and press that it was in Moscow. China's Ping-Pong team went ahead on the 18th with a call on Nixon at the White House. Kissinger, returning from a secret trip to Moscow, reported that if Moscow was not set to help end the war, it would at least acquiesce "in pushing [North Vietnam] to the limit."[49] Moscow and Beijing were willing to support Hanoi materially, but neither was willing to make any diplomatic sacrifice to avert U.S. punishment of their ally.

In late April, the PAVN tightened the noose around ARVN positions in the central highlands. Dak To, once the linchpin of U.S. outposts in western Kontum province, fell on the 24th. The PAVN 320th division chased the ARVN into Kontum city. Three days later, and further north, the PAVN began a two-pronged push against Dong Ha and Quang Tri city with heavy equipment trucked directly across the demilitarized zone. Dong Ha fell in a day. On May 1, some 8,000 ARVN troops fled Quang Tri and streamed southward on Route 1. Abandoning tanks, trucks, and armed personnel carriers (APCs) as they went, the berserk troops flooded Hue. In desperation, President Thieu fired the corps commander General Hoang Xuan Lam, a political appointee who had led the debacle in Laos the year before, and turned to General Ngo Quang Truong, the hero of Hue's defense in 1968. Truong hastily patched together a last line of defense on the south bank of the My Chanh River about thirty kilometers north of Hue. Fragile ARVN positions everywhere seemed on the verge of collapse.

From Saigon and Washington, it appeared that the Communists were bent on seizing Hue. But the Communists had not prepared to advance so far so quickly. Blaming "strategic commanders" (i.e., the high command in Hanoi) for lack of foresight that prevented "lower echelons" (himself) from achieving "certain victory," COSVN's General Tran Van Tra maintained that the ARVN's defeat in Quang Tri left Hue "practically wide open but we did not take advantage of that favorable opportunity."[50] The defense of Hue, however, did draw the ARVN

2nd division out of Quang Ngai province, leaving the province wide open to a rapid guerrilla recovery.

Further south, the effort to relieve An Loc sucked up the last ARVN reserves including Thieu's Palace Guard. In the Mekong Delta communist troop strength continued rising. Estimated at only 3,000 in 1971, communist forces in the delta would number between 20,000 and 30,000 by September 1972, as approximately 1 million persons came again under communist control.

Against this background, Kissinger and Le Duc Tho held another secret meeting in Paris on May 2. The United States was now prepared to waive its longstanding demand for total mutual withdrawal of "foreign forces" from the South, but Tho was in no mood to concede anything as long as military victory seemed imminent. Kissinger, thinking he had explored every diplomatic avenue, returned to Washington ready to support Nixon's wish for a massive blow.[51]

Nixon already had concluded that he could not survive politically if he accepted defeat.[52] The fact that it was an election year made it, to his way of thinking, more, not less, necessary to appear decisive. Moreover, he calculated, it was better to risk cancellation of the Moscow summit than to suffer the humiliation of negotiating with the Soviets at the same time that Soviet arms were crushing a U.S. ally.[53] With Congress debating "end-the-war" bills and withdrawals bringing the U.S. force level steadily down (to 47,000 by June 30), all of Nixon's remaining leverage over the course of the war would soon evaporate. If he were to end the war without defeat, this was his last best chance. Shunning the advice of Defense Secretary Melvin Laird, who warned of adverse domestic reaction, and of CIA Director Richard Helms, whose agency doubted the North could be deterred, Nixon on May 8 ordered his air armada to mine the North's harbors, cut all its communications and rail links, and intensify bombardment of military targets all over the North. For the first time in the war, newly developed laser and television guidance technology helped "smart bombs" find their targets with unprecedented accuracy.

Just how much the mining and bombing affected the PAVN's ability to sustain its offensive is difficult to say. Hanoi admitted that the blockade forced it to shift most of its import volume from sea to land routes.[54] But in the short run it was U.S. airpower in the South, not the North, that provided the margin of survival for shaky ARVN positions. The PAVN, too, had difficulty sustaining attacks on such far-flung fronts. During the first week of May, the weather cleared over Quang Tri, permitting U.S. air and naval bombardment to break up PAVN concentrations just north of the My Chanh River. A week later, hundreds of B-52s and fighter-bombers held off a PAVN attempt to penetrate An Loc. The Mekong Delta was subjected to the heaviest use of B-52s of the entire war, mainly over PAVN infiltration routes.

By mid-June, the PAVN's offensive had stalled, and on the 28th, behind a barrage of B-52 bombardments, the ARVN crossed the My Chanh River to inch back toward Quang Tri city (which it retook from a token communist regional force on September 16). The PAVN remained in control of northern Quang Tri province and had demonstrated that Vietnamization depended on the perpetual readiness of the United States to come to the ARVN's aid. But it had failed to dictate the peace.

BREAKTHROUGH AND BLITZ

By late summer, both sides were feeling the urge to compromise. Pressures were building in the U.S. Congress to cut off funds for the war, and Nixon knew he would not be permitted many more "savage, punishing blows." He also was increasingly impatient to remove the roadblock that Vietnam placed in the way of other objectives. As for Hanoi, its grasp at "decisive victory" had fallen short, its ports remained blockaded, and its allies had done nothing more than meekly protest. George McGovern's nomination as the Democratic candidate for president had strengthened Nixon's assurance of reelection. Hanoi may well have concluded that it would get better terms from Nixon before rather than after the November election.

The Kissinger-Tho talks resumed in July. The United States in 1971 already had expressed willingness to set a timetable for total withdrawal and, later, to let North Vietnamese troops remain in the South. Now Tho agreed to address military issues first and leave political settlement for later. Gone was the demand for Thieu's removal. Gone was the demand for a coalition government. By October 8, all the elements of agreement were in place: a standstill ceasefire over all of Indochina, U.S. withdrawal within sixty days, return of U.S. prisoners, and arrangements for the Vietnamese parties to consult among themselves about elections and the future of South Vietnam. As far as Kissinger and Tho were concerned, the two sides had made a deal.

But Kissinger had grossly underestimated his ally, Nguyen Van Thieu. For years Thieu had taken little interest in the negotiations, believing that Hanoi's intransigence would leave the United States no choice but to go on supporting him. Now, faced with a draft of the agreement between Hanoi and Washington, Thieu balked. The draft's requirement that he "consult" with the PRG while Northern troops remained in the South legitimized the threat to his existence. Articles that affirmed Vietnam's unity and recognized communist political rights in the South, echoing the Geneva Agreements of 1954, implied that the communist cause had been just all along. Furthermore, Washington's negotiation of this future for the South, accomplished with as little respect for Saigon's independence as Hanoi showed toward that of the PRG, placed Thieu in an intolerable position. Acceptance of the draft as written would have proved to himself as well as to the people he wished to lead that he was indeed a puppet.

Moreover, Thieu knew, as few U.S. leaders or advisers ever recognized, that compromise in Vietnam was a U.S. fantasy. Vietnam was like China—a society in which dogma had always ruled and only one dogma could rule at a time. In the colonial period, Vietnamese had slaughtered each other to determine which dogma and which party would lead Vietnam into the modern world. The French Sûreté had seen to it that only the most disciplined, unified, secretive, and ideologically implacable of these parties survived. It was hardly realistic to expect the surviving party, now holding the mandate of August 1945 and Dien Bien Phu, to share power with legatees of the colonial past. So Thieu assumed that if he did not eliminate the Communists, they would eliminate him. The "third force"—or "third segment," as presumably neutral opinion was called in the draft—would have to choose sides. A compromise as envisioned in the draft could only be a prelude to renewed struggle in the future.

As it happened, Nixon himself was having second thoughts. An agreement earlier would have helped his campaign, but a signing only a week or two before the November 7 election, by raising questions about his motives, could create, he said, a "messy situation." Nixon also saw Thieu's intransigence as an excuse to bargain for better terms. Kissinger was sent on another round of negotiations that Nixon knew was likely to result in postponement of the signing.[55] So it was that Hanoi, fearing the United States was backing away from the agreement, publicly revealed what had been secretly negotiated, forcing Kissinger, desperate to keep the negotiations going, to affirm on October 26 that "peace is at hand."

But it was not. When negotiations resumed after the election (which Nixon won in a landslide), Kissinger presented Thieu's demand for sixty-nine changes. Though he quickly withdrew half, which not even he took seriously,[56] the remainder were sufficiently substantive to raise doubts in Hanoi that the United States could be held to the October draft of the agreement. In view of rising congressional obsession with the fate of U.S. prisoners, Hanoi also apparently calculated that it had nothing to lose by postponing settlement. So Tho began introducing his own demands as the price for making changes demanded by Washington. Intensive negotiations brought the two sides very close to what had been agreed in October, but Hanoi's niggling convinced Kissinger that Hanoi was determined "not to allow the agreement to be completed."[57]

As for Saigon, Nixon offered $2 billion worth of military hardware and "absolute assurances" of "swift and retaliatory action" if Hanoi violated the agreement.[58] Washington also threatened to sign a separate peace. But to no avail. Thieu could not be budged any more than Hanoi could be pinned down. Pulled between adversary and ally alike, Washington resolved, as talks came to a close on December 13, to have an immediate final showdown with both.

Such was the background to Nixon's most splenetic decision of the war. After warning of grave consequences if "serious negotiations" did not resume within seventy-two hours, Nixon unleashed the full fury of all B-52s stationed in Southeast Asia against previously forbidden targets in Hanoi and Haiphong. He gave no public explanation. For how was he to tell the American people that it was he, not Hanoi, who had reneged on the October agreements and was now bombing Hanoi to make it agree to what it had once accepted?[59]

In the eleven days beginning December 18, with a day off for Christmas, 36,000 tons of bombs were dropped on railroad yards, bus stations, port complexes, factories, radio broadcasting stations, and warehouses—some of them square in the middle of densely populated areas. "Smart bombs" made the strikes the most accurate in the history of warfare. But even smart bombs could miss, and not all of the bombs dropped were smart. An entire string intended for the Hanoi railroad yards fell on the adjacent residential/commercial quarter of Kham Thien. Hits on the Cuban Chancery, Hanoi's largest hospital, and civilian housing were due, in the antiseptic language of Washington's military bureaucrats, to "accidents" and "bomb spillover." But the phrase that came to most tongues was "indiscriminate carpet-bombing."

Actually, the bombing was as discriminating as bombing could be, and Hanoi had prepared for it. The government had evacuated over half the city's poulation when bombing resumed in April, and on December 3, it had stepped up preparations for "disaster relief" and relocation of nonessential persons,[60] the day before Tho was to present new counterdemands to Kissinger. Kham Thien, an area of one square kilometer housing 30,000 people, had only a fraction of its normal population when the bombs fell on it. So had An Duong, another bombed neighborhood that normally contained 6,000 densely packed inhabitants. That the vast majority of Hanoi's buildings were never touched is plain today. The destruction was nothing compared to that inflicted on European and Japanese cities in World War II. Still, Hanoi on December 30 officially counted 1,318 dead and 1,261 wounded, later adjusting these figures to 2,196 dead and 1,577 wounded as more bodies were pulled out of the rubble.

B-52 FLIGHT PATHS

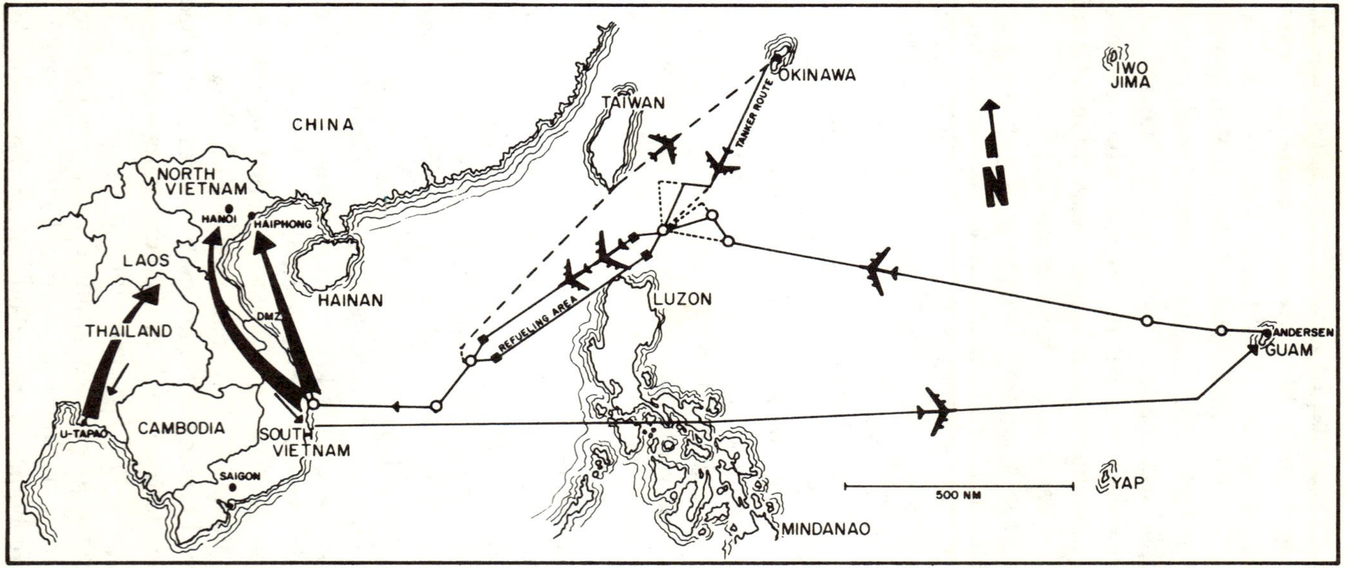

Map of the Western Pacific and Southeast Asia. The westbound route shows the general flight path taken by the B-52 forces to arrive at the mainland, from where they dispersed on a variety of routes into North Vietnam. Most sorties recovered to the South and back to Guam. Diversions from these basic routes were sometimes made to meet critical timing requirements or to perform supplemental inflight refuelings.

Source: From Brigadier General James R. McCarthy and Lieutenant Colonel George B. Allison, *Linebacker II: A View from the Rock* (Maxwell Air Force Base, Alabama: Airpower Research Institute, Air War College, 1979), p. 3.

What did the "December blitz" accomplish? The men who led the raids claimed to have cut the North's resupply—already reduced by the blockade of Haiphong harbor—from 160,000 to 30,000 tons per month. Furthermore, the North fired nearly its total supply of 1,000 SA-2 missiles, expending its most effective defense against the big planes. "Why are we stopping now?'" the B-52 pilots asked. "Another week of these missions . . . and the North Vietnamese would have been suing for peace on our terms."[61] But the United States also lost fifteen B-52s (Hanoi claimed thirty-four), or 10 percent of the force it had deployed, and ninety-two crew members. "Another week" may have been all the United States itself could have endured.

Just how much the bombing helped to sway Thieu is also open to question. The day after the bombing began, Nixon sent Thieu an ultimatum to "decide now whether you desire to continue our alliance or whether you want me to seek a settlement with the enemy which serves U.S. interests alone."[62] Thieu did drop his objections to the political provisions of the draft agreement, some believe, because the bombing made Nixon's reassurances credible.[63] But Thieu also restated his opposition to the continued presence of North Vietnamese forces in the South. Nor did his position change after Nixon, on January 5, 1973, put into writing his "assurances of continued assistance in the postsettlement period" and of response "with full force should the settlement be violated by North Vietnam." What finally made Thieu "close ranks" with the United States as Nixon demanded was a letter on the 16th that threatened "an inevitable and immediate termination of U.S. economic and military assistance."[64]

Indeed, the December bombing, by completing the alienation of Congress from the president, probably guaranteed that the last credible threat Nixon would ever be able to make regarding Vietnam was to cut off aid to Saigon. A poll of the newly elected Congress, taken as bombs fell, showed that most members now favored immediate legislation to end all U.S. involvement forthwith. As Congress returned to session in the first days of January, Democratic party caucuses in both the House and Senate voted by crushing margins to cut off all funds for military operations in Indochina, contingent only upon the safe withdrawal of the remaining 24,000 U.S. troops and return of U.S. prisoners. Nixon knew he had to wrap up the negotiations quickly, before Congress did it for him.

As for Hanoi, its official reply, which came on December 26 after eight days of bombing, was to accept the gist of what Nixon and Kissinger demanded. Talks would resume on the basis of what had been agreed, except for details, in October. Thus the United States got what it wanted, but by being careful not to ask for much.

The talks resumed in early January and moved swiftly to conclusion. Kissinger extracted wording changes that he claimed gave the United States the right to go on supplying Saigon with military assistance on an "unrestricted" basis. He also proudly claimed to have reduced the National Council of National Reconciliation and Concord—the mechanism for consultation among "three equal segments" on elections and on the South's political future—to "essential impotence."[65] More haggling reaffirmed the demilitarized zone in the precise terms of the Geneva accords of 1954, and though Kissinger expressed satisfaction, those terms defined the demarcation as "only provisional and not a political or territorial boundary," as Hanoi had steadfastly insisted. Joint military commissions were to oversee a standstill ceasefire, and a 1,160-person International Commission of Control and Supervision was set up to report on implementation of the agreement. "Foreign countries" were to end all their military activities in Laos and Cambodia, and a ceasefire was arranged for Laos. The "Red Prince" Souphanovong entered Vientiane to a tumultuous welcome and joined a coalition government dominated by the Pathet Lao a little later. But Hanoi confessed it lacked sufficient control over the Khmer Rouge to guarantee a ceasefire in Cambodia.

The ceasefire in South Vietnam went into effect on January 27, the day the agreement was signed in Paris. The representatives of Hanoi and the PRG signed on one page, the United States and Saigon on another, so that the signature of Tram Van Lam, Saigon's minister for foreign affairs, would not have to appear beside that of Nguyen Thi Dinh, the PRG's minister for foreign affairs. Prisoner exchanges began, the United States dismantled what remained of its bases, and on March 29, the last U.S.

soldier left for home. As far as the United States was concerned, the war was over.

But it was only a new phase of the war for the Vietnamese. The ceasefire—a standstill-in-place leaving hostile forces cheek-by-jowl—invited violation. Both sides ordered their armed forces to increase areas of control just before the ceasefire went into effect, enlarging claims that each was sure to contest. As for political settlement, the Paris Agreement proclaimed that "immediately after the ceasefire the two South Vietnamese parties will achieve national reconciliation and concord, end hatred and enmity, prohibit all acts of reprisal . . . assure . . . democratic liberties," as if miracles could be accomplished by decree. The agency of this miracle was to be the National Council of National Reconciliation and Concord, which Kissinger, anxious to avoid the appearance of mandating a coalition government, had proudly reduced to "essential impotence." Lastly, the Paris Agreement affirmed Vietnam's unity and territorial integrity and ordered North and South to move "step by step" toward reunification, but without obligating the two sides to anything more specific than "peaceful means." The Paris Agreement, from the U.S. point of view, was satisfactory in that it permitted the United States to complete its withdrawal and left Nguyen Van Thieu in power. Thus did the United States, not able to bring peace to Vietnam, exit from Indochina just as the French had done nineteen years before.

NOTES

1. Henry Kissinger, *White House Years* (Boston: Little, Brown, 1979), p. 1345.

2. Richard M. Nixon, "Asia After Vietnam," *Foreign Affairs* (October 1967), p. 111.

3. H. R. Haldeman, *The Ends of Power* (New York: Times Books, 1978), p. 81.

4. Phan Van Dong speech to the DRV National Assembly, April 8, 1965, Vietnam News Agency, in Wallace J. Thies, *When Governments Collide* (Berkeley: University of California Press), Appendix I, pp. 421–422.

5. Kissinger, *White House Years*, p. 228.

6. Henry Kissinger, "The Vietnam Negotiations," *Foreign Affairs* (January 1969), pp. 211–234.

7. Haldeman, *The Ends of Power,* p. 83.

8. J.L.S. Girling, "The Resistance in Cambodia," *Asian Survey* 12, no. 7 (July 1972), pp. 549–559.

9. The classic account is William Shawcross, *Sideshow: Kissinger, Nixon and the Destruction of Cambodia* (New York: Simon and Schuster, 1979).

10. Signs were given to presidential emissary Chester Bowles in January 1968. Just what Sihanouk said to Bowles and whether it constituted an invitation to bomb the sanctuaries is a matter of dispute. Compare Kissinger, *White House Years,* p. 250, with Shawcross, *Sideshow,* pp. 69–71.

11. Kissinger, *White House Years,* p. 249. Emphasis is in the original.

12. David E. Brown, "Exporting Insurgency: The Communists in Cambodia," in J. J. Zasloff and A. E. Goodman, eds., *Indochina in Conflict: A Political Assessment* (Lexington, Mass.: Heath, 1972), p. 126.

13. *Viet-Nam Documents and Research Notes* [hereinafter cited as *VNDRNs*], no. 88 (Saigon: U.S. Mission, January 1971).

14. War Experience Recapitulation Committee of the High-Level Military Institute, *The Anti-U.S. Resistance War for National Salvation 1954–1975: Military Events,* trans. by the Joint Publications Research Service, JPRS no. 80,968 (Washington, D.C.: GPO, June 3, 1982), p. 124. Text hereinafter cited as *The Anti-U.S. Resistance War.*

15. Ibid., p. 117

16. Jeb Stuart Magruder, quoting Nixon, cited in Tad Szulc, *The Illusion of Peace* (New York: Viking Press, 1978), p. 158.

17. "Report: Status of Deserters," *VNDRNs,* no. 56 (April 1969).

18. Author's interview with PAVN senior captain in December 1972 shortly after his defection in the Mekong Delta.

19. U.S. government sources, cited in Guenter Lewy, *America in Vietnam* (Oxford: Oxford University Press, 1978), p. 191.

20. Combined Intelligence Center Vietnam, Study ST70-05, "North Vietnam Personnel Infiltration into the Republic of Vietnam," U.S. Military Assistance Command Vietnam, J-2, Saigon, December 16, 1970, p. 59.

21. Tran Van Tra, *Nhung chang duong cua "B2"-Thanh dong": tap V. Ket thuc cuoc chien tranh 30 nam* [Stages on the Road of the B2-Bulwark, vol. V., Concluding the 30 Years War] (Ho Chi Minh City: Van Nghe Publishing House, 1982), p. 64.

22. Kissinger, *White House Years,* p. 272.

23. United States Arms Control and Disarmament Agency, "World Military Expenditures and Arms Transfers, 1968–1977" (Washington, D.C.: U.S. Department of State, October 1979), p. 152. Figures in current dollars.

24. Julian J. Ewell and Ira A. Hunt, Jr., *Sharpening the Combat Edge* (Washington, D.C.: Department of the Army, 1974), chart 25, p. 206.

25. Lewy, *America in Vietnam*, p. 92.

26. Michael Maclear, *The Ten Thousand Day War* (London: Thames Methuen, 1981), p. 259.

27. Lewy, *America in Vietnam*, p. 172.

28. Maclear, *The Ten Thousand Day War*, pp. 260–261.

29. James Pinckney Harrison, *The Endless War: Fifty Years of Struggle in Vietnam* (New York: Free Press, 1982), p. 271.

30. See Thomas C. Thayer, "On Pacification," in W. Scott Thompson and Donald D. Frizzell, eds., *The Lessons of Vietnam* (New York: Crane, Russak, 1977), p. 271.

31. Kissinger, *White House Years*, p. 441.

32. Ibid., p. 444.

33. *The Anti-U.S. Resistance War*, pp. 123–124.

34. Szulc, *The Illusion of Peace*, pp. 242–243; and Shawcross, *Sideshow*, pp. 112–123.

35. John J. Tolson, *Airmobility, 1961–1971* (Washington, D.C., 1973), pp. 215–233.

36. According to Saigon and U.S. officials interviewed by the author in 1973, General Quang headed a group of officers who enriched themselves from ARVN operations in Cambodia.

37. "Code of Conduct," dated April 27, 1970, *VNDRNs*, no. 88 (January 1971).

38. *The Anti-U.S. Resistance War*, p. 129.

39. To be exact, since 1947, when the French attacked Viet Minh redoubts from bases in Laos and Cambodia. The words "strategic unity, a single battlefield," are those of General Vo Nguyen Giap, from a pamphlet published in 1950. Vo Nguyen Giap, *Nhiem vu quan su truoc mat chuyen sang Tong phan cong* [The Military Mission in Transition to the General Offensive and Uprising] (Ha Dong Committee for Resistance and Administration, 1950), p. 14, in Library of Congress, Orientalia/South Asia 4 microfilm collection, *Vietnamese Communist Publications*, compiled by P. T. Chau, item 40.

40. Kenneth Quinn, "Political Change in Wartime: The Khmer Krahom Revolution in Southern Cambodia, 1970–1974," *Naval War College Review* (Spring 1976), pp. 3–31. Also see Timothy Carney, *Communist Party Power in Kampuchea (Cambodia: Documents and Dis-*

cussion) (Ithaca, N.Y.: Cornell University Southeast Asia Program Data Paper no. 106, January 1977), pp. 7–8.

41. See study document on COSVN Resolution 10, *VNDRNs,* no. 99 (October 1971); and *The Anti-U.S. Resistance War,* p. 123.

42. Colonel Hoang Co Quang, interviewed in Hanoi by the author on April 21, 1984.

43. *The Anti-U.S. Resistance War,* p. 138.

44. Hanoi later excoriated Beijing in a white book, "The Truth about Vietnam-China Relations over the Past 30 Years" (October 1979), and Beijing replied in *People's Daily* with "On the Vietnamese Foreign Ministry's White Book Concerning Viet Nam–China Relations" the next month. For analysis of Hanoi's role in the Sino-Soviet dispute, see W. R. Smyser, *The Independent Vietnamese: Vietnamese Communism Between Russia and China, 1956–1969* (Athens, Ohio: Ohio University Center for International Studies, Papers in International Studies, Southeast Asia no. 55, 1980).

45. *The Anti-U.S. Resistance War,* p. 138.

46. See David W.P. Elliott, "NLF-DRV Strategy and the 1972 Spring Offensive" (Ithaca, N.Y.: Cornell University, International Relations of East Asia Project, Interim Report no. 4, January 1974), especially pp. 39–54.

47. N. C. (pseud.), "Let Us Firmly Grasp This Strategic Opportunity, Intensify Our General Offensive and Uprisings, Defeat the Vietnamization Plan, Achieve a Decisive Victory, End the War, and Move Toward a Complete Victory," *Tien Phong,* no. 4 (internal magazine of the Region 5 party organization), translated in *VNDRNs,* no. 109 (December 1972).

48. Tactical data in this and the following paragraphs are taken from a U.S. Army intelligence study, "The Nguyen Hue Offensive," U.S. Military Assistance Command Vietnam-J2, Saigon, January 12, 1973.

49. Kissinger, *White House Years,* p. 1159.

50. Tra, *Ket thuc cuoc chien tranh 30 nam,* p. 101.

51. Kissinger, *White House Years,* pp. 1173–1174.

52. Seymour M. Hersh, *The Price of Power: Kissinger in the Nixon White House* (New York: Summit Books, 1983), p. 510.

53. Szulc, *The Illusion of Peace,* p. 550.

54. *The Anti-U.S. Resistance War,* p. 149.

55. For a detailed reconstruction of these negotiations, see Hersh, *The Price of Power,* pp. 589–609.

56. Allen E. Goodman, *The Lost Peace: America's Search for a Negotiated Settlement of the Vietnam War* (Stanford: Hoover Institution Press, 1978), p. 152.

57. Kissinger, *White House Years,* p. 1444.

58. Richard M. Nixon, *RN: Memoirs of Richard Nixon* (New York: Grosset & Dunlap, 1978), p. 718.

59. Nixon confirmed this in a television interview quoted in Hersh, *The Price of Power,* p. 619.

60. *Hanoi moi* [New Hanoi], December 5, 1972, p. 1.

61. James R. McCarthy et al., *Linebacker II: The View from the Rock* (Maxwell, Ala.: Air War College, Airpower Research Institute, USAF Southeast Asia Monograph Series Vol. 6, monograph 8, 1979), pp. 171–172.

62. Nixon's messages to Thieu are excerpted in Kissinger, *White House Years,* pp. 1459–1460, 1462, 1469.

63. Hersh, *The Price of Power,* p. 624.

64. Kissinger, *White House Years,* pp. 1459–1460, 1462, 1469.

65. Ibid, p. 1466.

8

Vietnam Without the United States

"We sincerely did not want a recurrence of the grievous naivete of the 1954–1956 period," wrote Tran Van Tra. Like many Southern party leaders, Tra believed it had been a mistake to make local cadres renounce violence as required by the Geneva accords. Ordered to continue "political struggle" after Ngo Dinh Diem unleashed his troops to exterminate them, recalled Tra, "many comrades had fallen in battle, . . . many local movements had drowned in blood."[1] This time the Communists were determined to defend and build upon their gains by whatever means were necessary.

The South had changed considerably since 1954, however. The Saigon government was no longer a fragile colonial rump but a fairly stable regime in possession of the world's fifth largest armed force. Whatever its weaknesses, it was no longer susceptible to overthrow by political turmoil or Southern-based insurgency. Although the Communists had added significantly to their military strength, they were not assured an easy victory by the U.S. withdrawal, and they knew it. The withdrawal had removed the screen behind which the Saigon regime had been built, but it also had removed a constraint on how Saigon used resources that the United States continued to supply. U.S. withdrawal left the Vietnamese free, for the first time in a century, to fight among themselves without much likelihood of foreign military intervention. Neither side was certain how the subtraction of U.S. power would affect the balance between them.

In one important respect, however, nothing had changed: The Communists were accustomed to fighting without a foreign guarantee but Saigon was not. Anticommunists in the South focused as much on U.S. rescue as on their own self-defense, partly from habit but also because no leader, party, or government, not even the idea of the "South" itself, commanded their collective loyalties. Although they clung to the belief that Washington could not remain completely idle, Saigon leaders felt abandoned by their ally, a feeling that gave way to paralysis as U.S. actions fell short of Saigon's hopes.

FROM CEASELESS FIRE TO POSTWAR WAR

The Paris Agreement recognized two administrations, two armed forces, and two zones of control in the territory of South Vietnam. But Thieu stood firm on "four no's"—no negotiations with the enemy, no communist activity in the South, no coalition government, no surrender of territory. The "four no's" ruled out implementation of the Paris Agreement's political articles, mocked the idea of compromise, and invited the Communists to respond in kind. Despite negotiations on a National Council of National Reconciliation and Concord, which were deadlocked from beginning to end in May 1974, it was quickly plain to most Vietnamese that the purpose of the agreement was to let the United States withdraw and leave the Vietnamese to resolve their irreconcilable differences as they saw fit. Vietnamese with U.S. connections began asking anxious questions or arranging study abroad for their children. Others renewed contact with family members on "the other side" and began openly discussing what life would be like under communist rule. Journalists, artists, writers, and disaffected professionals who for years had admired the Communists for their apparent probity or simply yearned for peace and social reform were increasingly attracted to the possibility of cooperation. As tension increased, the worldwise wags of Saigon dubbed the new conflict "the ceaseless fire," and later "the postwar war."

Meanwhile, the Communists had decided to respect the Paris Agreement precisely because they assumed that Thieu was determined to obstruct it. By respecting the Paris Agreement, they hoped to cast Thieu in the role of peacebreaker and isolate him from a war-weary population. But, remembering the mid-1950s, they were not prepared to rely solely on legalistic demands to achieve their aims.

In early fall 1972, as Le Duc Tho was preparing proposals he felt sure Kissinger would accept, orders had gone out to the Communists' Southern commands to prepare for a sharpening of conflict in the period between the announcement of agreement and the ceasefire.[2] The orders had assumed Saigon would try to enlarge its area of control, so those orders had called for preemptive uprisings. The objective was to expand the "liberated areas," break open refugee holding centers, and spark a "return to the village" that would repopulate the territory under communist control. By the Communists' own admission, the number of people in "liberated and contested areas" was still below the 4 million (in a population of 19.5 million) that they had controlled on the eve of the 1968 Tet Offensive.[3] That figure, they believed, needed raising if they were to support their ceasefire claims and win the struggles that were sure to follow.

Before the ceasefire went into effect, both sides attempted to plant their flags on as much territory as possible. In this, "the war of the flags," the Communists took an early lead and succeeded in raising their colors not only in "contested areas" but in some that had been under Saigon's control for years. They also invaded a portion of Tay Ninh city the day before ceasefire, provoking the ARVN to counterattack until well after the truce had begun. Each side resorted to "land grabbing" and "nibbling" to consolidate and expand their holdings. But the Communists, eager to make Saigon appear the aggressor, let the ARVN commit most of the transgressions. In June 1973, Kissinger and Tho met to reaffirm the Paris Agreement but succeeded in only briefly restoring a very wobbly truce. It was the last time that Hanoi and Washington would discuss ways to make the Paris Agreement work.

Most ARVN operations at first sought to recover areas the Communists had seized from Saigon just before ceasefire, but the ARVN soon encroached upon areas that traditionally had been under communist control. From January 1973 to mid-1974, out of 1,000 additional hamlets Saigon claimed to have placed under its control, it retook 300 the Communists had seized just before ceasefire and seized 90 they had controlled for a long time.[4] Thus began Thieu's drive to establish control over all South Vietnam. If a communist counterattack put him in trouble, he calculated, the United States, its prestige still at stake, would be certain to bail him out.

The Communists had fully anticipated Thieu's strategy but wished to avoid major fighting at that time. Hanoi had sought a halt to the bombing in 1968 partly so the North could support the Southern revolution more effectively, and a similar calculation had figured in Hanoi's decision to sign the Paris Agreement. The North's task, as a COSVN directive noted in March 1973, was "to heal the wounds of war, to build socialism with speed . . . and make a base for the task of liberating South Vietnam and unifying the nation."[5] The North was in no condition to apply the pressure Hanoi strategists thought would be necessary to compel Thieu to implement the Paris Agreement or face military defeat.[6] Some strategists also still believed the ARVN was superior to the PAVN and expressed concern for the morale of troops who had been in combat for years.[7] Although priority was given to Northern recovery, COSVN's initial orders had been to mobilize the people to demand enforcement of the Paris Agreement, clarify zones of control, withdraw from contested areas if necessary, and abstain from major use of force.[8]

Orders only to "defend the Agreement" seemed unwisely passive to some of Hanoi's field commanders, however. To older cadres in particular the strategy bore a haunting resemblance to the post-Geneva "political struggle" in which so many comrades had "drowned in blood." With the approval of COSVN's General Tra, the heads of Military Region 9, Vo Van Kiet and General Le Duc Anh, ignored orders and pushed the ARVN out of positions it had established before the Paris Agreement took effect. Tra candidly explained that

> the actions of the military forces of Region 9 were based on the view that there had been no agreement, that nothing had changed, and that it was necessary to keep on fighting. That was an incorrect understanding of the Paris Agreement and of the new strategic phase. But it correctly evaluated the obstinacy of the enemy, just like the Geneva Accords period, and it was resolute in preserving the gains the revolution had won. It was consistent with the actual situation, not illusory or utopian. "Luckily," it was a distant battlefield, so upper-echelon policies were often slow in arriving and rectification of errors was not always prompt.[9]

Ironically, some communist ceasefire violations were also violations of Hanoi's wish. It was "lucky" for Kiet, Anh, and Tra that Region 9's efforts were successful.[10] In a series of debates during mid-1973, their demand for vigorous action gained support, and in October, the 21st Plenum of the Central Committee affirmed that Thieu did not intend, and could not be made, to implement the Paris Agreement. The only recourse, the plenum concluded, was a "fierce revolutionary war to defeat the enemy and win complete victory." The plenum authorized immediate retaliatory strikes "based on the specific circumstances of each area" and preparations to resume large-scale warfare in the near future. Authorization also was given on October 24 for the PAVN to form its First Army Corps, based in the Tri-Thien zone.[11] (Three more corps would be organized between October 1973 and March 1975.)

As 1973 came to a close, the two sides observed an uneasy truce in Quang Tri, Thua Thien, and Quang Nam provinces where the PAVN held virtually all of the countryside, and the ARVN held Quang Tri city, Hue, and a narrow strip of coast. But elsewhere the skirmishing over hamlets gave way to maneuvers for strategic position. In the central highlands the ARVN extended its string of firebases to harass PAVN supply lines, and the PAVN began work on a new road, Corridor 613, running north-to-south through the mountains just inside the Vietnamese border. To cover its western flank, the PAVN left 15,000 troops in Laos to stiffen the Pathet Lao and another 35,000 to man the Ho Chi Minh Trail (in violation of the Paris Agreement) as Lao Communists peaceably joined the new Provisional Government of National Union. Ostensibly in retaliation for ARVN "land grabbing," the PAVN overran half a dozen ARVN firebases in the highlands from September 1973 to April 1974. Eight thousand men died in these battles. North and west of Saigon, the ARVN went on the offensive to break up PAVN logistical bases. In the delta it attacked communist strongholds in an attempt to interdict infiltration from the Parrot's Beak. The Communists responded in the delta by destroying eighty small outposts between January and May 1974, and daylight ambushes began to occur again. In the first year of "peace," 80,000 Vietnamese including 14,000 civilians died in combat or crossfires.

THE MILITARY BALANCE

The Communists for a while considered themselves to be weaker than Saigon. The ARVN had grown, it had adequate reserves, and though U.S. aid was decreasing, that aid was still abundant. On the revolutionary side, "liberated areas" were thinly populated, many party cells were cut off from the people, and irregular forces were weak. "In continuous action since 1972," noted General Tra, "our cadres and men were tired. Nor had we had time to make up our losses. All our units were in disarray, we lacked manpower, food and ammunition were short, so it was difficult to cope with the enemy's attacks."[12] Coordination of the "three-pronged attacks" (military offensive, proselytization of enemy armed forces, and civilian uprising) was out of the question. "The enemy," said COSVN in February 1974, "temporarily has the upper hand." To tip the balance in their favor, the Communists counted on economic decline and political turmoil in Saigon, opportunities afforded by a rear linking the North, Laos, and Cambodia, and the rebuilding of both local and regular forces.[13]

In the year following the signing of the Paris Agreement, an estimated 100,000 to 120,000 PAVN troops infiltrated the South, raising their numbers after casualties and rotation to more than 150,000 men. Approximately 30,000 PLAF regulars and 50,000 guerrillas brought the total number of communist forces in the South to about 230,000. The heavy loss of tanks suffered in 1972 was quickly made up, and as PAVN armament approached parity with the ARVN, Soviet-built tanks began to appear in Binh Duong province near Saigon. The PAVN sharply increased its supply of 130-mm field guns to the South. Although by spring 1974 the PAVN still had only one-fourth the heavy artillery of the ARVN, its 130s were highly mobile, had longer range than most ARVN guns, and compensated for numerical inferiority with rapid deployment. The equipment build-up further required the PAVN to improve its logistical facilities in Laos and Cambodia, build a new road linking Route 9 and the central highlands, extend petroleum pipelines into Quang Tri and Quang Tin provinces, and install ground-to-air missiles and large calibre anti-aircraft weapons as far south as the Cambodian border of Tay Ninh province. A U.S. congressional staff report concluded in May 1974 that the effect of these developments was "to diminish significantly the logistical advantage which the South enjoyed in the past and to give the North Vietnamese a capability to move and mass troops in a manner hitherto impossible for them."[14]

However, the PAVN build-up came nowhere near giving it conventional capability equal to that of the ARVN. The ARVN main force grew from 223,000 to 320,000 in the year following the Paris Agreement. By spring 1974, including irregulars, Saigon had more than 1 million men in arms, or about four times the total number of communist forces in the South and roughly twice as many regulars.[15] Although U.S. aid had declined, the ARVN had huge stocks of equipment and ammunition that the United States had left behind or turned over just prior to signing the Paris Agreement. Last-minute infusions of U.S. aid, known as Operation Enhance and Enhance Plus, were valued at $753 million. Soviet and Chinese aid to the North in the same period was mainly economic. Of some $715 million worth of aid given to Hanoi in 1973, only $270 million was for the military. Although figures on Soviet, Chinese, and U.S. arms shipments are not fully comparable (communist aid consisted of arms, equipment,

Table 8.1
Value of arms shipments to North and South Vietnam, 1972–1975 (millions of current dollars)

	North	South
1972	775	1,300
1973	270	2,700
1974	220	835
1975	130	850

Source: U.S. Arms Control and Disarmament Agency, *World Military Expenditures and Arms Transfers 1968–1977* (Washington, D.C.: GPO, October 1979), p. 152.

and ammunition; U.S. aid included costly operating and maintenance programs), they remove any doubt about Washington's generosity by comparison with that of Moscow and Beijing (see Table 8.1). The much greater U.S. aid was necessary of course to sustain an army that had been organized and trained to fight with lavish use of ammunition, motorized transport, abundant aircover, and sophisticated equipment.

In 1974, the ARVN fired sixteen times as many artillery shells as the PAVN, a ratio that U.S. advisers regarded as excessive, even for defensive forces firing upon a highly mobile, unseen enemy.[16] Within the South alone, the balance in arms, men, and equipment was heavily in the ARVN's favor.[17] Saigon's real military vulnerabilities were strategic. Thieu's effort to extend Saigon's authority took the form of an order for the ARVN to penetrate and hold every corner of the South, which had not been done even with the help of 500,000 foreign troops. A much larger proportion of ARVN troops than of the PAVN was tied down in defense and logistics. With each advance, with the total defense of every point it held, the ARVN stretched itself more thinly against an enemy that could still choose the time and place of its response. While the Communists methodically improved their logistical system and stockpiled equipment, the ARVN began consuming more of its supplies than U.S. aid replaced. Gradually the military balance began to shift.

THE POLITICS OF DESPAIR

The postwar war dispirited ordinary citizens—and troops—on both sides. But on Saigon's side despair turned to disgust as the Thieu regime reverted to earlier ways. Exacerbated by economic decline, and without the United States to cajole or pay for compromise and reform, the divisiveness that had destroyed his predecessors stalked Nguyen Van Thieu.

For this divisiveness Thieu was partly to blame. Having wrested control of the military from Nguyen Cao Ky in 1967, Thieu had set out to construct an authoritarian state loyal only to himself. In August 1971, he had abolished elections for hamlet chiefs (reversing an earlier reform) and increased the authority of appointed province chiefs. In October, he had found a pretext to disqualify Ky from the presidential elections, Duong Van Minh had already dropped out of the race in protest back in August, and Thieu had run unopposed. In 1972, the year of the Spring Offensive, Thieu had declared martial law, and in place of civilian village security commissioners he had installed career police officers as deputy village chiefs. In March 1973, after restricting the number of political parties, he had inaugurated his own Dan Chu (Democracy) party. Unlike the other two legal parties, the Dan Chu was the political arm of the government (much as the Can Lao had been for Ngo Dinh Diem), and civil servants had to join. In July, Thieu had unveiled an "administrative revolution" whose purpose he claimed was to transform the "old individualistic mentality" of civil servants into a new "cadre spirit," but which in fact was to enable province chiefs to allocate development projects in exchange for political support.[18] Finally, in the August elections for the Senate, the two pro-government slates won all thirty-one contested seats, reducing the opposition to one-quarter of the sixty-member body. A vote five months later in the National Assembly to amend the constitution so Thieu could run for a third term in 1975, which passed by a margin of 153 to 52, came as no surprise.

These moves—toward single-party, authoritarian, bureaucratic rule—were hardly novel for Vietnam nor exceptional for Asia.

But they were inaugurated by a man who had never really won broad popular acceptance. In a culture that measured legitimacy by the effortlessness of its attainment, Thieu had reached the top with transparent maneuver, sheer doggedness, and the support of a foreign power. His mandate could never be anything but dubious, and so his efforts to consolidate power were resented. Local officials chafed at the intrusive presence of policemen chosen for them as deputy village chiefs. Civil servants balked at Dan Chu membership and felt demeaned by retraining sessions. The administrative revolution grated on senior civilian officials who regarded Thieu as a low-status military upstart. The chronically discontented intelligentsia, who were anti-military anyway, grew rebellious at the exclusion of their cliques from the list of approved parties. Where the regime did succeed in establishing its writ in rural areas, old self-destructive practices reappeared. Land reform began to reverse in some secure areas as plantation owners induced local officials to pressure peasants into relinquishing titles given them only a few years before.[19] Hoa Hao protested Thieu's efforts to absorb its private militia (which had been a haven for Hoa Hao males evading the draft).[20] In Darlac province, a Jarai tribal leader succeeded in stirring rebellion among montagnards who, previously sheltered by U.S. Special Forces and aid programs, resented Thieu's efforts to populate the hills with lowland Vietnamese.[21]

Political tensions were made worse by an agonizing economic transition. From 1966 to 1972, U.S. troops, contractors, and official agencies had spent $2 billion on the local economy, mostly on services. At one time, domestics, repairmen, taxi drivers, bar girls, and guards were earning 35 percent of the South's total income, with public services responsible for another 20 percent.[22] The U.S. presence created an estimated 300,000 jobs.[23] Inflation had been controlled—and revenue raised—by U.S. agreement (the Commodity Import Program) to exchange dollars for piastres and thus facilitate imports. Along with cement and steel for development had come motorbikes, stereos, and cognac for consumption. Also to preserve urban tranquillity, the regime had held down the price of rice to about one-half the world level, to the detriment of peasant incomes and per capita agricultural production.[24] Little money flowed into savings or investment. What observers saw as wealth (TV antennas, Honda motorbikes) was a fragile bubble. In 1973, U.S. withdrawal combined with rising world prices for commodities (e.g., oil) produced 65 percent inflation and 40 percent urban unemployment in a matter of months. Living standards declined. Several individuals protested the futility of trying to support their families by immolating themselves in the streets. A tripling of patients at a mental hospital near Saigon was attributed to mental stress caused by economic and other war-related difficulties.[25]

With much of the work force on public salaries of diminishing value, corruption became more visible and pervasive. Corruption was not new. Even the puritanical Diem had tolerated corruption. But Thieu had found that the loyalty of subordinates depended on it. Some of Thieu's province chiefs had bought their posts for 30 to 50 million piastres (at a time when the official rate was 118 piastres to the dollar), district chiefs for 15 to 25 million, and they had recovered many times these amounts from graft. Vast sums had been made "taxing" military convoys, scrapping spent artillery shells, "protecting" gambling dens and whore houses, and smuggling. Under the twin impact of economic decline and political challenge, corruption had become the glue that held the Thieu regime together. A large majority of National Assembly deputies was said to be in Thieu's pay to assure its complicity in repressing the opposition.[26] At the bottom of the pyramid, petty officials increased their exactions to make ends meet and to meet the exactions of superiors. Even policemen operating traffic lights at Saigon intersections turned their tiny domains to advantage, with results that could be seen in their girth. The powerless grew thinner. To public criticism, Thieu responded by closing down twenty-four news agencies for operating without government permission and supplying "libelous stories."[27]

Protest finally broke out behind the unlikely leadership of a right-wing Redemptorist priest and frequent lecturer at the ARVN military academy, Father Tran Huu Thanh. Heading a movement that had gestated in the Redemptorist order, Thanh issued a six-count "indictment" of Thieu's government in September 1974, and three newspapers published it. The indictment charged

Thieu with perverting anticommunism for personal and corrupt purposes. It specifically charged his wife with profiting from a private charity, cited other instances of corruption by his relatives and associates, and hinted at his own links to the heroin trade. Thieu denied all charges and ordered police to confiscate copies of the three newspapers.

Father Thanh's movement was not the only focus of dissent. Another priest, Father Chan Tin, led demonstrations on behalf of political prisoners and prison reform. Madame Ngo Ba Thanh, a U.S.-trained lawyer sympathetic to the NLF, headed a women's movement for peace. Journalists spearheaded attacks on press censorship and Information Minister Hoang Duc Nha, Thieu's cousin. But the regime could not brush off the vociferously anticommunist Father Thanh as a neutral or communist dupe as it did the others, and the dissidence gained momentum. The suddenly strong opposition moved Thieu in late October to accept the resignations of four cabinet ministers including Nha, to dismiss 377 field grade officers for corruption, and to transfer three of the four corps commanders. However, police continued to arrest students and journalists and to confiscate newspapers, and oppositionists demanded the departure of Thieu himself. Though the Phuoc Long province capital fell to communist forces in January 1975, Thieu went on closing newspapers, Father Thanh accused Thieu of "high treason,"[28] and Duong Van "Big" Minh denounced the regime as "nothing but tyranny."[29]

Significantly, the anti-corruption movement remained predominantly Catholic, revealing the persistence of division and disunity on the noncommunist side. Journalists protested repression, Minh called Thieu a "great obstacle to peace" in a speech at An Quang pagoda,[30] and non-Catholics expressed sympathy with Father Thanh's aims. But most non-Catholics stood aside, suspicious that the anti-corruption theme disguised a Catholic grab for power. There was quite simply neither the unity nor a personality outside the regime strong enough to present a credible alternative to Thieu. Yet Thieu was losing his grip: Only after agreeing to a larger share of power for Premier Tran Thien Khiem was he able, in late November 1974, to reform his cabinet with little-known figures, most of whom were Khiem's chums.

The United States continued to distance itself from Thieu as his regime decayed. But Thieu's problems were more an excuse than the cause of U.S. detachment. More important was the sense in Washington that "our war" was now "their war." Even Kissinger confessed that "we have succeeded not in guaranteeing necessarily a permanent peace but in moving the decision to a Vietnamese decision."[31] Furthermore, the last shred of congressional tolerance for presidential war-making had evaporated in July 1973 with the revelation of the secret bombing of Cambodia to the Senate Armed Services Committee by Air Force Major Hal Knight. The bombing, Congress was incensed to learn, had been conducted on Nixon's orders, and the Pentagon had falsified or destroyed the records. The War Powers Act, a ban on bombing in Cambodia, and a spate of amendments prohibiting any kind of U.S. combat activity in Indochina had quickly followed.[32] Frustrated by Saigon's insatiable dependence on U.S. support, Congress was averse to huge, open-ended aid commitments. In May 1974, it cut $474 million from an administration proposal of $1.6 billion for military assistance. Finally, nearly two years of skirmishing between Nixon and Congress over the Watergate scandal came to a head. On August 9, 1974, the president resigned. Two days later, President Gerald Ford sent a letter to Thieu reaffirming the commitment made by his four predecessors and assuring Thieu that U.S. support would be "adequate." But that was a promise no U.S. president henceforth would be able to keep. Tragically, Thieu and his generals never grasped how weak the U.S. president really was in the face of congressional opposition to the war and went on policing villages, expending supplies, and depleting reserves assuming that Ford's commitment was the only one that really mattered.[33]

RACE AGAINST THE ENEMY AND HEAVEN

The Communists assessed the prospects of U.S. reintervention rather differently—and more accurately. In April 1973, Party Secretary Le Duan opined that a defeated United States had withdrawn "never to return."[34] Washington's disarray in the face of recession, the oil crisis, Watergate, Nixon's resignation, and revolutionary advances in Laos and Cambodia further convinced Hanoi leaders that they had little to fear. "The U.S. imperialists would find it very difficult to intervene directly," the Political Bureau concluded in October 1974. "If the puppets are in danger of a complete collapse, we must be on guard against the U.S. intervening with its air force or navy, not to expand the war but to save the Saigon regime. There is little possibility that they will use infantry, but we must continually monitor their plots, be vigilant, and be prepared to react. No matter how they intervene, we will be fully determined and able to defeat them, and they cannot save the Saigon regime from collapse."[35]

By then preparations for the last offensive were well under way. The decision to abandon the Paris Agreement had been ratified at the Central Committee's 21st Plenum in October 1973. Thieu's adamant refusal to implement the agreement's political provisions had supplied the rationale, and plans for a violent showdown had been set in motion. Le Duan and Le Duc Tho had spelled out the details for military cadres in March 1974. PAVN successes later that year—destroying a district capital in Military Region 5, overrunning ARVN firebases in the highlands—had overcome the reservations of some party and military leaders about PAVN capability.

The plan adopted by the Political Bureau at year's end envisioned a two-year, two-step campaign. Main forces were to mount continuous attacks in 1975, paving the way for a general offensive and uprising in 1976. The Communists had learned from previous experience not to expect an uprising until the "puppet army" had been smashed. "Only then could favorable conditions be created for uprisings by the urban masses."[36] However, the plan acknowledged that these steps might be compressed into one and victory achieved in 1975 if opportunities were properly exploited.

The major role assigned to conventional forces encouraged the high command to plan a military conquest. Generals in the map rooms of Hanoi, given the task of organizing, supplying, and deploying multidivision armies for the first time in their lives, naturally focused on the military dimensions. Many also were skeptical that the chronic "imbalance" between main forces and guerrillas and between military and political struggle could be quickly corrected.[37] Such perspectives certainly dominate the account by General Van Tien Dung, PAVN chief of staff and overall commander of the offensive.[38] But at the opposite end of the country, COSVN leaders had somewhat different concerns. A campaign that consisted only of regular forces attacking in the highlands and advancing on Saigon, they pointed out, ran the risk of driving the enemy into an enclave consisting of Saigon and the richest rice-growing portions of the delta. Such an enclave could be easily supported by U.S. air and naval power and had been proposed by General James Gavin, once in 1966 and again in 1972. Wouldn't that leave Thieu with control over 10 million people? Hadn't the French considered possession of the delta the key to possession of Indochina, asked COSVN commander General Tran Van Tra? "Colonialists' views of things differed very little."[39] COSVN, according to Tra, was more confident than Hanoi that the political situation could be exploited to bring victory in 1975.

To preempt an enclave strategy, COSVN requested three to four more divisions for the B2 theatre. Supplied with intelligence from agents planted in ARVN headquarters, it also drew up plans to soften Saigon's outer rings of defense and demoralize the ARVN in advance of main force attack. The theatre's plan, said Tra, "was based on the assumption that B2 itself would have to carry out a general offensive and uprising in Saigon and that each military region and province would have to take care of their own battlefield needs without waiting on forces from the upper echelon."[40] Thus did COSVN dust off plans it had carefully revised since the 1968 Tet Offensive and send out feelers to dissident groups. However, only after intense lobbying—and a military victory—did COSVN extract consent from Hanoi to its attack plans and authorization to use tanks and artillery. For the attention of the high command was fixed on provinces farther north and on conserving forces for the final push in 1976.

Meanwhile a massive logistical effort was funnelling the PAVN's equipment into the South. "Great quantities of materiel such as tanks, armored cars, missiles, long-range artillery and antiaircraft weapons which the U.S. imperialists had sought unsuccessfully to destroy during their twelve-day B-52 blitz against the North, gradually were sent to the various battlefields."[41] Some 30,000 troops and "assault youths" worked feverishly to extend the new road—Corridor 613—from Route 9 to the edge of eastern Nam Bo, 1,000 kilometers to the south. Over this two-lane road, by early 1975, 10,000 trucks were shuttling both ways, fueled by a 5,000-kilometer pipeline that ran from Quang Tri to Loc Ninh. With connecting routes, the PAVN logistical network now had 20,000 kilometers of communications and supply lines, which Dung likened to "sturdy hemp ropes being daily and hourly slipped around the neck and limbs of a monster who would be strangled with one sharp yank when the order was given."[42]

The Communists felt by late 1974 that the situation had turned decisively in their favor. They had tested themselves against the ARVN in set-piece battles in the highlands, and they had blunted ARVN "nibbling operations" in the delta. Many areas where revolutionary forces had been heavily suppressed between 1968 and 1972 had fallen again under their control. As for Saigon, economic troubles, political malaise, and cuts in U.S. aid were beginning to take their toll. The ARVN's morale was low, desertions were high, and stocks of bombs, ammunition, and petrol were running down. No longer could the ARVN squander supplies in large-scale sweeps, airborne mobility, and the policing of every village. As Dung put it, "Nguyen Van Thieu had to make his army switch to 'poor man's war'"—not in the sense that U.S. aid was meager but that it was inadequate to support the strategy Thieu unwisely had chosen.[43]

Scanning the South for its first target, the PAVN high command decided against the northern provinces because there the ARVN had concentrated five strong divisions in a small territory.[44] It decided against ARVN III Corps because the ARVN's three divisions there could be easily reinforced. The delta was out because it was too far from the main supply lines. This left the central highlands, a vast area over which just two ARVN divisions were thinly scattered. The highlands' relatively open terrain also permitted rapid deployment of tanks and artillery and easy access to the PAVN's much enhanced logistical base in the B3 "western highlands front." If the initial attacks were successful, large forces could move quickly toward the coast and south over existing roads. To the PAVN general staff, the central highlands presented the greatest contrast between thin ARVN defenses and PAVN offensive strengths.

But even as generals in Hanoi were weighing options, mixed regular, regional, and guerrilla forces seized Route 14 and an ARVN garrison overlooking Phuoc Binh city, capital of Phuoc Long province. On January 7, 1975, the province capital, then the whole province, fell to PAVN and PLAF units supported by tanks and a company of 130-mm artillery. The victory suddenly gave the Communists unobstructed access to the lowlands northwest of Saigon. It also vindicated COSVN's persistent demand for a strong attack in the B2 theatre. Officials in Washington considered diverting a navy task force to Vietnam that was then sailing between Subic Bay and the Indian Ocean. Though U.S. planes flew over the South, Cambodia, and the North on reconnaissance missions, administration spokesmen were constrained to deny any intent to intimidate. At the same time, the Ford administration request for $1.3 billion in military aid for Saigon encountered stiff opposition in Congress. A special session of the Political Bureau, meeting in Hanoi since December 18, closed on January 8 with the conclusion that the signs for victory had never been more propitious.

The next day, the Central Military Party Committee joined by COSVN's Vo Chi Cong and generals Chu Huy Man, Hoang Minh Thao, and Le Trong Tan met to select the first target. By that time the PAVN had deployed five divisions in the central highlands, compared with two regular divisions, seven Ranger regiments, and one armored brigade for the ARVN. As the ARVN had taken no steps to reinforce now dangerously vulnerable positions, the committee was sure PAVN preparations so far had gone undetected. After heated debate, the committee decided to launch the offensive with an attack on Ban Me Thuot, a city of about 100,000, capital of Darlac province, and headquarters of the ARVN 23rd division. Ban Me Thuot was less well-defended than Pleiku and Kontum, where the ARVN II Corps command thought that attack was more likely to come.

More important, seizure of Ban Me Thuot would isolate the other two cities and connect the PAVN supply lines with roads leading out of the hills.

On February 5, General Dung left Hanoi and travelled to Dong Hoi by air, to Quang Tri by car, up the Ben Hai River by motorboat, and down Corridor 613 to the western highlands to assume supreme command of the campaign. The situation he found was more complicated than he had expected. Large units could not move easily without detection, and information on conditions inside Ban Me Thuot was unreliable. A cadre sent to reconnoiter was surprised by the bright lights and tall (over two stories) buildings and reported the city was almost as big as Haiphong. Admitting that "to attack a big city was still new to us," Dung decided to use the "blooming lotus" tactic (bypassing outer defenses with sappers to attack the center, then "blooming" outward to meet regiments attacking from outside), which he had concocted for a raid in 1952 on Phat Diem, a Catholic community in the North.[45]

But in all other respects Dung found reason for satisfaction. The ARVN II Corps commander, Major General Pham Van Phu, had deployed the bulk of his forces to protect his corps headquarters at Pleiku, leaving only one regiment of the 23rd division and three territorial battalions to defend Ban Me Thuot, despite ample evidence of PAVN intentions. To attack the city, Dung had the entire 316th division reinforced by one infantry regiment, one sapper regiment, two anti-aircraft regiments, two artillery regiments, two engineering regiments, an armored regiment, and a communications regiment.[46] Dung calculated that although in the entire central highlands his forces were "not much superior to the enemy's," at Ben Me Thuot he had 5.5 times as many troops, 1.2 times as many tanks and armored vehicles, and 2.1 times as much artillery. His main concern was to prevent the ARVN from reinforcing the city before he was ready to attack, a concern that was much alleviated by General Phu's deep reluctance to move troops away from his own command post, which was under harassment anyway.[47]

To keep Phu off balance, Dung ordered diversionary attacks north of Ban Me Thuot, destroying two ARVN outposts on Route 19 west of Pleiku. On March 4, the PAVN attacked positions on the same route east and west of An Khe and on Route 21. Though the ARVN moved to clear the roads, the highlands were now cut off. Only Route 14 between Pleiku and Ban Me Thuot remained open, as the 320th division sought to avoid revealing its position just four kilometers off the road. But encounters with ARVN patrols forced the 320th to seize that road, too, and by March 9, Ban Me Thuot was effectively encircled. That evening, Dung recalled, officers in his staff could not conceal their "joy and emotion" as "tens of thousands of men moved toward their targets."[48]

At two in the morning, sappers attacked the city's two airfields, a logistic facility, and a storage depot. Long-range artillery opened fire on 23rd division headquarters. Tanks left hiding places forty kilometers away with infantry and armored cars falling in behind to converge on the city from four directions. At 7:25 A.M. on March 10, the artillery ceased, and tanks and infantry raced toward the 23rd division's main installations. The large part of the city was in PAVN hands by late afternoon. Resistance weakened as it became clear that neither aerial reinforcements nor tactical air support could easily penetrate PAVN anti-aircraft fire. One plane dropped a bomb on the 23rd division command post, severing communications and ending organized defense. The division commander, Brigadier General Le Trung Tuong, had already escaped in a helicopter after diverting a Ranger Group to secure a landing zone so he could pick up his family.[49] By 10:30 A.M., March 11, the 23rd division command post, the division's deputy commander, and the chief of Darlac province were in PAVN hands.

Communist commanders were surprised by the ease of victory at Ban Me Thuot as compared with the hardships of 1968, and they pursued the ARVN cautiously. But Dung demanded speed, as any pause risked prolonging the campaign into the rainy season. Now that the PAVN was organized into mechanized battle groups equipped with heavy weapons, it, like the ARVN, needed dry ground. The rest of the campaign, thought Dung, would be "a race against the enemy and heaven."[50]

Dung's forces could barely keep up with their enemy's collapse. An ARVN attempt to relieve Ban Me Thuot bogged down for lack of helicopters. Worse, the relief force was the 23rd division's

44th regiment, which had been stationed at Pleiku although dependents remained in Ban Me Thuot, and when men of the regiment saw civilians leaving the city, they threw down their weapons to join their wives and children in flight. General Tuong checked into a hospital with a slight facial wound "to avoid responsibility," said a fellow officer, "for [the] certain defeat of his division."[51]

As the United States failed to respond, it became apparent to Thieu that not only would the United States not return to combat, but Congress was unlikely to approve the $300 million supplemental military assistance that Ford had requested ("the minimum needed to prevent serious reversals," Ford had said in January).[52] On March 10, Thieu ordered the airborne division to return from I Corps to defend theatened Tay Ninh (and, some said, to guard against a coup, which indeed had been proposed by Nguyen Cao Ky). On the 11th, he called a meeting of his chief advisers to discuss what he had vowed never to do, namely, to surrender territory. A general redeployment was ordered to defend III and IV Corps, a move Thieu described as "lightening the top to keep the bottom." Lieutenant General Ngo Quang Truong, I Corps commander, learned on the 13th that he was to keep only Danang. On March 11, Thieu met General Phu at Cam Ranh to plan a retreat of ARVN regulars from Pleiku and Kontum for regroupment to retake Ban Me Thuot. Montagnard regional and popular forces were to stay behind to screen the move. The United States was not to be told. Phu argued that with reinforcements and supplies he could hold Pleiku for a month but was overruled. To evade communist forces, he suggested withdrawing by Route 7-B, a narrow unmaintained dirt track from Pleiku to the coast at Tuy Hoa, 225 kilometers away.

Just what Phu's orders were and what he meant to do on his return to Pleiku on March 15 is disputed. He is widely accused of precipitously ordering total withdrawal. Certainly there was no planning.[53] But it hardly mattered; as Phu, his senior officers, and their families boarded planes, the 6th air division had its men lifted out by C-130s (leaving sixty-four of their own aircraft on the ground), and army trucks headed out of town. To montagnard irregulars, government administrators, and civilians, the move meant abandonment. Troops with dependents bolted to find their families, and a panicky mass streamed out of Pleiku to follow the army convoy down Route 7-B.

The withdrawal route did catch the Communists by surprise. Dung severely reprimanded the 320th division commander for having no plan to block the road. But the retreating column was slowed to a crawl by fallen bridges and old land mines, and the division easily overtook it. Regional forces and mutinous montagnards joined the PAVN in raking the retreat with small arms, machine guns, and mortars. One group of refugees, halted by a blown bridge and closely circled by PAVN troops, was bombed by Saigon's air force. On the 22nd, stunned and starving survivors poured out of the hills with tales of horror, spreading panic to the lowlands.

By that time the PAVN 2nd army had retaken Quang Tri city and surrounded Hue. On March 22, PAVN tanks crossed the My Chanh River. ARVN and U.S. aircraft had successfully defended the river in 1972, but without U.S. air support, the elite ARVN 1st division disintegrated. Thousands of deserting troops fell back on Hue to join the scramble for transport to the sea. The PAVN entered Hue four days later. Meanwhile the PAVN 2nd division and regional forces had routed the ARVN in Quang Ngai and Binh Dinh provinces and taken possession of the former U.S. Marine base at Chu Lai. Danang was isolated.

Thieu thought Danang was defensible as a coastal enclave. With a population of more than 500,000 (the South's second largest city), Danang was many times larger than Ban Me Thuot. The ARVN marine and 3rd infantry divisions were stationed there, thousands more troops were streaming in from the countryside, food and ammunition could be supplied by air and sea. But the avalanche of refugees from the highlands had swept through provinces on both sides of Danang and was now rushing into the city. More than 1 million refugees swarmed in the streets, food reserves dwindled, and deserters turned to looting. The evacuation of U.S. Consulate personnel on March 26 ignited hysterical fury in the huge crowd gathered at the airport. As PAVN artillery began to shell the airfield and military installations on March 28, panicky mobs surged into the center of the city. A despairing General Ngo Quang Truong, his communications cut and staff deserting, ordered his troops to evacuate by sea. Less than one-half the marine division and only 1,000 troops of the 3rd division succeeded in boarding ships, the rest having deserted or been left on the beach. Three PAVN divisions and assorted regional and technical units entered the city unopposed on March 29.

In just two weeks, twelve provinces and nearly 8 million people had come under communist control. The ARVN had lost 35 percent of its troop strength and 40 percent of its weapons. Having expended little of its own supplies and lost few troops, the PAVN now enjoyed a significant materiel and manpower advantage. But these were not solely the achievements of communist arms. The ARVN had been deployed in far-flung positions that had permitted each communist success to place another ARVN outpost in jeopardy. Fantasizing U.S. rescue, officers had abandoned their troops when reinforcements and air cover failed to appear. Abandoned by their officers, troops had left their units. Personal ties between superiors and subordinates, so essential to solidarity among Vietnamese, had dissolved. Though some units had fought bravely and well, many had broken up, sometimes without fighting at all. Never planned, retreat had turned into panic. Fearing the unknown and not wanting to be left behind, great masses of civilians had fled.

As Danang was falling, President Ford dispatched General Frederick Weyand to see what military assistance Saigon needed. Weyand reported that an emergency infusion of $722 million—the value of materiel lost in the retreat thus far—could stave off defeat. But Weyand's professional overoptimism was obvious. Even the Pentagon's own Defense Intelligence Agency predicted defeat within a month. For once the Pentagon agreed with the Communists, who concluded during a Political Bureau meeting on April 1 that "the U.S. has proved to be completely impotent, and even if it increased its aid it cannot save the puppets from collapse."[54] Ford's insistence on the emergency allocation, placed before Congress on April 10, was widely seen as a cynical attempt to hold Congress responsible for the inevitable. There could be no rescue now, and each day's news confirmed this fact.

Having decided to strike for complete victory by May, the Communists raced to occupy all of ARVN I and II Corps and to shift forces southward. A new army corps, the 3rd, was created. The 1st army, dispatched from Ninh Binh province in the North, arrived via Route 9 and Corridor 613 at the southern edge of the highlands in mid-April. The 2nd army left Danang in the hands of reserves to advance 900 kilometers down Route 1. The PAVN rolled through coastal cities, crushing hastily regrouped ARVN units at Phan Rang on April 16 and reaching Phan Thiet on the 19th. Supplies began arriving at Danang, Qui Nhon, and Cam Ranh by sea. Meanwhile sizeable communist units had moved by boat and foot into the Mekong Delta and linked up with local forces to menace Route 5, Saigon's main link to the delta. At Xuan Loc, a province capital at an intersection 30 kilometers northwest of Saigon, the ARVN 18th division, supported by air from nearby Bien Hoa airbase, held out for ten days against three PAVN divisions. But with reinforcements and heavy shelling of the airbase, the PAVN overwhelmed Xuan Loc on the 20th, and the way to Saigon was open.

Saigon was not to be the first capital "liberated," however. In neighboring Cambodia, land routes to Phnom Penh had been cut for over a year. Supplies had reached the city by barge up the Mekong River or by air. No longer supported by the Vietnamese, the Khmer Rouge had formed a siege line around the city in early January, and ill-aimed 107-mm rockets had crashed randomly in its streets. Under the desperate illusion that Lon Nol's departure would clear the way to negotiations, government leaders and allies demanded his resignation. On April 1, the Marshall left via Bali for Hawaii. The Khmer Rouge ignored appeals for talks, the U.S. Embassy pulled out on the 12th, and Phnom Penh's army collapsed on the 17th.

In South Vietnam, murmurs of a second partition or another attempt at "reconciliation" were silenced by the relentless communist advances. U.S. Embassy dependents quietly departed. Pressure grew on the U.S. Embassy to begin evacuating staff, Vietnamese employees, and "high-risk" government officials. Ambassador Graham Martin suggested to Thieu that he appoint a premier who could negotiate with the Communists. Then, in the early evening of April 21, police loudspeakers announced that curfew would be set forward one hour to 8 P.M. to herd people before their radio and television sets. For the next hour President Thieu spoke to them in a voice filled with anger, sorrow, and tears. "If the Americans do not want to support us any more," he railed, "let them go, get out!" The beginning of the end, in Thieu's opinion, had been the Paris Agreement: "Kissinger didn't see that the agreement led the South Vietnamese people to death. Everyone else sees it, but Kissinger does not see it. . . . I said at the time, we must fight. No coalition! If there is a coalition, South Vietnam cannot stand. I never thought a man like Mr. Kissinger would deliver our people to such a disastrous fate." Thieu then announced that he was stepping down ("I resign but do not desert"), taunting those who had called him an obstacle to U.S. aid on the one hand and to a negotiated peace on the other, to do better.[55] His successor, the aged, nearly blind, asthmatic Vice President Tran Van Huong, was immediately pressured to hand over the government to General Duong Van "Big" Minh, whom many believed, or wished to believe, was somehow "acceptable" to the Communists. Minh's most avid supporter, French Ambassador Jean-Marie Merillon, persuaded Ambassador Martin that Hanoi was willing to cut a deal with Minh for a ceasefire and transitional government.[56]

THE HO CHI MINH CAMPAIGN

But it made no difference to the Communists who occupied Independence Palace. They had firmly believed ever since Ngo Dinh Diem's demise that any successors would be, in General Dung's words, "docile and faithful henchmen" of the United States. "The Huong administration was only the Thieu administration without Thieu."[57] As for General Minh, whom many in Saigon believed to be acceptable to the Communists, he was, said Dung, just another "stubborn ringleader."

The Communists moreover were too far advanced with their own preparations and too near total victory to indulge any offer but surrender. Since March, Dung and his staff had been drawing up a plan to attack the city. On April 7, Le Duc Tho had arrived at B2 headquarters to represent the Political Bureau in last-minute discussions, and on the 14th, the bureau had given final approval to what it dubbed the Ho Chi Minh Campaign. A special campaign command headed by General Dung and staffed by Pham Hung, Tran Van Tra, and Le Duc Anh was told to launch the attack during the last ten days of April.

The PAVN divisions, tanks, and artillery then massing on Saigon's outskirts provided the means of frontal assault if this proved necessary. But Danang's extraordinary collapse had strengthened faith in the contribution that political conditions could make to taking a large city. Turbulence or paralysis, it seemed to the Communists, would in fact be necessary to take Saigon, which was five or six times as large as Danang and would have time to prepare a defense. The Communists were particularly keen to avert an ARVN withdrawal into the city, where it might stage a last-ditch defense. The campaign therefore was to be a general offensive and uprising, a combination of military thrusts and political agitation to induce the ARVN to crumble and the "people" to seize power. More concretely, the plan called for cutting off the retreat of ARVN units from the outer perimeter, deep penetration by mechanized units to government "nerve centers," and the emergence of clandestine organs from hiding to lead the people in asking ARVN troops to lay down their weapons. Nguyen Van Linh, COSVN deputy secretary, was placed in charge of organizing mass uprisings, and political cadres joined throngs of refugees entering the city.

Maneuvering into position took the Communists several days, during which large units had to enter areas long held by Saigon. B2's Military Region 8 contained "highly populated areas," noted General Tra, "in which supporters of the revolution were not necessarily more numerous than the families of puppet troops. The masses were not awakened. Here was an operation where we had to attack and move, where we had to open a way in order to advance."[58] The column assigned to attack Saigon's National Police Headquarters had to "wipe out" forty-five outposts and "liberate" twelve villages on the way to its position. The column commander's aide recorded in his diary: "Passed through a populated area. Most of the people stayed put." Yet at another place he wrote, "When they awoke in the morning and saw the liberation troops everywhere, the people were extremely enthusiastic. One old woman went out into the field and dug up a red flag with a gold star. I don't know when it had been buried, but it looked very new."[59]

By April 26, fifteen communist divisions and assorted regional and guerrilla forces were set to launch the final attack. Against them, in isolated positions on a tattered perimeter around Saigon, stood about five ARVN divisions. The first assaults cleared roads and bottled up the ARVN 25th division in Tay Ninh. An attempt to move artillery up to hit Tan Son Nhut airfield ran into stiff resistance, so on April 28, the base was struck by U.S.-made A-37 jet fighters recently captured at Phan Rang and led by a defector from Saigon's air force. General Minh assumed the presidency in Saigon the same day. Ordering the troops to keep fighting, Minh announced he would seek "to arrive at a ceasefire, at negotiations, at peace on the basis of the Paris Accords. I am ready to accept any proposal in this direction."[60] But the general offensive went ahead on the 29th as planned. "Our soldiers and people, squashing Duong Van Minh's plot to call for a ceasefire and negotiations to turn over the government, resolutely carried out the order of the Political Bureau and the campaign command: 'Continue to advance into Saigon according to plan, advance with the greatest possible vigor, liberate and occupy the city, disarm the enemy troops, dissolve the enemy's administration at the various levels, and thoroughly smash all enemy resistance.'"[61] A delegation sent by Minh to parlay with Hanoi's representatives to the Joint Military Commission at Tan Son Nhut (housed there since 1973 under terms of the Paris Agreements to handle ceasefire matters) wound up staying the night in the Communists' bunker. As the delegation arrived, PAVN 130-mm shells began to fall on the airfield, and PAVN columns closed in from five directions.

The PAVN 3rd army seized the 25th division headquarters at Cu Chi on the 29th and sent one division toward Tan Son Nhut. Fifty kilometers north, the 1st army surrounded the ARVN 5th division at Lai Khe, and a division headed toward the ARVN general staff compound. The 4th army took Bien Hoa airbase and ARVN III Corps headquarters as its 7th division crossed the Dong Nai River. The 2nd army closed on approaches over the Saigon River and quickly overcame remnants of the ARVN 18th division. South of the city, the army-strength 232nd group broke up what remained of the ARVN 22nd division.

Where isolated ARVN units resisted effectively, they were bypassed. Others were overrun, or they crumbled at the approach of superior force. The commander of the ARVN 5th division committed suicide. Approaching an ARVN artillery base near Go Vap, General Tra observed that "the puppet troops had lost morale and some had fled, but the 81st Airborne Ranger Group continued stubbornly to defend the gates." A communist regiment attempted unsuccessfully to storm the rangers on the 30th. A team finally broke through using a gun from an abandoned tank, seized the post computing center (with everything intact), and turned to staff headquarters. "All enemy troops had fled except a corporal who greeted the team and turned over a bunch of keys with all documents and property. That puppet corporal was comrade Ba Minh, a regional intelligence agent who had been planted in the staff headquarters long before."[62] Behind every military advance, political cadres stepped out to gather supporters, track down ARVN stragglers, and take over administrative offices.

Most members of the ARVN high command had fled. General Cao Van Vien, the chief of staff, had left on the 28th without resigning. His replacement, General Vinh Loc, broadcast an impassioned speech on the "dishonor" of flight, and then he too had fled. Police Chief Nguyen Khac Binh had taken an armed guard to the airport and commandeered a plane for Thailand. By the morning of April 30, the ARVN 5th, 18th, 22nd, and 25th divisions had quit fighting or broken up into fugitive groups. Fearing that troops who remained in Saigon might barricade themselves for a futile last stand, General Minh went on radio at 10:20 A.M. and ordered them to lay down their arms. Most obeyed, some turning over their weapons to youthful activists who encouraged surrender. Before PAVN spearheads could reach the city's center, thousands of ARVN troops shed their uniforms and headed for home in their underwear. In government ministries, military headquarters, even the Central Intelligence Organization, small numbers of civil servants and officers revealed to bewildered colleagues that they always had served the revolution and then took charge. Resistance sputtered at Can Tho and other points in the delta, but in Saigon the Second Indochina War was already over when at 10:45 A.M. a Soviet-made T-54 tank, the number 843 stamped on its turret, bashed down the gates of Independence Palace.

NOTES

1. Tran Van Tra, *Nhung chang duong cua "B2-Thanh dong": tap V, Ket thuc cuoc chien tranh 30 nam* [Stages on the Road of the B2-Bulwark, vol. V, Concluding the 30 Years War] (Ho Chi Minh City: Van Nghe Publishing House, 1982), p. 83.

2. "Plan of General Uprising When a Political Solution is Reached," October 4, 1972, in *Viet-Nam Documents and Research Notes* hereinafter cited as *VNDRNs*], no. 109 (December 1972). Also see "Directive 20/H," October 15, 1972, in *VNDRNs,* no. 108 (November 1972).

3. Tra, *Ket thuc cuoc chien tranh 30 nam,* pp. 128, 133.

4. Allen E. Goodman, *The Lost Peace: America's Search for a Negotiated Settlement of the Vietnam War* (Stanford: Hoover Institution Press, 1978), p. 168.

5. "Directive 03/CT 73," March 30, 1973, in *VNDRNs,* no. 115 (September 1973).

6. The Central Committee Report to the 4th Party Congress in 1978 acknowledged that war damage had nullified ten to fifteen years of growth. Agricultural output increased 4 percent between 1965 and 1975—no mean accomplishment under the circumstances—but population grew 23 percent. Equally disturbing was the loss of control over the economy due to prolonged dispersal. See William S. Turley, "Vietnam Since Reunification," *Problems of Communism* (March-April 1977), pp. 45–46.

7. Tra, *Ket thuc cuoc chien tranh 30 nam,* pp. 82–83.

8. "Directive 02/73," January 19, 1973, in *VNDRNs,* no. 113 (June 1973); also see Tra, *Ket thuc cuoc chien tranh 30 nam,* p. 88.

9. Tra, *Ket thuc cuoc chien tranh 30 nam,* p. 88.

10. Vo Van Kiet went on to become deputy head of the Saigon–Gia Dinh Military Management Committee in 1975 and chairman of the Municipal People's Revolutionary Committee (in effect "mayor") in January 1976; at the 4th Party Congress in December, he was made an alternate member of the Political Bureau. Le Duc Anh was placed in command of PAVN forces in Cambodia in 1979 and given a seat in the Political Bureau in 1982. But Tra, after serving as Kiet's

superior on the Saigon–Gia Dinh Military Management Committee, faded from view in late 1977 and was dropped from the Central Committee at the 5th Party Congress in 1982.

11. War Experience Recapitulation Committee of the High-Level Military Institute, *The Anti-U.S. Resistance War for National Salvation 1954–1975: Military Events*, trans. by the Joint Publications Research Service, JPRS no. 80,968 (Washington, D.C.: GPO, June 3, 1982), pp. 160–162. Text hereinafter cited as *The Anti-U.S. Resistance War.*

12. Tra, *Ket thuc cuoc chien tranh 30 nam*, p. 54.

13. "Political Reorientation and Training Materials for Infrastructure Cadres and Party Members," *VNDRNs*, no. 117 (April 1974).

14. U.S., Congress, Senate, Richard M. Moose and Charles F. Meissner, *Vietnam: May 1974*, 93rd Cong., 2nd sess., August 5, 1974 (Washington, D.C.: GPO, 1974), pp. 4–5.

15. The Communists estimated revolutionary forces "at most one-third those of the enemy," according to Tra, *Ket thuc cuoc chien tranh 30 nam*, p. 55.

16. Moose, *Vietnam: May 1974*, p. 22.

17. In all of Indochina, the PAVN had 900 tanks to the ARVN's 600, but only 40 armored personnel carriers compared with the ARVN's 1,000. The PAVN's total inventory of 122-mm and 130-mm field guns was nearly 1,200; the ARVN possessed 1,500 105-mm and 155-mm howitzers and 175 self-propelled guns of 175-mm calibre. The North's 200 combat aircraft never dared to venture over the South, which had 500. The North's equipment was deployed along the Ho Chi Minh Trail as well as in defense of the North and in combat in the South, and the South's deployment was generally confined to Southern territory that the ARVN controlled. International Institute for Strategic Studies, *The Military Balance 1974–1975* (London: International Institute for Strategic Studies, 1974), pp. 60–61.

18. Jerry M. Silverman, "Local Politics and Administration in South Vietnam," paper presented at the annual meeting of the Association for Asian Studies, Boston, April 3, 1974, p. 55.

19. *New York Times*, January 14, 1974, p. 1.

20. *New York Times*, July 6, 1974, p. 2; February 2, 1975, p. 9; and February 15, 1975, p. 2.

21. *New York Times*, November 2, 1974, p. 4. For the bizarre background and details of this rebellion, see Gerald Cannon Hickey, *Free in the Forest: Ethnohistory of the Vietnamese Central Highlands 1954–1976* (New Haven, Conn.: Yale University Press, 1982), pp. 266–271

22. Moose, *Vietnam: May 1974*, pp. 27–29.

23. Allen E. Goodman, "South Vietnam: War Without End?" *Asian Survey* 15, no. 1 (January 1975), p. 76.

24. Moose, *Vietnam: May 1974*, p. 27.

25. *New York Times*, January 22, 1975, p. 8.

26. Viet Tran, *Vietnam: j'ai choisi l'exil* [Vietnam: I Have Chosen Exile] (Paris: Editions du Seuil, 1979), pp. 33–34.

27. *New York Times*, August 9, 1974, p. 17.

28. *New York Times*, February 4, 1975, p. 1.

29. *New York Times*, February 6, 1975, p. 10.

30. *New York Times*, November 2, 1974, p. 1.

31. *New York Times*, January 27, 1974, p. 24.

32. The War Powers Act, passed over Nixon's veto on November 7, 1973, prohibited the president from committing U.S. troops abroad for more than sixty days without specific congressional authorization. The Cambodian bombing ban was an amendment to an appropriations bill that required the president, who signed the bill on July 1 after a compromise, to discontinue the bombing after August 15. Other action broadened the ban, e.g., the Military Procurement Authorization passed on November 16, which said in part: "No funds heretofore or hereafter appropriated may be obligated or expended to finance the involvement of United States military forces in hostilities in or over or from off the shores of North Vietnam, South Vietnam, Laos, or Cambodia, unless specifically authorized hereafter by Congress."

33. Stephen T. Hosmer et al., *The Fall of South Vietnam: Statements of Vietnamese Military and Civilian Leaders* (New York: Crane, Russak & Company, 1980), pp. 10–11 and passim.

34. *The Anti-U.S. Resistance War*, p. 160.

35. Ibid., pp. 166–167.

36. Ibid., p. 167.

37. Communist sources confirm that Southern regional forces and militia, and coordination between military and political struggle, had remained weak since 1968. See *The Anti-U.S. Resistance War*, p. 162.

38. Van Tien Dung, *Dai thang mua xuan* [Great Spring Victory] (Hanoi: People's Army Publishing House, 1976).

39. Tra, *Ket thuc cuoc chien tranh 30 nam*, p. 145.

40. Ibid., pp. 147–148; on intelligence plants, p. 102.

41. Dung, *Dai thang mua xuan*, pp. 19–20.

42. Ibid., p. 21.

43. Ibid., p. 25.

44. The following paragraphs on communist planning and assault on Ban Me Thuot are based on Dung, ibid., pp. 23–99 unless otherwise indicated.

45. Dung regarded this tactic as something of a personal hallmark. General Tra's memoir, however, derides the tendency to use the "blooming lotus" everywhere, a tendency based on "the subjective thinking of one person or another." As for Dung's unfamiliarity with attacks on "a big city," Tra implies this was because Hanoi-based commanders lacked the experience of those like himself who had fought for years in the South's more urbanized milieu. Tra, *Ket thuc cuoc chien tranh 30 nam,* pp. 178–179.

46. Hoang Minh Thao, *Chien dich Tay nguyen dai thang* [The Great Victorious Western Highlands Campaign] (Hanoi: People's Army Publishing House, 1977), p. 56.

47. Hosmer, *The Fall of South Vietnam,* p. 169.

48. Dung, *Dai thang mua xuan,* p. 79.

49. Hosmer, *The Fall of South Vietnam,* p. 171.

50. Dung, *Dai thang mua xuan,* p. 95.

51. Hosmer, *The Fall of South Vietnam,* p. 174.

52. *New York Times,* January 28, 1975, p. 1.

53. Tran Van Don, in *Our Endless War* (San Rafael, Calif.: Presidio Press, 1978), p. 224, asserts that Phu "unilaterally ordered the withdrawal of his headquarters with all its supporting forces from Pleiku to Nha Trang." Also see Hosmer, *The Fall of South Vietnam,* pp. 177–178.

54. *The Anti-U.S. Resistance War,* p. 179.

55. Thieu quoted in John Clark Pratt, *Vietnam Voices: Perspectives on the War Years 1941–1982* (New York: Penguin Books, 1984), pp. 611–612.

56. Don, *Our Endless War,* pp. 249–251, 254; Frank Snepp, *Decent Interval* (New York: Random House, 1977), pp. 324–325.

57. Dung, *Dai thang mua xuan,* p. 249.

58. Tra, *Ket thuc cuoc chien tranh 30 nam,* pp. 263–264.

59. Ibid., pp. 270, 271.

60. Quoted in Tiziano Terzani, *Giai Phong: The Fall and Liberation of Saigon* (New York: St. Martin's Press, 1976), p. 41.

61. *The Anti-U.S. Resistance War,* p. 182.

62. Tra, *Ket thuc cuoc chien tranh 30 nam,* p. 288.

9

Of Lessons and Their Price

As South Vietnam was falling, Thieu had lobbied Ford and Ford had lobbied the U.S. Congress for supplemental military assistance. The two presidents had argued that without increased aid the ARVN would be unable to withstand the PAVN's assault. If the supplement were not approved and Saigon collapsed, they averred, it would be the result of insufficient aid, and responsibility would belong to those who opposed the aid. Similar arguments were made for airstrikes against the PAVN's massing armies.

In a narrow military sense, the arguments had merit. For years the security of the Saigon regime had depended principally on military strategy, and that strategy had depended on the regular ARVN. The ARVN had been trained and organized to rely on firepower superiority, which in turn made the ARVN dependent on a constant flow of equipment, weapons, and ammunition. Because South Vietnam manufactured no military goods, the ARVN required continuing and voluminous U.S. military assistance (roughly $1 billion a year) to sustain combat during communist offensives (just as the Communists needed substantial, if less, assistance from their allies to mount them). Even with that assistance, it was doubtful the ARVN, due to unwise strategy, could long have withstood a concerted PAVN push without U.S. aircover. That strategy had been to enlarge Saigon's zone of control, with the result that, when the Communists pushed, the ARVN was seriously overextended. Once the PAVN had defeated the ARVN in the highlands, the ARVN's unorganized retreat guaranteed a rout. Without a massive infusion of U.S. aid and reinvolvement in combat, Saigon was doomed.

In the long run, however, the argument for rescue was vulnerable to severe and justifiable criticism. The fact that the argument was made at all simply spotlighted the twenty-five years of U.S. aid that had left the anticommunist regimes dependent, seemingly forever, on U.S. support. If emergency aid were given to help stave off defeat in 1975, what guarantee was there that aid would not have to be given again in 1976 and in every year thereafter? The material dimensions of that dependency in fact had grown over the years, not diminished. The record, not to mention unfolding events on the battlefield, provided convincing evidence that the United States had to accept Saigon's defeat if it wished to disengage from Indochina's wars.

Still, it has been asked, wasn't there something the United States could have done earlier to win militarily? The hypothetical answer is yes if, for example, the United States had been willing to deploy 1 million men and indefinitely support the ARVN in occupying every village as U.S. and ARVN forces completed the destruction of the North, perhaps with nuclear weapons. For obvious political, economic, and moral reasons, however, these options could not be seriously considered. More realistically, would it have been sufficient to have given General Westmoreland the 206,000 additional troops and permission for an "amphibious hook" around the demilitarized zone that he requested? How would the Communists have responded, and what would have been the outcome? Though even a PAVN officer would have to reply speculatively, the answers given to the author by a colonel in the PAVN Military History Institute were sobering:

> Look what happened in 1970. Americans and ARVN forces did cross the border into Cambodia, but it was easier for us to fight in Cambodia than in South Vietnam. The fighting showed that

> the PAVN could adapt to the expansion of the war. In fact, the expansion of the war into Cambodia helped us because it laid a basis for us to stage even bigger battles later inside the South. As for an American strike into the North, this would have taken place in an area that had been well-prepared to wage people's war and where our ability to provide material support to the main forces was much greater than anywhere else. So such a strike would have been blunted by popular resistance and then have faced a powerful main force counterattack, like what the Chinese encountered along the northern border in 1979. The PAVN's victories against a strike into the North would have been greater than the ones scored in southern Laos in 1971. A small number of American troops made a difference in Korea, but not in Vietnam where everything is different. So you see, Westmoreland's plan could not have changed the essentials of the strategic situation.[1]

Of course, at the time the Joint Chiefs forwarded Westmoreland's request (1968), Hanoi might have felt pressed to compromise. But considering Hanoi's strategic doctrine and resolve, it seems more likely Hanoi would have temporarily dispersed the PAVN all across Indochina and braced for invasion of the North. That invasion would have had to take place in areas where 10–40 percent of village populations were enrolled in the militia. Furthermore, by that time the war was impinging on U.S. ability to meet commitments in more vital areas, such as Western Europe. Even supposing that popular support for mobilizing the reserves and instituting a universal draft had been present, the United States could not significantly have enlarged its involvement in Indochina without further distracting it from other pressing issues, thinning resources needed elsewhere (e.g., Europe, the Middle East), and undermining the confidence of important allies. A further turn of the screw was plausible only in a world where other problems did not exist.

The reasons had little to do with inadequacies of U.S. military strategy or prowess, however. U.S. arms could only forestall Saigon's defeat; they could not guarantee its long-term survival. For the war, contrary to official propaganda, required the United States not simply to defend one-half of a "divided state" from attack by the other (as in Korea), but to defend a specific elite against an ongoing revolution that had begun in all parts of Vietnam decades before. That elite was suffering a terminal illness when the United States took over sponsorship of it from France. Not only was South Vietnam's elite the heir of colonial rule, but it was largely composed of landowning and urban upper classes. Outside its own very restricted membership, the elite had little legitimacy; what little it had was squandered through incompetence, corruption, and short-sightedness. In stark contrast to the Communists, the Saigon elite had no background of common effort, sacrifice, or doctrine to lend cohesion, no sensational victories to capture the imagination, no striking achievements or personalities to inspire loyalty, and no party organization aside from patronage-based cliques. Moreover, it was quite isolated—politically and often physically—from the vast majority of the South's population that lived in rural villages, many of which had been bastions of Viet Minh resistance against the French. Though the elite contained honorable and capable individuals, it was internally divided and had no momentum to match that of the communist-led revolution. As a ruling group, the elite may have survived the turbulent 1950s only because the Communists, bent on reconstruction in the North and "political struggle" in the South, refrained from exercising their full potential to bring it down. Certainly the Communists had no trouble becoming a serious threat almost as soon as they commenced "armed struggle." Collapse of the South Vietnamese government was imminent when the United States intervened massively in 1965.

Against that unpromising background U.S. involvement must be credited with placing some major obstacles in the path of communist victory. The military elite that replaced Diem let itself be used as an instrument of experiment in counterinsurgency. U.S. spending significantly increased the number of people who depended on Saigon's war effort for their income. ARVN expansion drew young men into the ranks of Saigon's military and away from the PLAF. The fighting drove hundreds of thousands of people from contested areas into refugee camps and squatter settlements where they could be kept under watch. The sheer intensity of combat combined with the Communists' overexertion in 1968 increased the risk of supporting the revolution. Lastly, President Thieu consolidated a personal hold on the government and army and introduced administrative and agrarian reforms.

For a time the proverbial sea in which revolutionary fish were supposed to swim seemed to dry up. Evidence of this "drought" was provided by the Communists themselves in the offensive of 1972 that relied on main forces led by PAVN regulars to restore village political and guerrilla movements to their former strength. But any impression of profound or permanent improvement in Saigon's political resilience was illusory. The stability among the South's political elite that Washington worked so diligently to nurture during the 1960s came apart as U.S. interest in enforcing that stability waned. U.S. effort to impose stability in fact had been self-defeating because it confirmed the popular impression—which of course the Communists most happily encouraged—that the Saigon government was the creature of a foreign power. However people in the South felt about communist rule, they weren't likely to question the Communists' patriotism. The same cannot be said of the public attitude toward the ARVN generals.

Also illusory was the perception that popular support for the revolution had dried up. Political cadres were sometimes cut off from access to the people or were themselves exterminated ("hundreds of thousands of cadres and party members sacrificed their lives or were sent to prison," Le Duc Tho told the 4th Party Congress in 1976[2]), but it is unlikely that the sentiments of several million people whose families had identified with and sacrificed for the revolution since the 1940s had changed much. Significant, too, was the growth in party membership in the South from just 5,000 in 1959 to about 200,000 by war's end, despite the risks.[3] In the overall equation of power, party membership in the South not only added to the resources of the North but subtracted from what was available to Saigon, whose strength was further depleted by the indifference of many people to anything but peace. The war, long by military standards, was far too short by political ones to bring about lasting change in the underlying weaknesses of the Saigon side.

A number of lessons for the United States have been drawn from the Second Indochina War. A popular argument among

U.S. military officers who fought mainly PAVN units in conventional combat was that the root of war was North Vietnam. It followed that if the United States could not destroy the North, it at least should have cut off access to the South by naval and ground blockade, permitting the protected regimes to resolve their internal problems by themselves.[4] In the same vein, it is broadly accepted in the armed forces that the United States should not have fought far from home without firm public support, a formal declaration of war, a clear objective, and license to employ whatever means necessary to achieve that objective. However, officials charged with responsibility for the "other war" as exemplified by "accelerated pacification" and Vietnamization have argued that these programs did turn the political tide and should have been given higher priority from the beginning.[5] Still another view was held by Nixon and Kissinger, who tended to emphasize the need for a credible threat to use force, the efficacy of sudden and massive (as opposed to gradual) escalation, and linkage with other issues to entice the Soviet Union and China into helping negotiate a settlement. Implicit in such arguments was the belief that U.S. involvement, if conducted differently, could have brought a favorable result. Contrarily, three-quarters of the people who came to maturity (and, for males, to draft eligibility) during the war years believed it had been a mistake to intervene in the first place and remain deeply skeptical of interventionism of any kind.[6] This lesson is encapsulated in the phrase "no more Vietnams."

Whether these are really lessons worth applying elsewhere is properly the subject of a different book. The present work more modestly suggests that in Indochina the United States made commitments out of proportion to its interests. This was done in the belief that maintaining the credibility of commitments required defending them everywhere. But placing credibility at stake in a region that was not vital to U.S. interests undermined the conviction of the American people that the commitment had to be kept. Neither U.S. enemies, U.S. allies, nor its own people believed that the United States, for the sake of Indochina, would long sacrifice its effectiveness in other parts of the world. Thus, an appearance of unconditional commitment to the Saigon regime—to which the United States was never bound by formal treaty or alliance—actually undermined U.S. credibility.

The United States also trapped itself by supporting political groups that lacked the confidence of their own people. Unstinting support of such groups raised doubts that the United States had any interest in "self-determination" for the people in question and invited cynicism about U.S. intentions. It also required the United States to involve itself deeply in stabilizing fragile governments and in "nation-building," which cast the United States in a quasi-colonial role. Having adopted chronically weak clients to fight a long-established, well-organized, deeply entrenched adversary, the United States had to substitute its own resources and purpose for those of the regimes it purported to defend. These in turn were robbed of initiative and stigmatized by dependency. Under the circumstances, the United States could not intervene without perpetuating conditions that U.S. leaders believed required them to intervene in the first place. Finally, a succession of U.S. leaders grossly miscalculated many things: the historical context of the war itself; the efficacy of military power; U.S ability to rehabilitate friends; and the skill, adaptability, and resolve of the enemy.

The cost was extremely high. For the United States, the direct budgetary cost of the war has been variously estimated at between $112 billion and $155 billion. Other and future costs (e.g., sacrificed earnings, veterans benefits, war-related recession) have been estimated to bring the grand total as high as $925 billion.[7] No less damaging was the political cost of rancor between the executive and legislative branches over the war-making powers of the president and the alienation of a generation from its government. And the United States had its dead: 45,943 killed in action, 10,298 dead from noncombat causes, and nearly 2,477 missing in action and presumed dead—a total of 58,718.[8] Also dead were 4,407 troops from South Korea, 468 from Australia and New Zealand, and 351 from Thailand.

These losses pale beside those suffered by the countries of Indochina. U.S. sources estimated the total number of communist troops (Northern and Southern) killed in action between 1965 and 1974 at 950,765.[9] Though such "body count" figures were notoriously inflated, communist spokesmen admit their losses were high. Hanoi may never release comprehensive figures of its own, but it has released sketchy information on a few, mostly Southern localities: 26,719 revolutionary combatants dead and 4,858 living wounded in An Giang province (which comprises Chau Doc since administrative reorganization in 1976); 42,000 families of dead combatants, over 50 families with 5 to 9 members who died in combat, and 3,200 orphans in Quang Nam–Danang (which since 1976 includes Quang Tin province); 13,000 families of dead combatants in Dong Thap (formerly Kien Phong) province; over 200 families in a single village of the North's Thanh Hoa province with members dead or wounded;[10] 125,000 veterans (one-fifth of them invalids) in Nghe Tinh province.[11]

Not much can be made of such figures except that the number of communist combatants killed in An Giang—an area of relatively low intensity combat during the war—equalled 2 percent of that province's 1976 population; that 6 percent of the families in Dong Thap and 15 percent in Quang Nam–Danang lost members fighting on the communist side; and that PAVN veterans make up over 4 percent of the population of Nghe Tinh province today (which would extrapolate to over 1 million for the North as a whole). Certainly, to fight on the revolutionary side involved extreme personal risk. As for civilians, U.S. intelligence estimated that 52,000 people perished in the bombing of the North, not including the renewed bombing of 1972.[12] The bombing also made the North's railroads impassable and turned its roads into cratered tracks. Hanoi and Haiphong were spared, but twenty-nine out of thirty provincial capitals were heavily damaged, and nine were completely levelled.[13]

In the South, the physical damage was less severe. Bombs and artillery fell mostly in rural areas, not on cities, roads, and facilities needed for postwar reconstruction. But it was in the South that heaviest use was made of chemical defoliants, which destroyed roughly one-fifth of all timberlands and bled into waterways to contaminate croplands and food supplies. As of late 1974, the number of ARVN killed in action was put at 220,357,[14] and about 500,000 ARVN had been wounded. Figures on the number of civilian casualties in the South are hardly more reliable than those for the North but run from 247,600 to 430,000 dead and approximately 1 million wounded.[15] Needless to say, both the communist and noncommunist sides had countless thousands missing in action, of whom an accounting can never be made. Though not on a par with the world wars or China's civil wars in absolute terms, the period of "interstate war" from 1965 to 1975 for Vietnam alone has been judged the fourth most "severe" in proportional impact on the society involved of all such wars since 1816. In battle deaths per capita, this war ranked sixth, while the period 1960 to 1965 ranked seventh among civil wars.[16]

As for Laos and Cambodia, information is too fragmentary other than to suggest damage proportional to that experienced by Vietnam.[17] Laos was spared a cataclysmic last offensive by the ceasefire and neutral coalition government of 1973. The Pathet Lao, however, proceeded with local seizures of power by "people's committees" and with elections to engineer the abdication of King Savang Vatthana and the installation of a People's Democratic Republic on December 2, 1975. In Cambodia, the victorious Khmer Rouge, vengeful toward former enemies and unsure of their hold on power, launched a reign of terror that caused the deaths of perhaps 2 million people—roughly one-third of the population. The Khmer Rouge were also unable to reconcile differences with the Vietnamese, whom the Khmer leader Pol Pot suspected of seeking dominion over Cambodia, and sought security in support from China. As Vietnam's own ties with the Soviet Union were incurring intense hostility from Beijing, Hanoi sought to remove the threat of a Chinese-backed regime in Phnom Penh by invading Cambodia in December 1978. China in turn mounted a punitive attack on Vietnam in February 1979 and began a long campaign, with approval from the United States and Thailand, to "bleed" Vietnam by means of diplomatic isolation and arms supplies for Khmer resistance forces. Thus for a third time since World War II, Indochina was swept into a vortex of conflict with Vietnam at the center.

NOTES

1. Interview with Colonel Hoang Co Quang, Hanoi, April 21, 1984.

2. Radio Hanoi broadcast, December 17, 1976 in Foreign Broadcast Information Service, *Daily Report: Asia and the Pacific*, December 26, 1976.

3. The official figure for Southern party membership in 1978 was 273,000. Alexander Casella, *Foreign Policy* (Spring 1978), p. 72; and *Los Angeles Times*, October 18, 1978. Total party membership in 1976 was 1,533,500.

4. See Harry G. Summers, Jr., *On Strategy: The Vietnam War in Context* (Carlisle, Pa.: Strategic Studies Institute, U.S. Army War College, April 1981).

5. See for example, Robert Komer, "Was There Another Way?" in W. Scott Thompson and Donald D. Frizzell, eds., *Lessons of Vietnam* (New York: Crane, Russak, 1977), pp. 211–223.

6. A Gallup poll for *Newsweek* magazine in 1985 indicated that 63 percent of a national sample and 76 percent of college graduates in the 30–39 age bracket believed the war to have been a "mistake." In answer to the question whether the United States should make greater use of military force abroad, 75 percent of the national sample and 90 percent of the Vietnam-era college graduates answered no. See *Newsweek*, April 15, 1985, p. 37.

7. Robert Warren Stevens, *Vain Hopes, Grim Realities: The Economic Consequences of the Vietnam War* (New York: New Viewpoints, 1976), p. 187.

8. Attention given in the United States, unlike attention following any previous war, to the U.S. MIAs and to spurious reports that some are still alive might suggest that their number was comparatively large. The facts are these: The 78,751 MIAs at the end of World War II represented 27 percent of that war's U.S. battle deaths and 0.4 percent of the 16 million servicemen in the military during it. The 8,177 MIAs of the Korean War equalled 15.2 percent of the U.S. battle deaths and 0.14 percent of the era's 5,720,000 U.S. servicemen. In Vietnam, the 2,477 MIAs were just 5.4 percent of the war's U.S. battle deaths and 0.028 percent of the 8 million persons who served in U.S. armed forces from 1964 to 1973 and 0.095 percent of the 2,594,200 who were actually sent to South Vietnam. By comparison with other major conflicts in which the United States has been involved, the Indochina War produced by far the fewest MIAs in both absolute and proportional terms—0.3 percent of the number that resulted from World War II and less than one-third the number from Korea. As for POWs, the House Select Committee on Missing Persons in Southeast Asia concluded in December 1976 that "no Americans are still being held alive as prisoners in Indochina, or

elsewhere, as a result of the war in Indochina," and no credible evidence has subsequently been adduced to show otherwise. It must be remembered, too, that firm evidence of death (e.g., the 436 air force pilots who were shot down over the sea and 647 cases, mostly dead or wounded, who could not be recovered from the battlefield) is absent for very few MIAs considering the nature, duration, and magnitude of the conflict. Figures on servicemen and battle deaths are from Department of Defense, Office of the Assistant Secretary of Defense (OASD) (Comptroller), "Selected Manpower Statistics," March 1979, p. 83. For figures on MIAs in other wars and discussion, see James Rosenthal, "The Myth of the Lost POWs," *The New Republic* (July 1, 1985), pp. 15–19; and Bill Herod, "America's Missing: A Look Behind the Numbers," *Indochina Issues,* no. 54 (February 1985).

9. Office of the Assistant Secretary of Defense (OASD) (Comptroller), *Southeast Asia Statistical Summary,* February 18, 1976, cited in Guenter Lewy, *America in Vietnam* (Oxford: Oxford University Press, 1978), p. 450.

10. *Nhan dan* [The People], July 20, 27, 1983; *Quan doi nhan dan* [People's Army], July 21, 1983.

11. Barry Wain, *Wall Street Journal,* April 11, 1985, p. 1.

12. National Security Study Memorandum 1 (1969), cited in Lewy, *America in Vietnam,* p. 451.

13. See "Report of the United Nations Mission to North and South Viet-Nam," March 1976, in U.S., Congress, Senate, *Aftermath of War: Humanitarian Problems of Southeast Asia,* Staff Report for the Subcommittee to Investigate Problems Connected with Refugees and Escapees, Committee on the Judiciary, 94th Cong., 2nd sess., May 17, 1976, pp. 153, 163.

14. OASD, *Southeast Asia Statistical Summary,* cited in Lewy, *America in Vietnam,* p. 451.

15. Lewy, *America in Vietnam,* p. 445.

16. Melvin Small and J. David Singer, *Resort to Arms: International and Civil Wars, 1816–1980* (Beverly Hills, Calif.: Sage Publications, 1982), pp. 102, 238.

17. See U.S., Congress, Senate, "Humanitarian Problems in Indochina," Hearings before the Subcommittee to Investigate Problems Connected with Refugees and Escapees, Committee on the Judiciary, 93rd Cong., 2nd sess., July 18, 1974.

Chronology

1954

May 7. French surrender at Dien Bien Phu.
May 8. Geneva conference on Indochina opens.
June 26. Ngo Dinh Diem, premier-designate of the State of Vietnam, arrives in Saigon.
July 21. Geneva conference ends with signing of three ceasefire agreements and issuance of one unsigned final declaration.
September 8. United States, France, Britain, Australia, New Zealand, the Philippines, Thailand, and Pakistan sign the Southeast Asia Collective Defense Treaty, which establishes the Southeast Asia Treaty Organization (SEATO) and extends protection to Cambodia, Laos, and "the free territory of the state of Vietnam."
October 23. President Eisenhower promises Diem that henceforward U.S. aid for Vietnam will be channelled directly to the Saigon government.

1955

January 1. U.S. aid begins flowing directly to Diem government.
February 12. U.S. advisers replace French in training Diem's army.
March. Sectarian resistance collapses, private armies dispersed.

June 28. Secretary of State John Foster Dulles declares United States not a party to the Geneva "armistice agreements."

August 9. Diem government refuses to negotiate with the Democratic Republic of Vietnam (DRV) on elections for reunification.

August 31. Dulles declares support for Diem's position on negotiations with the DRV.

October 23. Fraudulent referendum on whether to establish a republic (98.2 percent of ballots in favor) paves way to depose Emperor Bao Dai and make Diem chief of state.

October 26. Republic of Vietnam (RVN) proclaimed, with Diem its first president.

1956

April 6. RVN declares it is under no obligation to abide by the Geneva Agreements as it is not a signatory, turns down Hanoi offer to negotiate.

April 28. U.S. Military Assistance Advisory Group officially takes over responsibility for training the Army of the Republic of Vietnam (ARVN) from departing French.

July 21. Time limit stipulated by Geneva Agreements for holding referendum on reunification passes.

September. With land reform completed, 10th Plenum of the Vietnam Workers' (Communist) party Central Committee announces "rectification" of land reform "errors," forecasts "long, arduous, complicated struggle for unification."

December. Instructions from Political Bureau in Hanoi tell Southern cadres to persist in "political struggle" while preparing for "self-defense" and "armed propaganda."

1957

March. Twelfth Plenum of the Central Committee adopts three-year plan to restore production to 1939 level and begin transition to socialism.

May 5–19. Diem visits the United States, addresses joint session of Congress.

October. Communists in the South assemble first battalion-sized armed force from ex–Viet Minh fighters, armed propaganda teams, and sect remnants.

November 2. Royal Lao Government and Pathet Lao agree to form coalition government and integrate their armed forces.

November 19. Lao National Assembly chooses Souvanna Phouma to head first neutral coalition government.

1958

July 23. U.S.-supported rightist elements force Souvanna Phouma to resign.

August 18. Pro-U.S. faction in Vientiane forms new cabinet without Pathet Lao and arrests Pathet Lao leaders, ending the first neutral coalition government in Laos.

1959

March. Political Bureau authorizes "limited guerrilla warfare" in the South's central highlands.

May 6. Diem government issues Law 10/59, which sets up military tribunals to mete out harsh penalties for involvement with the revolutionary movement. U.S. advisers are assigned to ARVN infantry at regiment level, marines at battalion level.

May. Fifteenth Plenum of the Central Committee approves plan for limited armed struggle in the South, foresees possibility of "protracted armed struggle," and commissions transportation groups to infiltrate men and supplies.

August 28. Party cadres stir ethnic minority dissidence in highlands of Tra Bong district, Quang Ngai province.

August. Group 559 of the People's Army of Vietnam (PAVN) delivers first load of arms to the South.

1960

January 17. Armed struggle is kicked off in the Mekong Delta with "uprisings" in Ben Tre province.

January 26. Communist-led forces attack ARVN 5th regiment near Tay Ninh city.

August 9. Neutralist military coup restores Souvanna Phouma to power in Vientiane. U.S.-backed rightists counterattack, and Laos slides into civil war.

September 5–10. 3rd National Congress of the Vietnam Workers' party adopts dual objectives of socialist construction in the North and struggle for reunification in the South, chooses new (3rd) Central Committee, elects Le Duan as party first secretary.

November 8. John Kennedy elected president.

December 20. National Liberation Front (NLF) is unveiled at Congress of People's Representatives in the South.

December 31. U.S. military personnel in Vietnam total about 900.

1961

January 1. Pathet Lao and PAVN "volunteers" evict Royal Lao armed forces from the Plaine des Jarres.

February 15. Southern revolutionary armed forces "unified" to form People's Liberation Armed Force (PLAF), military wing of the NLF.

May 13. Ceasefire in Laos. Three days later, fourteen-nation conference opens in Geneva to restore neutral coalition government.

June 19. Kennedy adviser Dr. Eugene Staley arrives in Saigon to assess Diem's military assistance needs.

October 19–25. Presidential advisers Walt Rostow and General Maxwell D. Taylor visit South Vietnam; plans for enhanced assistance are drawn up on their return to Washington.

December 31. U.S. military personnel in Vietnam total 3,200.

1962

February 8. United States appoints General Paul D. Harkins to head a reorganized military aid mission dubbed the U.S. Military Assistance Command–Vietnam (MACV).

February 16. NLF holds its 1st Congress.

May. Following rightist military probes, joint Pathet Lao and PAVN forces extend control in Laos; Kennedy dispatches troops to Thailand.

July 23. Geneva conference concludes with signing of treaty to restore the neutrality of Laos.

December 31. U.S. military personnel in Vietnam total 11,300.

1963

May 8. Government troops fire on marchers in Hue protesting ban on public celebration of Buddha's birthday, kill nine.

July 17. Police use clubs to break up Saigon Buddhist demonstration against religious discrimination.

August 21. Special Forces under direction of Diem's brother Ngo Dinh Nhu raid pagodas, arrest 1,400; martial law declared.

August 28. U.S. Ambassador Henry Cabot Lodge recommends Diem's overthrow in cable to Kennedy.

October. Major Generals Duong Van Minh and Tran Van Don request, and receive, assurance through CIA contact that United States will support a coup.

November 1–2. Military coup ousts Diem; Diem and Nhu are killed.

November 22. Kennedy assassinated; Lyndon Johnson becomes president.

December. Ninth Plenum of the Central Committee in Hanoi criticizes "revisionism," lays basis for increasing Northern involvement in the war in the South.

December 31. U.S. military personnel in Vietnam total 16,300.

1964

January 30. Major General Nguyen Khanh ousts Minh and Don in another military coup; subsequent rivalry and ineptitude of military leaders alienates civilians.

April 25. General William Westmoreland is appointed to replace General Hawkins as MACV commander in June.

May 27. Second Lao coalition government collapses; Pathet Lao retake Plaine des Jarres.

July 30–31. South Vietnamese naval forces carry out raids on islands near the coast of North Vietnam.

August 1–2. U.S.-supplied Laotian planes bomb two villages in the North's Nghe An province.

August 2, 4. North Vietnamese patrol boats menace the U.S. destroyers *Maddox* and *C. Turner Joy;* President Johnson orders airstrikes against the patrol boats and their support facilities.

August 7. By a vote of 88–2 in the Senate and 416–0 in the House, the U.S. Congress passes the Tonkin Gulf Resolution allowing the president to use "all necessary steps . . . to prevent further aggression."

December 4. PLAF defeats larger U.S.-trained and equipped ARVN force at Binh Gia village.

December 8–20. Student and Buddhist demonstrations threaten stability of Saigon's military government.

December 14. U.S. warplanes begin bombing the Ho Chi Minh Trail in Laos.

December 31. U.S. military personnel in Vietnam total 23,300.

1965

February 7. Communist attack on U.S. advisers' compound near Pleiku kills nine U.S. servicemen; U.S. planes make "reprisal airstrikes" against targets in the North.

February 18. Military coup ousts General Khanh.

February 28. U.S. officials reveal that "reprisal airstrikes" on the North will occur on a continuous basis (Operation ROLLING THUNDER) to pressure Hanoi into a negotiated settlement.

February 29. Hanoi government orders evacuation of the North's cities.

March 9. First U.S. ground combat troops land in Vietnam at Danang.

April 8. Hanoi issues four-point statement advocating peace in the South "in accordance with the program of the National Liberation Front."

June 14. Saigon's ruling committee of generals, headed by Nguyen Van Thieu, chooses Air Vice Marshall Nguyen Cao Ky as premier. Ky's cabinet is the ninth to hold office since November 1963.

November 14–16. U.S. and PAVN units have first major encounter in Ia Drang valley.

December 31. U.S. military personnel in Vietnam total 184,000.

1966

March 10. Dismissal of I Corps Commander Nguyen Chanh Thi sparks demonstrations in Hue and Danang.

March 16. Demonstrations spread to Saigon, spearheaded by Buddhist monks demanding return to civilian rule.

March 23. General strikes occur in Hue and Danang with cooperation of local authorities.

May 15. Ky dispatches two battalions of ARVN marines to seize I Corps headquarters in Danang.

September 11. RVN Constituent Assembly is elected from officially approved slates and denounced by South's Buddhist leaders.

December 31. U.S. force level in South Vietnam reaches 362,000. Contingents from South Korea, the Philippines, Thailand, Australia, and New Zealand total about 50,000.

1967

April. Massive anti-war demonstrations occur throughout the United States.

June. PAVN General Nguyen Chi Thanh presents draft plan for general offensive and attacks on cities in the South.

June 30. Under pressure from other military rulers, Ky withdraws from the presidential race and agrees to run as vice presidential candidate with Thieu.

September 3. Thieu-Ky ticket wins election with 34.8 percent of the vote.

October. Anti-war rally in Washington concludes with march on Pentagon.

November 21. In a speech to the National Press Club, General Westmoreland claims the end of the war is in sight.
December 31. U.S. military personnel in Vietnam total 485,600.

1968

January 21. Siege of Khe Sanh begins.
January 30–31. Communist forces launch coordinated attacks on the South's major cities and penetrate the U.S. Embassy compound in Saigon.
February 7. PAVN overruns Lang Vei camp near Khe Sanh.
February 24. Communist troops are driven out of Hue after twenty-five days of heavy fighting.
February 27. Joint Chiefs of Staff forward Westmoreland's request for 206,000 additional troops to the president.
February. Senate hearings on the 1964 Tonkin Gulf Incident cast doubt on accuracy of Johnson administration's account of this pivotal event.
March. Clark Clifford replaces Robert McNamara as secretary of defense; General Creighton Abrams replaces Westmoreland as MACV commander.
March 31. Johnson announces he will not seek reelection, suspends bombing of the North except near the demilitarized zone, and calls for peace talks.
May 3. Hanoi and Washington agree to hold preliminary talks in Paris.
May. Weaker, second round of communist attacks on cities is beaten back in a few days.
October 31. Johnson orders all bombing of North Vietnam halted effective November 1 to meet Hanoi's condition for productive discussions; bombing intensifies in Laos.
November 6. Richard Nixon elected president.
December 31. U.S. military personnel in Vietnam total 536,100.

1969

January 25. Four-party peace talks open in Paris.
February 23. Nixon approves Abrams' request to bomb communist sanctuaries in Cambodia with B-52s.

March 18. B-52s make the first secret MENU strikes on Cambodian bases. These strikes continue for the next fourteen months.

May 8. NLF unveils ten-point peace plan that demands unconditional U.S. withdrawal and coalition government excluding Thieu.

May 14. With U.S. troop strength in Vietnam at its peak of 543,400, Nixon calls for withdrawal of "all non-South Vietnamese forces" and announces U.S. troops will be gradually withdrawn.

June 10. NLF and allied organizations form Provisional Revolutionary Government of South Vietnam (PRG).

August 4. Henry Kissinger meets Xuan Thuy in Paris to propose compromise.

September 3. Ho Chi Minh dies.

October 15 and November 15. Nationwide "moratorium" demonstrations in the United States are the biggest to date.

November 3. Nixon's second major statement on the war conjures vision of disasters that would follow a communist victory, appeals to "silent majority" for support.

December. Articles by top PAVN leaders concede Southern revolution is "temporarily" in a defensive position.

December 31. U.S. military personnel in Vietnam total 475,200.

1970

February 21. Kissinger and Le Duc Tho hold first secret meeting.

February. PAVN and Pathet Lao forces drive Royal Lao, Thai, and CIA-backed H'mong troops off the Plaine des Jarres and Xieng Khoang airfield, enlarging secure logistical corridor through southern Laos.

March 12. With Prince Sihanouk out of the country, Phnom Penh government demands the immediate withdrawal of Vietnamese communist troops from Cambodian territory.

March 18. Cambodian National Assembly deposes Sihanouk, installs General Lon Nol as chief of state. Sihanouk, in Beijing, forms "national union government" with the communist Khmer Rouge.

March 27–28. U.S.-supported ARVN forces attack communist base areas in Cambodia.

April 11. Cambodian government troops and police participate in massacres of Vietnamese civilian residents of Cambodia.

April 28. Joint U.S.-ARVN force attacks communist bases in Cambodian Parrot's Beak.

April 29. Joint U.S.-ARVN force attacks communist bases in Cambodian Fishhook.

April 30. Nixon reveals U.S. troops are participating in "incursions" into Cambodia. Protests erupt in the United States.

June 24. U.S. Senate repeals the Tonkin Gulf Resolution in vote of 81–0.

June 29. U.S. ground combat troops pull out of Cambodia, leaving ARVN units to continue operations.

June 30. U.S. Senate passes Cooper-Church Amendment barring U.S. military personnel from further combat or advisory roles in Cambodia.

October 7. Nixon proposes standstill ceasefire in all three countries of Indochina.

December 31. U.S. military personnel in Vietnam total 334,600; ARVN total nears 1 million.

1971

February 8. With U.S. air and logistical support, the ARVN begins Operation LAM SON 719 to disrupt PAVN supply lines in southern Laos, but encounters stiff resistance.

March 24. LAM SON 719 comes to an end as battered ARVN forces flee or are airlifted out of Laos.

May. Communist party Political Bureau resolves to achieve "decisive victory" in 1972.

August 20. Duong Van Minh withdraws from South Vietnam presidential race, leaving Thieu, after disqualifying Ky, to run unopposed.

October 3. Thieu elected to another four-year term.

December 31. U.S. military personnel in Vietnam total 156,800; ARVN exceeds 1 million.

1972

March 30. PAVN troops cross the demilitarized zone to launch the largest offensive of the war since 1968; they quickly overrun northern Quang Tri province.

April 6. As communist forces open a second front close to Saigon, U.S. warplanes resume bombing of the North.

April 7. Loc Ninh falls to PAVN and PLAF troops; An Loc is besieged.

April 15. B-52s join strikes on "military targets" in the North.

May 1. PAVN occupies Quang Tri city.

May 2. In secret meeting with Tho, Kissinger indicates United States is prepared to drop its demand for withdrawal of Northern troops from the South; public talks are suspended on the 4th.

May 8. Nixon orders mining of North's harbors and waterways and destruction of all its transportation and communications.

June 28. Behind U.S. aircover, ARVN forces cross the My Chanh River and inch back toward Quang Tri city.

June 30. U.S. military personnel in Vietnam drop to 47,000.

September 16. ARVN retakes Quang Tri city.

October 8. Tho presents Kissinger with "breakthrough" draft peace plan.

October 26. Hanoi reveals contents of tentatively agreed plan; Kissinger proclaims "peace is at hand."

December 13. Further talks concerning changes in peace plan demanded by Thieu break down.

December 18–30. B-52s and tactical aircraft heavily bomb targets in and around the North's major cities.

December 26. Hanoi agrees to resume talks on basis of principles agreed in October.

December 31. U.S. military personnel in Vietnam total 24,200.

1973

January 5. Nixon letter assures Thieu of "continued assistance in the postsettlement period."

January 8. Kissinger and Tho resume negotiations in Paris.

January 16. Nixon threatens Thieu with aid cutoff if Saigon refuses to "close ranks" with Washington on peace agreement.

January 23. Kissinger and Tho reach initial agreement; a separate ceasefire for Laos is concluded.

January 27. Agreement on Ending the War and Restoring Peace in Vietnam is signed in Paris by representatives of the DRV, SRV, PRG, and United States. Ceasefire goes into effect. ARVN continues to reoccupy villages seized by communist forces just before the ceasefire deadline.

March 29. The last U.S. troops in Vietnam depart for the United States.

April–May. Hanoi, Saigon, and Washington trade charges of ceasefire violations.

June 6–13. Kissinger and Tho meet in Paris, agree on measures to improve observance of ceasefire.

June 29. Compromise legislation passed in the House fixes August 15 deadline for cessation of bombing in Cambodia.

July 10. Thieu launches "administrative revolution" to consolidate his government in the South.

July 14. Air Force Major Hal Knight reveals documents falsified to cover up bombing of Cambodia.

August 26. Pro-Thieu slates win all contested seats in RVN Senate elections.

October. Twenty-first Plenum of the Central Committee concludes that Thieu cannot be made to implement the Paris Agreement, resolves to achieve reunification by military means.

November 7. War Powers Act passes over Nixon's veto.

November 15. Military Procurement Authorization passed by Congress prohibits use of funds for any U.S. military action in any part of Indochina.

1974

January 19. South Vietnam National Assembly special session votes to amend constitution so Thieu can run for third term; opposition legislators protest.

February. ARVN offensive operations encroach upon areas long under communist control; Communists retaliate.

March. Heaviest fighting since ceasefire.

April 4. House rejects Nixon administration request for $474 million increase in military aid to South Vietnam, reaffirms cut on May 22.

April 12. RVN withdraws from Paris talks on political reconciliation with PRG.

May 13. PRG delegation withdraws from Paris talks protesting Saigon's withdrawal and ARVN operations in communist zones of control.

August 6. House cuts military aid appropriation for South Vietnam from $1 billion to $700 million.

August 9. Nixon resigns; Gerald Ford becomes president.

August 11. Ford letter to Thieu reaffirms U.S. commitment, promises "adequate support" for Saigon.

September 20. Antigovernment demonstrations erupt in Saigon following confiscation of newspapers that publish Father Tran Huu Thanh's six-count "indictment" of corruption in the Thieu regime and family.

December 18. Hanoi Political Bureau, in session until January 8, assesses situation as highly favorable, adopts plan for military campaign to defeat Thieu regime in two years.

1975

January 1. Khmer Rouge in Cambodia launch final offensive from siege ring around Phnom Penh.

January 8. Communist forces seize Phuoc Long province north of Saigon.

February 5. General Van Tien Dung leaves Hanoi to take command of offensive in the South.

March 9. PAVN opens offensive with attack on Ban Me Thuot, which falls the next day.

March 14. Thieu orders redeployment to defend III and IV Corps, abandonment of Pleiku and Kontum.

March 15. ARVN retreat from central highlands turns into a rout.

March 22. PAVN crosses the My Chanh River to move on Hue, which falls on the 25th.

March 28. PAVN artillery opens fire on Danang airfield; communist troops enter Danang the next day.

April 1. Marshall Lon Nol leaves for Hawaiian exile as his troops fall back on Phnom Penh.

April 10. Ford requests $722 million emergency military assistance for Saigon. Congressional reaction is overwhelmingly negative.

April 14. Political Bureau gives its approval for Ho Chi Minh Campaign to take Saigon.

April 17. Lon Nol's army collapses; Khmer Rouge enter Phnom Penh.

April 20. PAVN breaks stiff resistance of ARVN 18th division at Xuan Loc, thirty kilometers from Saigon.

April 21. Thieu announces resignation in televised address, is replaced by Vice President Tran Van Huong.

April 26. Fifteen PAVN divisions plus auxiliaries begin maneuvers for final push on Saigon.

April 28. Duong Van Minh takes over presidency from Tran Van Huong.

April 30. Minh issues radio appeal for ARVN troops to lay down their arms. PAVN advance elements enter Saigon.

December 2. Following local seizures of power by "people's committees" and elections in November, Lao Communists declare the establishment of the Lao People's Democratic Republic.

Suggested Readings

The following list is neither a bibliography of works cited in the notes nor a rigorous selection of recommended readings. The purpose, rather, is to point broadly in essay form to other books and documentary materials, with emphasis on recent titles and those from the past that have had lasting influence or value.

BIBLIOGRAPHIES

Extensive if not exhaustive guidance to additional materials in English can be found in the well-organized Richard Dean Burns and Milton Leitenberg, *The Wars in Vietnam, Cambodia and Laos, 1945–1982: A Bibliographic Guide* (Santa Barbara, Calif.: ABC-Clio, 1984). Covering English, French, and Vietnamese language sources of the Echols Collection at Cornell University, Christopher L. Sugnet and John T. Hickey, *Vietnam War Bibliography* (Lexington, Mass.: Heath, 1983) is a fairly lengthy list alphabetized by author or originating agency. The sole but now somewhat dated guide to materials in several languages on all aspects of communism in Vietnam is Phan Thien Chau, *Vietnamese Communism: A Research Guide* (Westport, Conn.: Greenwood, 1975).

Other research tools for the serious scholar can be found in Michael Cotter, *Vietnam: A Guide to Reference Sources* (Boston: Hall, 1977).

DOCUMENTARY SOURCES

The forty-seven-volume study known as *The Pentagon Papers* that was commissioned by Secretary of Defense Robert McNamara, xeroxed surreptitiously by Daniel Ellsberg, and synopsized in the *New York Times* is a gold mine of U.S. government internal documents. The official version, Department of Defense, *U.S.-Vietnam Relations, 1945–1967,* 12 vols. (Washington, D.C.: Government Printing Office, 1971) is a disjointed compendium of documents and staff papers. Senator Mike Gravel tidied up a large portion of these for publication as the Senator Gravel edition, *The Pentagon Papers,* 5 vols. (Boston: Beacon, 1971). Casual readers can get the flavor, analysis, and commentary in the one-volume work compiled by Neil Sheehan et al., eds., *The Pentagon Papers* (New York: Quadrangle, 1971) as serialized in the *New York Times.* More recently, the documentary deluge has continued with the release of State Department Central Files, National Security Council classified histories, transcipts of the Paris peace talks, and CIA Research Reports through the "Indochina Research Collections" microfilm series (Frederick, Md.: University Publications of America, various dates).

Of course, U.S. government-generated documents can be considered primary sources only with respect to the U.S. side of the war. The nearest equivalent for any other side would be the huge trove of communist documents captured by U.S., South Vietnamese, and "allied" forces and stored on microfilm. Someday an enterprising, abundantly funded scholar will exploit this film, on deposit at the National Archives. Meanwhile, readers with a command of Vietnamese must content themselves with the Douglas Pike collection (Chicago: Center for Research Libraries, items 1–850, 1966; and Ithaca, N.Y.: Cornell University Library, items 856–1120, 1967) and the eighty documents and thirty interviews of the Jeffrey Race collection (Chicago: Center for Research Libraries, 1968). Selected translations of captured documents released by the U.S. Information Service, *Viet-Nam Documents and Research Notes,* nos. 1–117 (Saigon: U.S. Mission, 1967–1972) may be found in a few major research libraries. A few of these documents along with an extensive selection of materials mainly from U.S. official sources are arranged chronologically in Gareth Porter, ed., *Vietnam: The Definitive History of Human Decisions,* 2 vols. (Stanfordville, N.Y.: Coleman Enterprises, 1979). A one-volume abridgement, Gareth Porter, ed., *Vietnam: A History in Documents* (New York: New American Library, 1981), serves as a compact documentary history though heavily weighted toward U.S. sources. The defunct noncommunist regimes are very poorly represented in the war's publicly available records and are likely to remain so.

GENERAL HISTORIES

Readers interested in the historical and cultural currents that lay behind the war are strongly advised to consult Alexander B. Woodside, *Community and Revolution in Modern Vietnam* (Boston: Houghton Mifflin, 1976). Other works on the prewar context include John T. McAlister, Jr., *Viet Nam: The Origins of Revolution* (New York: Knopf, 1969); Ralph Smith, *Vietnam and the West* (Ithaca, N.Y.: Cornell, 1971); William J. Duiker, *The Rise of Nationalism in Vietnam, 1900–1941* (Ithaca, N.Y.: Cornell, 1976) and *Vietnam: A Nation in Revolution* (Boulder, Colo.: Westview, 1983); and David G. Marr, *Vietnamese Tradition on Trial, 1920–1945* (Berkeley: University of California, 1981). The presently most authoritative study of the implantation of communism in Vietnam is Huynh Kim Khanh, *Vietnamese Communism 1925–1945* (Ithaca, N.Y.: Cornell, 1982). Helen B. Lamb, *Vietnam's Will to Live* (New York: Monthly Review, 1972) is an amiable recital of Vietnam's "resistance to foreign aggression from early times through the 19th century."

Turning to the war itself, James Pinckney Harrison, *The Endless War: Fifty Years of Struggle in Vietnam* (New York: Free Press, 1982) is a scholarly treatment by an eminent sinologist. George C. Herring, *America's Longest War: The United States and Vietnam, 1950–1975* (New York: Wiley, 1979) focuses on U.S. policies, politics, and perspectives, as the title implies. The "anti-war" (that is, anti–U.S. policy) interpretation is presented in Committee of Concerned Asian Scholars, *The Indochina Story* (New York: Bantam, 1970). For a collection of critical reflections with a "revisionist" bent, see Peter Braestrup, ed., *Vietnam as History* (Lanham, Md.: University Press of America, 1984).

The most comprehensive popular history to date is the chunky volume by the journalist Stanley Karnow, *Vietnam: A History* (New York: Viking, 1983), which overshadows, in balance and thoroughness, the thirteen-part PBS television series it was written to accompany. Michael Maclear, *The Ten Thousand Day War* (New York: St. Martin's, 1981) also grew out of a television project (for Canadian Broadcasting Corporation). A glossy, ambitious treatment for the mass audience is the fifteen-volume series, *The Vietnam Experience* (Boston: Boston Publishing, 1981–1985). Still the best "read" and most devastating description of Americans in Vietnam is Frances Fitzgerald, *Fire in the Lake* (Boston: Atlantic Monthly Publications, 1972), though her interpretation of Vietnamese society and culture tends to strike specialists as eccentric, precious, and out of date. The classic by Bernard Fall, *The Two Viet-Nams* (Boulder, Colo.: Westview, 1985), remains a useful source on the consolidation of separate regimes in North and South up to the fall of Diem.

JOURNALISM

To the consternation of U.S. embassies in Indochina, journalists, including American ones, were poor team players compared with correspondents in previous wars. The note of skepticism is struck early by David Halberstam, *The Making of a Quagmire* (New York: Random House, 1965). Robert Shaplen's *The Lost Revolution* (New York: Harper and Row, rev. ed., 1966) and *The Road from War* (New York: Harper and Row, 1970) record copiously what a veteran correspondent considers to be missed opportunities for the United States. Bitter indictments of both the United States and its South Vietnamese allies can be found in Gloria Emerson's award-laden *Winners and Losers* (New York: Random House, 1976). Jonathan Schell, *The Military Half* (New

York: Knopf, 1968), clinically describes destruction in two provinces. Don Oberdorfer, *Tet!* (Garden City, N.Y.: Doubleday, 1971), dissects the 1968 offensive; and Robert Pisor, *The End of the Line* (New York: Norton, 1982), provides a detailed account of the siege of Khe Sanh based on U.S. sources and interviews with some of the (noncommunist) participants. An excellent retrospective, filled with the anecdotes that journalists excel at telling, is Arnold R. Isaacs, *Without Honor: Defeat in Vietnam and Cambodia* (Baltimore, Md.: Johns Hopkins, 1983); in a similar vein, see Peter Scholl-Latour, *Death in the Rice Fields: An Eyewitness Account of Vietnam's Three Wars, 1945–1979* (New York: Orbis, 1981). As for journalism itself, former journalist Peter Braestrup, *Big Story,* 2 vols. (Boulder, Colo.: Westview, 1977; abridged ed., New Haven, Conn.: Yale, 1983) blames an erroneous media image of Tet 1968 for turning this pivotal event into a political defeat for the United States and Saigon.

THE SOUTH

Journalists have done the bulk of writing on politics in Saigon (see above). One example is Denis Warner, *The Last Confucian* (New York: Macmillan, 1963), in which two solid chapters on Ngo Dinh Diem, his regime, and his family appear alongside weaker sections. A scholarly analysis of the Diem regime's consolidation, ideology, and disintegration, based on the author's experience as a member of the Michigan State University Vietnam advisory group, is Robert Scigliano, *South Vietnam: Nation Under Stress* (Boston: Houghton Mifflin, 1964). Influential in shaping French opinion, Jean Lacouture, *Vietnam: Between Two Truces* (New York: Random House, 1966) contains valuable insights on Saigon politics by an experienced observer who believed the war was essentially a civil conflict among diverse groups of southerners. Dennis J. Duncanson, *Government and Revolution in Vietnam* (New York: Oxford, 1968) is a Cold Warriorish interpretation by a professional Asianist who headed the British advisory mission to the Diem government. A collection of journal articles by Charles A. Joiner, *The Politics of Massacre* (Philadelphia: Temple, 1974) makes for tedious reading but contains useful material on Saigon elections, parties, and personalities. A simple narrative description of Saigon politics is provided in a Keesing's Research Report, *South Vietnam: A Political History 1954–1970* (New York: Keesing's, 1970). Allan E. Goodman, *Politics in War: The Bases of Political Community in South Vietnam* (Cambridge, Mass.: Harvard, 1973) is a systematic and surprisingly sanguine analysis of Saigon's efforts to develop effective representative institutions. Also see Howard R. Penniman, *Elections in South Vietnam* (Washington, D.C.: American Enterprise Institute, 1973). The case for seeing things as ordinary Vietnamese saw them is made eloquently by Don Luce and John Sommer, *Vietnam: The Unheard Voices* (Ithaca, N.Y.: Cornell, 1969). The blend of pain, rage, alienation, and patriotism behind the Buddhist uprisings can be sensed in the pages of Thich Nhat Hanh, *Lotus in a Sea of Fire* (New York: Hill and Wang, 1967). The war is brought to a close in Tiziano Terzani, *Giai Phong!* (New York: St. Martin's, 1976), written by a journalist who stayed in Saigon as communist forces approached and who rather admired the victors for a time.

On the countryside, Jeffrey Race, *War Comes to Long An: Revolutionary Conflict in a Vietnamese Province* (Berkeley, Calif.: University of California, 1972) is "must" reading for anyone who wants to know how the Communists, starting from nothing, gained ascendancy over Saigon forces in the Mekong Delta. Another delta province study, more impressionistic and less schematic than Race, is Harvey Meyerson, *Vinh Long* (Boston: Houghton Mifflin, 1970). For portrayal of a different war in a different region, see James Walker Trullinger, Jr., *Village at War* (New York: Longman, 1980), based on the author's observations while a voluntary aid worker near Hue. The thesis that tenancy and inequality of land distribution drove peasants into the arms of the Communists is contested in Robert L. Sansom, *The Economics of Insurgency in the Mekong Delta of Vietnam* (Cambridge, Mass.: MIT Press, 1970). Historical perspective on the political economy of peasant society in Vietnam is provided by Samuel L. Popkin, *The Rational Peasant* (Berkeley, Calif.: University of California, 1979). The highland minorities, or "montagnards," neglected in so many ways, are the subject of Gerald

Hickey, *Sons of the Mountains* (New Haven, Conn.: Yale, 1982) and *Free in the Forest* (New Haven, Conn.: Yale, 1982), two monumental ethnographic histories of cultures the war destroyed.

Southern anticommunist leaders have been more successful at publicizing their views in English since the war's end than during it. Tran Van Don, *Our Endless War* (San Rafael, Calif.: Presidio, 1978) is (for the genre) an uncommonly dispassionate memoir by one of the generals who organized the coup against Diem. The memoirs of Nguyen Cao Ky, *Twenty Years and Twenty Days* (New York: Stein and Day, 1976), have yet to be answered by memoirs from the reclusive Nguyen Van Thieu. A number of memoirs and studies of specific campaigns by ARVN officers have been published under the auspices of the U.S. Army Center of Military History, most notably Cao Van Vien and Dong Van Khuyen, *Reflections on the Vietnam War* (Washington, D.C.: Center of Military History, 1980); Cao Van Vien, *The Final Collapse* (Washington, D.C.: Center of Military History, 1982); and Hoang Ngoc Lung, *The General Offensives of 1968–69* (Washington, D.C.: Center of Military History, 1981). Excerpts from interviews with these and other Saigon figures are quoted at length, with insightful commentary, in Stephen T. Hosmer, Konrad Kellen, and Brian M. Jenkins, eds., *The Fall of South Vietnam: Statements by Vietnamese Military and Civilian Leaders* (New York: Crane, Russak, 1980).

The revolutionary side in the South receives attention in some of the works above (especially Race). It is the exclusive focus of Douglas Pike, *Viet Cong* (Cambridge, Mass.: MIT Press, 1966), and *War, Peace, and the Viet Cong* (Cambridge, Mass.: MIT Press, 1969), by an official of the U.S. Information Agency. More systematic analyses of the organization and motivation of Southern communist armed forces (the PLAF) are Paul Berman, *Revolutionary Organization* (Lexington, Mass.: Heath, 1974), and William Darryl Henderson, *Why the Vietcong Fought* (Westport, Conn.: Greenwood, 1979). Southern communist militant and colonel in the PLAF, Madame Nguyen Thi Dinh describes the origins of revolutionary armed struggle in the Mekong Delta in the translation of her memoir, *No Other Road to Take* (Ithaca, N.Y.: Cornell University Southeast Asia Studies Program, 1976).

THE NORTH

A number of journalists visited the North during the war and wrote accounts that are best forgotten. An important exception is Gerard Chaliand, *The Peasants of North Vietnam* (Baltimore, Md.: Penguin, 1969). The North's internal response to U.S. bombardment is described in mind-numbing detail in Jon M. Van Dyke, *North Vietnam's Strategy for Survival* (Palo Alto, Calif.: Pacific Books, 1972), which should be read in conjunction with the bombing study by the Air War Study Group, Cornell University, *The Air War in Indochina* (Boston: Beacon, rev. ed., 1972). For scholarly studies of DRV politics and society that include commentary on the impact of war, see William S. Turley, ed., *Vietnamese Communism in Comparative Perspective* (Boulder, Colo.: Westview, 1980). Hanoi's attempt to remain neutral between Moscow and Beijing while preserving the support of each is analyzed in Donald Zagoria, *Vietnam Triangle* (New York: Pegasus, 1967), and W. R. Smyser, *The Independent Vietnamese* (Athens, Ohio: Ohio University Center for International Studies, 1980).

Of course, Hanoi has its own spokesmen. The ablest writer for foreign audiences is Nguyen Khac Vien, *Tradition and Revolution in Vietnam* (Berkeley, Calif.: Indochina Resource Center, 1974) and *The Long Resistance 1958–1975*) (Hanoi: Foreign Languages Publishing House, 1975), both of which emphasize the continuity of Vietnam's anticolonial and reunification struggles with its previous struggles against foreign rule. As for military strategy, it must be remembered when reading Vo Nguyen Giap, *People's War, People's Army* (New York: Praeger, 1962) that this work anthologizes articles about the war with France; it is not necessarily the blueprint for the war with the United States. Giap's later *Big Victory, Great Task* (New York: Praeger, 1968), written on the eve of the Tet Offensive, attempts in the manner of generals everywhere to apply the lessons of the past to the present. That the Southern revolution was "temporarily" on the defensive is conceded in Giap, *Banner of People's War, the Party's Military Line* (New York: Praeger, 1970), which also contains an insightful introduction by French scholar Georges Boudarel.

Articles by several PAVN commanders, in which a debate over military strategy can be discerned, are translated and analyzed in Patrick J. McGarvey, ed., *Visions of Victory* (Stanford, Calif.: Hoover, 1969). Hanoi's official account of the 1975 offensive is the memoir of PAVN Chief-of-Staff General Van Tien Dung, *Our Great Spring Victory* (New York: Monthly Review, 1977). A somewhat different account by a COSVN commander who none too subtly criticizes the high command in Hanoi is General Tran Van Tra, *Vietnam: History of the B2-Bulwark Theatre, vol. V, Concluding the 30 Years War* (Springfield, Va.: Joint Publications Research Service, translation no. 82,783, 1983), a work (cited in the notes above as *Ket thuc cuoc chien tranh 30 nam*) that was withdrawn from Vietnam's book stalls almost immediately upon publication. The authoritative secondary source on the evolution of Hanoi's strategy is William J. Duiker, *The Communist Road to Power in Vietnam* (Boulder, Colo.: Westview, 1981).

CAMBODIA

Amidst the dearth of work on Cambodia in English, David P. Chandler, *A History of Cambodia* (Boulder, Colo.: Westview, 1983) stands out as the essential concise introduction. Milton E. Osborne, *Before Kampuchea* (Boston: Allen Unwin, 1979) is a retrospective tour of the horizon on the eve of war by a former Australian diplomat. The primary source on the regime of Prince Sihanouk up to the time of its overthrow is, of course, Norodom Sihanouk, *My War with the CIA* (New York: Pantheon, 1973), to which the chastened follow-up is Sihanouk, *War and Hope* (New York: Pantheon, 1980). The classic account of Cambodia's slide into war and the "secret bombing" is William Shawcross, *Sideshow: Kissinger, Nixon and the Destruction of Cambodia* (New York: Simon and Schuster, 1979), to which Kissinger responds at length in his memoirs (see below). Also see Peter A. Poole, *The Expansion of the War into Cambodia* (Athens, Ohio: Ohio University Center for International Studies, 1970), and the left perspective of Malcolm Caldwell and Lek Tan, *Cambodia in the Southeast Asian War* (New York: Monthly Review, 1973). The war in Cambodia is brought to its ominous end in Francois

Ponchaud, *Year Zero* (New York: Holt, 1977), an account by a Catholic priest who was there of Phnom Penh's last days and the Khmer Rouge takeover.

Study of the Khmer Rouge suffers for lack of documentation, access, and attention. For once the adjective "shadowy" seems deserved. Just about everything that was known in the West at war's end is synopsized in Timothy Carney, *Communist Party Power in Kampuchea (Cambodia)* (Ithaca, N.Y.: Cornell University Southeast Asia Studies Program, 1977). Ben Kiernan and Chanthou Boua, eds., *Peasants and Politics in Kampuchea, 1943–1981* (New York: Sharpe, 1982), brings substantially more to light in diverse articles and documents, including items by Khmer Rouge leaders whom Pol Pot liquidated. Attempt at systematic interpretation of the revolution in Cambodia by scholars with appropriate experience and linguistic training begins with David P. Chandler and Ben Kiernan, eds., *Revolution and Its Aftermath in Kampuchea: Eight Essays* (New Haven, Conn.: Yale University Southeast Asia Studies, 1983), and Michael Vickery, *Cambodia: 1975–1982* (Boston: South End, 1984). Craig Etcheson, *The Rise and Demise of Democratic Kampuchea* (Boulder, Colo.: Westview, 1984) is the first serious history of Khmer communism from 1930 to the present.

LAOS

The valuable introduction by Arthur J. Dommen, *Laos: Keystone of Indochina* (Boulder, Colo.: Westview, 1985), builds upon the equally useful Arthur J. Dommen, *Conflict in Laos* (New York: Praeger, rev. ed., 1974). Earlier writing by other authors tends to focus on the themes of coalition, neutrality, and foreign intervention. Bernard Fall, *Anatomy of a Crisis* (Garden City, N.Y.: Doubleday, 1967) thoroughly dissects the U.S. role in the events of 1960–1961. Marek Thee, *Notes of a Witness* (New York: Random House, 1973) records the impressions of a member of the International Control Commission who worked in Laos during the Kennedy administration. By British scholar Hugh Toye, *Laos: Buffer State or Battleground* (New York: Oxford, 1968) is an authoritative overview. Nina S. Adams and Alfred W.

McCoy, eds., *Laos: War and Revolution* (New York: Harper and Row, 1970) gathers important articles written from an "anti-war" perspective for the Committee of Concerned Asian Scholars. For a meticulous analysis of U.S. policy toward Laos since 1954, based on a Harvard Ph.D. dissertation, see Charles A. Stevenson, *The End of Nowhere* (Boston: Beacon, 1972). An interpretation of the collapse of neutralism and the civil conflict by Australian journalist Wilfred Burchett, *The Furtive War* (New York: International Publishers, 1963) is sympathetic to Hanoi and the Pathet Lao.

The Lao Communists attracted attention from oddly few serious analysts. The subject is nearly monopolized by Paul F. Langer and Joseph J. Zasloff, *North Vietnam and the Pathet Lao* (Cambridge, Mass.: Harvard, 1970), and Joseph J. Zasloff, *The Pathet Lao: Leadership and Organization* (Lexington, Mass.: Heath, 1973). Even more odd is the dearth of writing on the Royal Lao government and the fighting from an RLG perspective. For a rightist view, but unfortunately very dated, one must consult Sisouk Na Champassak, *Storm over Laos* (New York: Praeger, 1961). On the later military campaigns from a Royal Lao Army perspective, see Soutchay Vongsavanh, *Royal Lao Government Military Operations and Activities in the Laotian Panhandle* (Washington, D.C.: U.S. Army Center for Military History, 1981).

AMERICAN POLITICS AND DIPLOMACY

The problem here is not dearth but surfeit. George McT. Kahin and John W. Lewis, *The United States in Vietnam* (New York: Dial, 1967) is a powerful criticism of U.S. diplomacy up to the time of large-scale intervention though unreliable as regards the origins and leadership of the revolution in the South. Wallace J. Thies, *When Governments Collide* (Berkeley, Calif.: University of California, 1980) shows meticulously that coercion was ineffective against Hanoi in the period 1964–1968. Allan E. Goodman, *The Lost Peace* (Stanford, Calif.: Hoover, 1978) contrasts the U.S. search for compromise with Hanoi's refusal to make concessions. Quite a different view by a scholar who had access to officials in Hanoi is Gareth Porter, *A Peace Denied* (Bloomington, Ind.: Indiana University Press, 1975). The sage observations of an early State Department dissenter can be found in Paul M. Kattenburg, *The Vietnam Trauma in American Foreign Policy, 1945–1975* (New Brunswick, N.J.: Transaction Books, 1980). Other important insider accounts are Townsend Hoopes, *The Limits of Intervention* (New York: McKay, 1969), and Chester L. Cooper, *The Lost Crusade* (New York: Dodd, Mead, 1970). Ex–CIA analyst Frank Snepp, *Decent Interval* (New York: Random House, 1977), vividly recounts Saigon's collapse and accuses U.S. officials of deceit, perfidy, and incompetence. Michael Charlton and Anthony Moncrieff, *Many Reasons Why* (New York: Hill and Wang, 1978) quotes principal actors at length and informatively from interviews conducted for a BBC radio program. For a vigorous defense of U.S. involvement and military conduct based on an analysis of U.S. statistics, see Guenter Lewy, *America in Vietnam* (New York: Oxford, 1978). A more sober retrospective by prominent figures in the planning and execution of the war is W. Scott Thompson and Donald D. Frizzell, eds., *Lessons of Vietnam* (New York: Crane, Russak, 1977).

The war is the obsession of memoirs by wartime presidents Lyndon Johnson, *The Vantage Point* (New York: Holt, 1971), and Richard Nixon, *RN: The Memoirs of Richard Nixon* (New York: Grosset, 1978). The masterpiece of rationalization by a top policymaker, however, is Henry Kissinger, *White House Years* (Boston: Little, Brown, 1979) and *Years of Upheaval* (Boston: Little, Brown, 1982), which contain much valuable information on the negotiations and the beleaguerment of the Nixon administration. The best commentaries are Doris Kearns, *Lyndon Johnson and the American Dream* (New York: Harper and Row, 1976); Tad Szulc, *The Illusion of Peace* (New York: Viking, 1978); Seymour M. Hersh, *The Price of Power* (New York: Summit, 1983); and Herbert Schandler, *Lyndon Johnson and Vietnam: The Unmaking of the President* (Princeton, N.J.: Princeton, 1983). The fantasies, foibles, and self-deception of presidential advisers under Kennedy and Johnson are unmasked in David Halberstam, *The Best and the Brightest* (New York: Random House, 1969).

The length, documentation, and divisiveness of the war are rich terrain for the student of U.S. decisionmaking. Against the "quagmire hypothesis" that the United States could not easily back out of a war it had stumbled into, Daniel Ellsberg, *Papers on the War* (New York: Simon and Schuster, 1972) argues in a chapter on "the stalemate machine" that the war was prolonged by the need of successive presidents to get elected. Robert L. Gallucci, *Neither Peace Nor Honor* (Baltimore, Md.: Johns Hopkins, 1975) plumbs *The Pentagon Papers* to analyze the impact of bureaucratic procedures and infighting. Leslie Gelb and Richard Betts, *The Irony of Vietnam* (Washington, D.C.: Brookings, 1979) comes to the curious conclusion that the policymaking system "worked" in the sense that it sustained the commitment of six administrations to prevent the loss of Vietnam to communism. Larry Berman, *Planning a Tragedy* (New York: Norton, 1982) uses documents from the LBJ Library to examine Lyndon Johnson's halting steps toward escalation in 1965. Former pacification chief Robert Komer, *Bureaucracy at War* (Boulder, Colo.: Westview, 1985) indicts the military for failure to adapt to an atypical conflict. For an exhaustive survey of the war's impact on executive-legislative relations commissioned by the Senate Committee on Foreign Relations, see Congressional Research Service, *The U.S. Government and the Vietnam War,* 4 vols. (Washington, D.C.: Government Printing Office, 1984).

Was it legal in international law? Informed judgment begins with reading the essential background provided in Robert Randle, *Geneva 1954—The Settlement of the Indochinese War* (Princeton, N.J.: Princeton, 1969). The Lawyers Committee on American Policy Toward Vietnam, *Vietnam and International Law* (Flanders, N.J.: O'Hare, 1967); Richard A. Falk, comp., *The Vietnam War and International Law,* 4 vols. (Princeton, N.J.: Princeton, 1968–1976); John Norton Moore, *Law and the Indo-China War* (Princeton, N.J.: Princeton, 1972); and Peter D. Trooboff, ed., *Law and Responsibility in Warfare: The Vietnam Experience* (Chapel Hill, N.C.: University of North Carolina, 1975) reveal many ambiguities, not only in the Geneva Agreements but in the application of the laws of war to an unconventional conflict.

On the broader effects of the war on U.S. society and politics, see John E. Mueller, *War, Presidents, and Public Opinion* (New York: Wiley, 1973); Robert Warren Stevens, *Vain Hopes, Grim Realities: The Economic Consequences of the Vietnam War* (New

York: New Viewpoints, 1976); Anthony Lake, ed., *The Vietnam Legacy: The War, American Society and the Future of American Foreign Policy* (New York: Council on Foreign Relations, 1976); Thomas Powers, *Vietnam: The War at Home* (New York: Grossman, 1973); and Alexander Kendrick, *The Wound Within* (Boston: Little, Brown, 1974).

U.S. ARMED FORCES

Writing on U.S. armed forces, strategies, and experience has been left largely to people who served in the armed forces or who could be regarded as part of the military establishment. The official summary of U.S. strategy and operations through the Tet Offensive is Admiral U.S.G. Sharp and General William C. Westmoreland, *Report on the War in Vietnam* (Washington, D.C.: Government Printing Office, 1969), which can profitably be compared with the more bitter memoir of General Westmoreland, *A Soldier Reports* (Garden City, N.Y.: Doubleday, 1976). Other personalized accounts from the command level, but composed with greater detachment, are General Bruce Palmer, Jr., *The 25-Year War* (Lexington, Ky.: University of Kentucky, 1984), and D. R. Palmer, *Summons of the Trumpet* (San Rafael, Calif.: Presidio, 1978). Stuart A. Herrington, *Silence Was a Weapon* (Novato, Calif.: Presidio, 1982) and *Peace with Honor* (Novato, Calif.: Presidio, 1983) recount the personal experiences of a U.S. Army intelligence officer in the period 1970–1975. The first in the U.S. Army's own history series, *United States Army in Vietnam*, is Ronald H. Spector, *Advise and Support: The Early Years 1941–1960* (Washington, D.C.: Government Printing Office, 1985). Passed over in the present work but not to be forgotten is the infamous My Lai massacre, on which readers may find all they can stomach in Seymour Hersh, *My Lai 4* (New York: Random House, 1970), and, by the officer who conducted the official inquiry, W. R. Peers, *The My Lai Inquiry* (New York: Norton, 1979).

In the category of attempts to draw lessons for the future, Douglas Kinnard, *The War Managers* (Hanover, N.H.: University Press of New England, 1977) analyzes what the war meant to army general officers who commanded in it. Douglas Blaufarb, *The Counterinsurgency Era* (New York: Free Press, 1977) finds performance falling short of doctrinal claims. Pacification has sturdy defenders in Richard A. Hunt and Richard H. Shultz, Jr., *Lessons from an Unconventional War* (New York: Pergamon, 1982). By a former member of McNamara's Systems Analysis team and "whiz kid," Thomas Thayer, *The U.S. in Vietnam: War Without Fronts* (Boulder, Colo.: Westview, 1985) provides a quantitative analysis of data collected by the U.S. military command in Vietnam to show that flawed strategies led inevitably to failure. The work that has had by far the most influence on thinking inside the U.S. Army, however, is Colonel Harry G. Summers, Jr., *On Strategy* (San Rafael, Calif.: Presidio, 1982), which pins the blame for defeat on failure to respect the rules of classical military strategy. As for the controversy of the war's impact on the army internally, see Richard Boyle, *The Flower of the Dragon* (San Francisco: Ramparts, 1972), and Zeb B. Bradford, Jr., and Frederic J. Brown, *The United States Army in Transition* (Beverly Hills, Calif.: Sage, 1973).

Index